M W
& R

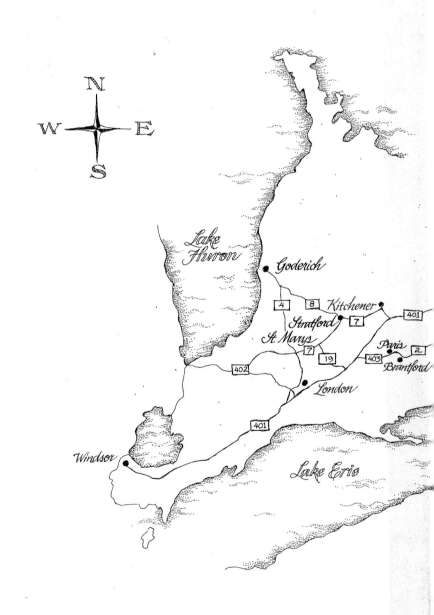

Going to Town

Architectural Walking Tours
in Southern Ontario

Katherine Ashenburg

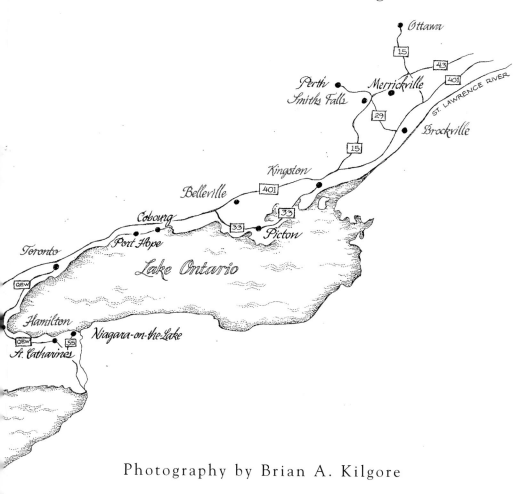

Photography by Brian A. Kilgore

Macfarlane Walter & Ross
Toronto

Macfarlane Walter & Ross
37A Hazelton Avenue
Toronto Canada M5R 2E3

Canadian Cataloguing in Publication Data
Ashenburg, Katharine
Going to town : architectural walking tours in Southern Ontario
Includes bibliographical references and index.
ISBN 0-921912-95-1

1. Architecture – Ontario, Southern – Guidebooks.
2. Ontario, Southern – Buildings, structures, etc. –
Guidebooks.   3. Historic buildings – Ontario, Southern –
Guidebooks.   4. Ontario, Southern – Tours.   I. Title.

NA746.05A75   1996   720'.9713   C96-931285-7

Quotations on page 164, from *Away* by Jane Urquhart,
and page 183, from *Water Street Days* by David Donnell,
are used by permission of the Canadian Publishers,
McClelland & Stewart, Toronto.

The publisher gratefully acknowledges the support
of the Canada Council and the Ontario Arts Council.

Printed and bound in Canada

To Elsie and Norman Ashenburg
who taught me to love old buildings

Contents

A Note on Towns, Buildings, and Dates

If comparisons are odious, choices can be agonizing. The ten towns in this book were, as it turned out, more easily chosen than the buildings. I wanted to map the most architecturally interesting small towns in Ontario, towns whose history was still relatively visible and that could be apprehended more or less completely in a walk of two to three hours. Stratford, the largest, has a population of 27,000; Merrickville, the smallest, has 1,000 inhabitants but a disproportionately high number of intriguing buildings.

Obviously, the older and better preserved the town, the more architectural styles there are to be seen. Perth, Merrickville, Picton, Cobourg, Port Hope, and Niagara-on-the-Lake were not difficult choices. The younger, mid-nineteenth-century towns appealed for a variety of reasons: Paris for its cobblestone buildings, Goderich for its history and unusual town plan, St. Marys for its limestone, Stratford for its downright market-town personality.

My practice in a strange town was to walk and re-walk its streets without much method, taking hundreds of photographs of interesting buildings. In the simplest possible terms, a building had to be visually appealing, a telling example of its type, or historically significant to be considered; a locally important house whose original charm had been effaced by misguided renovations was usually not good enough. When the walk was decided, candidates were eliminated, with reluctance, if they were blocks away from the nearest building on the route; others were cut because the chapter was growing to unmanageable lengths. Every town has scores of attractive buildings not on the walk: keep looking, keep walking.

There are various ways to date an old building: through assessment rolls; local newspapers' reports of architectural commissions, building tenders, and finished buildings; architects' and builders' office records; gazetteers, almanacs, and local histories. Many of the dates in the book derive from the files of the Local Architectural Conservation Advisory Committees (LACACs) and the

Architectural Conservancy of Ontario, whose members make use of all those sources. Others have been gleaned directly from the contemporary sources. But, as in many subjects, experts differ, researchers sometimes nod, and even assessment rolls can be open to interpretation. The credit goes to those patient searchers in the original sources; the errors are my own.

Acknowledgments

This book owes its existence to the kindness and expertise of strangers, many of whom did not stay strangers. It began when I walked the chapters of Patricia McHugh's *Toronto Architecture: A City Guide*, and wondered if I could do the same for Ontario's towns. Her example and encouragement were crucial.

Rob Mikel knows more about Cobourg than any living person, perhaps more than any person who has ever lived. He first contacted me when I wrote an article about Cobourg in the *New York Times* and misidentified the house where Katharine Cornell was married; he has been patiently correcting my mistakes ever since.

Dorothy Wallace, Goderich's pre-eminent architectural historian, read the Goderich chapter, as did Cindy Fisher, Paul Scholten, Roslyn Campbell, and Lucinda Jerry.

In Merrickville, Larry Turner saved me from many errors, and Shirley Watton conjured up dates and the life histories of buildings with remarkable speed.

Peter John Stokes, one of Ontario's most accomplished restoration architects and the author of a fine book on Niagara-on-the-Lake's buildings, graciously gave permission for the use of the glossary he wrote for *Rogues' Hollow*. Also in Niagara-on-the-Lake, William Severin, the curator of the Niagara Historical Society Museum, let me rummage in the museum storage room; Cathy Macdonald provided me with much valuable information about the designated properties; and Joy Ormsby read the Niagara chapter with her keen historian's eye.

In Paris, help came from Norman Derrick and the town historian, Fred Bemrose. Margaret Deans, the owner of a cobblestone house, gave me a tour of the town's cobblestone architecture.

In Perth, John J. Stewart made time for a stranger on a busy workday and gave her several pieces of good advice. One of those pieces led to Susan Code, who unsnarled tangles and tracked down elusive dates.

David Taylor shared his considerable knowledge of Picton with me and greatly improved that chapter. Tom Kuglin, then the curator of the Prince Edward County Museum, made the museum's architectural files available.

In Port Hope, Amy Quinn left me alone for several happy days in the local office of the Architectural Conservancy of Ontario, and Tom Cruickshank was reliably generous with his expertise. Thanks are also due to Marion Garland, who provided part of this book's glossary, and to Darrell Leeson, who solved some Dorset Street mysteries.

Mary Smith, the curator of the St. Marys Museum, brought me coffee, cookies, and the museum's files on designated buildings one cold September day in 1992, and has been answering my questions at intervals ever since. As tour guide, researcher, and all-round St. Marys expert, Larry Pfaff was invaluable. Thanks also to the museum's 1995 summer intern, Jessica Baarda.

At the Perth County Archives in Stratford, archivists Luitzen Reidstra and Carolynn Bart Reidstra preside over their beautifully organized files and gladly undertake to answer queries. Carolynn Bart Reidstra in particular was a careful reader of the Stratford chapter, and dated several buildings. The Toronto architect S. Kent Rawson helpfully shared his research on Stratford's city architect, Alexander Hepburn.

In Toronto, I benefitted greatly from the thoughtful readings that Stephen Otto and Roger Hall gave my book. Thanks also to Robert Hill, who identified several architects of hitherto unclaimed buildings, to Gary Ross, who supplied the title, and to John Macfarlane, Paul Kennedy, Bella Pomer, Brian Kilgore, Mary Hanson, Sybil Carolan, and Hannah Carolan for much welcome advice and encouragement.

Barbara Czarnecki, a woman who knows the exceptions to the obscurest rules and has a mean way with a palimpsest, has more than earned my gratitude. And finally, my thanks to Jan Walter, a publisher who literally walked the walk – all ten chapters, and frequently. An unflappable source of intelligent questions, subtle suggestions, and not-bad directional skills, she remains my ideal reader.

How to Read an Ontario Town

In the middle of World War II, the poet John Betjeman published a slim, affectionate book called *English Cities and Small Towns*. Written from memory, at a time when "Mr. Betjeman's present work has taken him temporarily out of England," as the jacket copy rather coyly puts it, the book begins with the poet's way of deciphering a strange town. It's an unhurried piece of detective work that takes him from the railway station to the ancient alleys that radiate from the parish church and the High Street; to the stationer's shop, where he buys postcards of the neighbourhood wonders, a relentlessly enthusiastic guide, and local newspapers full of parish news; past the backs of houses in the High Street, which reveal their origins far more honestly than their fronts; searching for a key to the eighteenth-century Unitarian church; attending morning service in the sadly renovated Anglican church; listening to the local talk in the "Family and Commercial" hotel properly redolent of HP sauce and brown wallpaper, and so on.

By the time I discovered Betjeman's book, I was a *habitué* of Ontario's small towns, from the heavy-lidded railway station to the "best street," from the bank-turned-country-inn to the local authors' shelf in the oak-lined Carnegie Library. I knew that a locked church can often be entered through the parish office, and that the antiques-shop proprietor, having a vested interest in the past, is frequently a good source of information about the town. There are no Tudor churches or eighteenth-century Corn Exchanges in Ontario and the visitor's path is more solitary and less systematic, but Betjeman's and my methods were remarkably similar. Had he found himself in Perth or Cobourg, he would have known how to proceed.

After, perhaps, an initial discouragement. Secretive and proud, in the Upper Canadian way that masquerades as self-effacement, Ontario towns would have you believe there is very little to read in their regular streets and handsome, plainish houses. One of the first things the curious visitor learns is that an interest in the cobblestone houses of Paris or the Crystal Palace in Picton is likely to be met with blank bewilderment or jocular indifference.

Like Betjeman, I tried to begin with a local guide, however sketchy and flattering. In Ontario, when they exist, they tend to be leaflets whose location is idiosyncratic – at the Town Hall here, the Chamber of Commerce there, the museum, even the local constituency office in one town. The cards, maps, and books on local subjects that Betjeman found reliably at the stationer's shop surface here in odd nooks and crannies. In Picton it was a camera store where I found *The Settler's Dream*, the invaluable architectural survey of Prince Edward County; in Napanee, the local history is for sale in the public library, in Stratford at the Perth County Archives, in Paris at the stationer's shop.

But, grudgingly or not, Ontario rewards patience, resourcefulness, and the ability to smile vaguely at scoffers. The traveller who tours a nineteenth-century town at the deliberate pace for which it was designed (walking when not on a slow horse) finds instant gratification in the details – terracotta plaques, bombastic keystones, leafy capitals. The occasional interiors available to the walker can be almost spookily evocative: the sculpted Victorian fittings in Andrews Jeweller (now Anstetts) in St. Marys, the more workaday look of Hall's House of Quality Linens in Paris, the gloriously churchy courtroom in Stratford's Perth County Courthouse. As for the real churches, when the parish office is locked, before or after the 11 a.m. Sunday service is a good time to admire the Anglicans' hammerbeam ceilings, the Catholics' stained-glass fantasias, and the Methodists' sloping floors, which direct all eyes to the pulpit.

When you first savour an Ontario town, its particularity is striking. Frequently it's a result of the available building material, which in the nineteenth century was difficult to transport even short distances. The buttery sandstone that makes Perth look like Perth does not appear in Merrickville, thirty minutes away by car. The terrain, the settlers' social and geographical origins, the date of settlement also determine a town's character: Perth, a Scottish settlement dominated by lawyers and retired military officers, presents a very different face from Merrickville, a limestone village settled by American, English, and Scottish small-scale industrialists.

When each town is a social history to be decoded, the architectural alphabet becomes a rich source of information. The presence of Greek Revival buildings, a republican style much favoured by Yankees, usually indicates American settlers, as in Paris. The virtual absence of Second Empire buildings suggests a town that had finished growing before the 1870s, when that showy style arrived, peaked, and declined: Cobourg is a case in point. Towns that began in the mid-nineteenth century, such as St. Marys or Stratford, missed the Loyalist, Greek Revival, and Regency styles almost altogether.

If the individual distinctiveness of the towns impresses a visitor first, a deeper acquaintance unmasks the common elements. There remains something very Ontario about Ontario towns, most obviously a plainness in the buildings that ranges from elegant to dour. The prevailing Scottish ethos, which distrusted display and prized straightforwardness, was influential here; so was the settlers' poverty and the dearth of easily workable stone. Using the repertoire of nineteenth-century styles common to Britain and the United States, Ontarians built more simply (and often smaller, because of the cold and the relative lack of servants). Compared with those of Australia, a sister colony with workable stone, abundant convict labour, and a certain national *joie de vivre*, Ontario's Gothic Revival and Italianate buildings can look downright severe. Commodity and firmness were in good supply, to cite two of Vitruvius's criteria for architecture; his third, delight, is here too, but most characteristically it is a delight that arises from proportion and restraint.

Ontario towns in the main were the creation of builders, not architects. And those builders could be stubbornly conservative, constructing a Gothic villa forty years after the style's peak in the U.S. or Britain. Next door to the villa the same builder might build an up-to-the-minute Queen Anne house, based on the latest pattern book from Britain or the U.S. Next door to that he might concoct a patchwork of a house from two or three styles. Just because a new style was à la mode was no reason to jettison an old favourite, and the builders' reliance on pattern books left them free to mix, match, and improvise when they saw fit. All of which makes Ontario buildings maddening to date, bewildering for the purist, and diverting for the walker.

In 1789 Lord Dorchester, governor general, prescribed that inland settlements in Upper Canada be laid out in a prim gridiron, and many towns obediently tried to impose that regularity on hill and dale and river. The flatter the terrain the better it worked, as in Niagara-on-the-Lake and Merrickville. A hilly town like Port Hope was by necessity laid out more naturally. A town's first buildings were close to the all-important Great Lake or river, as at St. Marys and Port Hope, but the water meant industry and transportation to the nineteenth century, not leisure or a picturesque view. Prosperity, as in the case of both St. Marys and Port Hope, often entailed a move away: the "best streets" are high above the water.

Even the street names of Ontario towns are suggestive. Queen, King, Victoria, and Church Streets cross-stitch their way across the province, constant reminders of church and state. St. Patrick's Street will be close to the Catholic church or perhaps the Irish quarter, St. Andrew's to the Presbyterian church, St. George's to the Anglican. The plethora of streets dedicated to the heroes of the Napoleonic Wars – Wellington, Wellesley (the Duke's family name), Picton, Waterloo – commemorate one of the great settling forces of Upper Canada. Judging by the number of generals and administrators honoured by Ontario's surveyors and town fathers, it was a society that held them in much higher esteem than artists and thinkers. The exceptions are memorable because they are exceptions: in Perth, Herriott Street is a misspelled salute to George Heriot (1759–1839), a watercolour artist better known in Canada as head of the post office. Byron and Ricardo Streets in Niagara-on-the-Lake are anomalous tributes to a poet and an economist.

One of the most appealing things about the towns is their completeness. The limitations of nineteenth-century transportation and communication made, to paraphrase John Donne, one little town an everywhere, with poignant results. Small as it was, a town might have a Corktown or an Irish section, an upper town and a lower town, a fashionable side and an unfashionable side. In these Lilliputian kingdoms, two shopping streets perpendicular to each other could compete hotly for supremacy.

Along with the completeness came a self-importance and great expectations. With the single arguable exception of St. Marys, the towns in this book believed they were destined to become important cities, centres of industry and power. They were equally vain about their beauty, and the hyperbole with which the historian of Brant County described Paris was not unusual. The town was "beautiful from every point," its hills just high enough to be picturesque, its river rejoicing in "the Wordsworthian charm of *quiet*," even its gas-lit factories "starring with dancing lights the impetuous stream below." Paris was unique in managing to bill itself simultaneously "the Manchester of Ontario" and "the prettiest town in Canada," but each town was convinced that *it* was an unparalleled beauty spot.

Their dreams of power and influence came to nothing, fortunately as it turned out for their nineteenth-century aspect: charm and the keen sense of the past that these towns sustain have proved more durable. Their very lack of architectural masterpieces has helped in this regard. The walker who encounters the variety of Ontario's "derivative" and "typical" buildings encounters, in Alan Gowans's words in *Building Canada*, a popular architecture "in which the past exists most concretely and vitally." Which is not to say that an Ontario town is a poor thing but our own: it is our own, and a fascinating thing. And the ten here are only a beginning.

Going to Town

Victoria Hall

Cobourg

"A Select Society with Some Fine Houses"

When Charles Dickens saw Cobourg in 1842, he called it a "cheerful, thriving little town." Cobourg still looks cheerful enough, but its placid streets offer more than a few surprises: a magnificent Palladian town hall, the poignant ghost of a university, and well-preserved examples of practically every style of nineteenth-century housing, from workers' cottages to antebellum mansions. Look a little deeper, and there are two Cobourgs. One is a Tory town with great expectations and repeated frustrations. The other, more shadowy, is "Newport North," an American resort in the grand style.

Like most of Ontario's early towns, Cobourg began with wilderness, land grants, and Americans. Their very names – Asa Burnham, Eliud Nickerson, Samuel Ash, Elias Jones, Liberty White – suggest the Old Testament qualities that had formed New England and New York State. By 1798, impelled by Loyalist convictions or cheap Canadian land, or both, these five men were trying to wrest a living from the cedar swamp that is now Cobourg. Their settlement duties were straightforward: they had to choose their 100 acres, build a log cabin, and clear enough wood to make five large brush heaps. That done, a settler could pay £5 to £6 for the deeds, and he owned the land.

Jokingly called Hardscrabble, the little village grew slowly. When a settler named Catherine Chrysler White arrived in 1813, she found a few small clearings, three houses, and a rough log road to the lake. The block of land on King Street from Division Street to St. Peter's Anglican Church, now the town's commercial centre, could be had for the price of a saddle.

Cobourg's first "American period" lasted until the War of 1812. It was the aftermath of that war and of the Napoleonic Wars in general that accelerated the town's halting development and gave it its distinctive personality. The American immigrants who had originally peopled the place were now unwelcome. Britain, on the other hand, was faced with a postwar depression and thousands of unemployed officers and soldiers; it encouraged emigration to

1

Upper Canada with generous land grants. With its partially cleared lakeside setting and access to the presumably expanding north, Cobourg looked ideal.

Ordinary veterans settled in Cobourg as well as officers, but it was the officers, retired with half pay, who created the town's leisured, aristocratic society more or less from a standing start. The town that an English traveller named Frances Stewart visited in 1822 sounds more like one of Jane Austen's country neighbourhoods than a primitive settlement carved out of the wilderness. Mrs. Stewart noted "several Captains of the Navy," a book club, dancing, tea drinking, and much visiting. She was without her winter dresses and furs, and she felt their absence: "The Cobourg ladies dress in a very smart, suitable style. They think nothing of giving 50 or 100 guineas for a fur muff or tippet. Indeed fur is much used. The sleighs are delightfully lined with it and are so comfortable. On the evening of January 5th, Mr. Henry called and took us to return some visit. We went first to Coverts, who are very decidedly English; then to Cap. Boswells where we remained for tea; two other English families are here, the Faulkners and the Sowdens from Bath. They came to Cobourg a year and a half ago, and now have the nicest farm here with every comfort."

"Every comfort," of course, was relative. The gently reared Mrs. Stewart was being taught to make yeast and bread, and the members of the book society often experienced the "melancholy pleasure" of rereading familiar books. But the town, now officially named in a misspelled tribute to Princess Charlotte's marriage to Prince Leopold of Saxe-Coburg, was flourishing. In 1832, Catherine Parr Traill found "a very pretty church and a select society," several good stores, mills, a bank, and a staunchly Tory newspaper. Both the newspaper and the church – the *Cobourg Star* and St. Peter's Anglican – are still thriving.

Civilization proceeds erratically in a pioneer settlement: ritualistic rounds of tea drinking and Tory newspapers precede sidewalks and police protection. Cobourg became a college town while stray pigs and cows roamed its unpaved main streets. In 1831, in a signal mark of confidence in the little village, the Methodist Conference chose Cobourg as the site of Upper Canada Academy. Conceived as an egalitarian, non-denominational challenge to the Anglicans' Upper Canada College in York (later Toronto), the Academy opened in 1836 as a preparatory school. Five years later it changed its name to Victoria College and began granting BAs.

Victoria College rises up at the crest of College Street much as it did in 1840, when W.H. Bartlett centred his engraving of Cobourg on its eloquent Greek Revival silhouette. Architecturally it dominated the town until 1860, after which it shared the skyline with the town hall, Victoria Hall. The first university in Canada to confer degrees on women, the college was staffed by celebrated educators such as Egerton Ryerson and Nathaniel Burwash. Augusta Stowe, the first woman doctor in Canada, received a medical degree from Victoria in 1888. Today the democratic high-mindedness of the college and its Methodist sympathies with political reform strike a more contemporary note than the Tory town fathers' grandiose business schemes. And if Victoria College was ever so slightly peripheral in Cobourg, it was unquestionably prestigious. Town and gown coexisted cordially until 1892, when Victoria became part of the University of Toronto.

The town's leading citizens, the D'Arcy Boultons, the Beattys, and the Dumbles, were less interested in higher education than in their dream of Cobourg as a great city. By mid-century, their euphoria seemed perfectly plausible. With a population of 5,000, the busiest central Lake Ontario harbour, and the Cobourg Peterborough Railway to connect the town with the developing north, Cobourg was well on its way to national importance.

Looking back on the optimism and extravagance of those years, a Cobourgian named John Maw remembered "lots of champagne, sundry little parties every night somewhere, select balls at five dollars a head for the upper ten, dollar hops for mechanics." The hotels were crowded with sailors, shipwrights, and lawyers. Times were so good that labourers "turned up noses at pork and potatoes," and demanded beefsteak for breakfast and supper and poultry for dinner.

All Cobourg needed was a town hall to match its prestige. One of Ontario's most accomplished architects, the Irish-born Kivas Tully, won the design competition in 1852, but the distracted and increasingly ambitious town fathers delayed construction until Tully came up with something more grandiose than the original design. Work finally began in 1856. Both Cobourg's hopes of glory and the cost of the monumental Palladian structure escalated during the four years of construction. What had been planned as a $25,000 expenditure cost five times that amount by the time Victoria Hall officially opened.

Some of Cobourg's citizens thought the building extravagant, but few guessed the depth of their miscalculation. When the Prince of Wales inaugurated the building, on September 6, 1860, the little town indulged in an orgy of colonial adulation and civic pride. Native-born Canadians carrying torches pulled the Prince's carriage from the harbour to Victoria Hall. It passed under various ceremonial arches, including one made by the hardware merchant which featured ploughs, rakes, hoes, spades, pumpkins, and squashes. In spite of fears that the new ballroom floor might be dangerous, the Prince danced until dawn with fifteen carefully chosen local belles. The

Cobourg Star reported that the ballroom was perfectly safe, "except for bachelors," which would come as no surprise to "all who have seen the ladies of Cobourg."

A prescient American, seeing Victoria Hall's richly sculpted bulk, wondered, "That is indeed a splendid building, but where is the town for whose use it was built?" When the Cobourg Peterborough Railway's three-mile bridge across Rice Lake collapsed during the winter of 1861–62, Cobourg's great expectations were finished. For a while its entrepreneurs continued to hope, through a variety of railway and mining projects, but the town never really recovered. Its decline was compounded by the staggering cost of Victoria Hall, which was not finally paid for until 1938.

For decades Cobourg's next-door neighbour, Port Hope, had sneeringly called the town "Sleepy Hollow." (Cobourg retaliated with "Port Misery.") In the 1860s, perhaps the lowest point in its history, Cobourg justified its nickname. About 150 single men and several families left town in 1863 alone.

Relief arrived from an unlikely source. By the end of the decade, several Pittsburgh industrialists had gained control of the Cobourg Peterborough Railway and the iron mines at nearby Marmora. They liked Cobourg, with its maple-lined streets, fine houses, and genteel, rather English atmosphere. Led by Colonel William Chambliss, the managing director of the Marmora mines, they made the town "Newport North," one of the most fashionable resorts in North America. Wealthy Civil War veterans from both sides moved to Cobourg for long, luxurious summers that included balls, weddings, and garden parties furnished with Oriental carpets and upholstered chairs. For the Southerners, Cobourg was doubly attractive: they could escape the heat without spending their money in the Northern states. Both sides rejoiced in what they believed was the finest "ozone" on the continent.

By the turn of the century, Cobourg's summertime population had swelled by more than 2,000, and it was by far Canada's premier summer resort. More millionaires per capita were said to summer in Cobourg than anywhere else in the country. At first the Americans lived in hotels, especially the 150-room Arlington Hotel (now demolished), which Colonel Chambliss built in 1874. Gradually they enlarged existing houses and built lavish mansions along the lake. Cobourg took in its stride a social life that included a Saturday evening "Grand Hop" at the Arlington, the annual Cobourg Horse Show, an international polo match, and near-professional music and theatre.

The Cornells of Buffalo were part of the American colony, and Katharine Cornell spent her youthful summers organizing plays in the family garden. In 1921, she was married at her aunt Lydia Cornell's house at 139 Queen

Street (**18**). Cobourg has other unexpected show business connections: the comedienne Beatrice Lillie was born here in 1898, lived on George Street, and sang in the Presbyterian choir. The silent movie star Marie Dressler was born in Cobourg, and the Chamber of Commerce houses a small museum in her honour (**46**, 212 King Street West).

By the 1920s and '30s, the pace of resort life was recognizably modern. Carloads of treasure-hunters raced through Cobourg's once quiet streets in Duesenbergs, Stutz Bearcats, and Mercers. At one memorable party, the band playing on a raft in an orchid-filled swimming pool was submerged when enthusiastic women in formal dress jumped in and swam to the platform. In the '30s, the irrepressible Americans even made a movie in Cobourg, renting equipment from Hollywood. The American occupation ended with the Depression, and the local antiques dealers still talk about the estate sales that went on well into the 1940s.

Fortunately, in a place as small as Cobourg, there's no such thing as an American enclave. The most lavish mansions along the lake are within walking distance of older, simpler houses built when Cobourg seemed destined to become a great city. Ironically, the American showplaces have proved more vulnerable than Regency cottages or Greek Revival houses. Many have burned or been demolished; others have been transformed. Sidbrook (**25**, 411 King Street East) is now a private hospital, and Strathmore (**26**, 420 King Street East) is a school. The real, continuing life of a small Ontario town threads in and around and through the mansions the Americans left behind.

Architecturally, Cobourg's conservatism has served it well. The town's population remained about 5,000 from 1860 until the end of World War II. (It is now 15,000.) Because the townspeople often lacked the means, if not the desire, to alter their well-built houses, the central core has changed very little since the 1860s. A walkable sampler of nineteenth-century housing, Cobourg has a charm that is lived-in and unemphatic. It is, as the proverb says, *multum in parvo* – a great deal in a small compass.

Cobourg

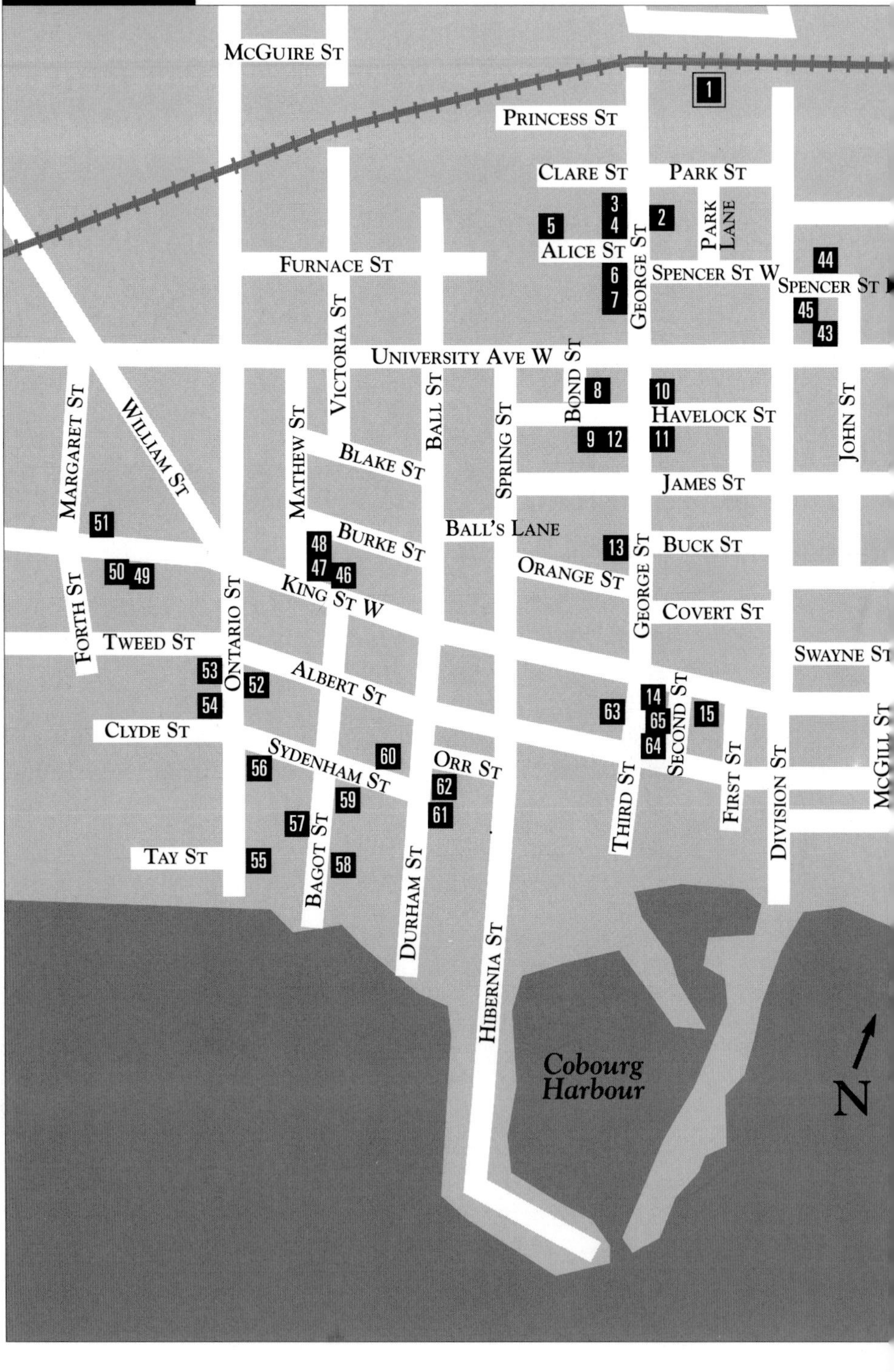

McGuire St

Princess St

Clare St   Park St

1

3
4

5

2

Park Lane

44

Alice St

6
7

George St

Spencer St W   Spencer St

45
43

Furnace St

Victoria St

University Ave W

Bond St

8

10

Havelock St

John St

Mathew St

Ball St

Spring St

9   12

11

Margaret St

William St

Blake St

James St

51

Ball's Lane

Burke St

48
47   46

13

Buck St

George St

50   49

Forth St

King St W

Orange St

Covert St

Tweed St

Ontario St

Albert St

Swayne St

53

52

54

63

14
65
64

15

Second St

Clyde St

Sydenham St

60

Orr St

Third St

First St

Division St

McGill St

56

59

62
61

57

Bagot St

58

Tay St

55

Durham St

Hibernia St

Cobourg
Harbour

N

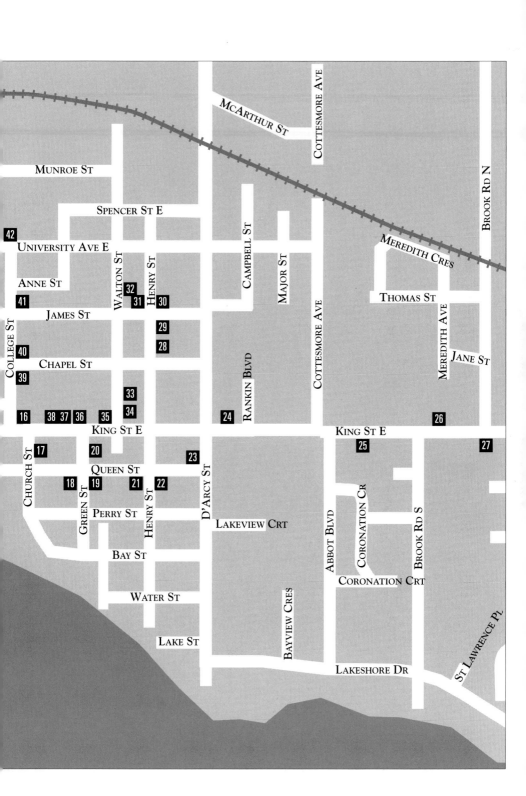

3 *475 George Street* 4 *465 George Street*

1 Cobourg pinned its hopes firmly on the railroad, and its low-slung **station** is a good starting point. Built about 1911 by the Grand Trunk Railway to one of its standard plans, it's a top-heavy red-brick depot with a rocky stone foundation and Romanesque-inspired window surrounds. From it, turn down George Street, which is lined with some grand houses on the right and more modest ones on the left. Cobourg's most interesting buildings seem to come in clumps, almost as if they enjoyed each other's company.

2 480 George Street, 1870s
Plainer and primmer than the High Victorian trio across the street (**3**, **4**, **6** below), this elongated brick box faces its extroverted neighbours with self-assurance to spare. A conservative builder's version of the Loyalist style, topped with an Ontario gable, this house is seen to better advantage in the fall and winter, when not overtaken by ivy. The brick is a soft weathered rose, except for the buff window trim and the quoins that emphasize the house's length and give it a gift-wrapped appearance. The wide eaves and the slim double windows above the door are typical of Cobourg. The original owner was a druggist named Johns.

3 475 George Street, ca. 1871,
  renovated in the 1890s
The original Gothic villa, as large-gabled

and bargeboarded houses like this were called, took on more eclectic airs with a *fin-de-siècle* renovation. The curvaceous two-tier porch, grafted a bit incongruously onto the brick house, is a plus. But the juxta-positions of scale in this house, although normal for its era, are unsettling: the Ionic pilasters that climb the walls and the dentils lining the central gable are extra-large, while the Ionic columns and finials decorating the porch are altogether daintier.

4 465 George Street, 1871
James Crossen was the founder of a railway car factory that at its peak employed 600 people. (The carriages that transported Princess Louise across Canada when her husband was governor general were built by Crossen Car Works.) Crossen's Gothic villa, called Cedar Hedge, bristles with emphatic wooden details, mostly medieval in origin. (Originally the yellow-brick house also sported finials in the peaks, wooden cresting on the gables, and a balcony above the main veranda. The Victorians were not given to understatement.) The heavy, assured bargeboard, the round windows with star tracery, and the bold, arched treillage on the front veranda are superb.

5 96 Alice Street, ca. 1870s
Like many Victorian industrialists, Mr. Crossen lived next to "the works." His fore-man's stern red-brick house was directly

[5] *96 Alice Street*   [9] *77 Havelock Street*

behind his, to the west, and the factory was to the north of that. The builder tried to soften the tall symmetry of the foreman's house with Italianate touches such as the curving roof over the main door, the double round-headed windows, and the painted brick swags framing the windows. But the unrelieved flatness of the façade defeated him: the house, now a tannery office, has a wide-awake and very businesslike look.

[6] 447 George Street, 1870s, remodelled 1895

When James Crossen's son William remodelled his house in 1895, he chose the profusion of materials and details that were essential for the Queen Anne style. Almost anything goes in this mixture of yellow brick and rough-cut stone, two kinds of shingles, leaded glass, Gothic windows, porches, projecting bays, and gently swelling Ionic columns. Nor was the source of the Crossen prosperity, the Crossen Car Works, forgotten in Fairlawn, as the house was called: the outsize projecting window facing south onto the front porch is the rear window of a railway car, and the billiard room is shaped and decorated like a railway car.

[7] 429 George Street, before 1874

Behind the monumental classical porch (which is newer than the house) sits a neat Ontario cottage on a high foundation. The effect, like a little girl in her mother's hat

and high-heeled shoes, is disproportionate but fetching. Note the Northumberland County wide eaves and the fine picket trim on the five-panelled door.

Continue south on George Street and turn right at Havelock Street.

[8] 80 Havelock Street, 1875

William Bond, a Cobourg contractor, built this glorified two-storey Ontario cottage with a central peak and double bay windows. (Bond Street, to the west of the house, is named after him.) The grandiose cast-stone quoins and window surrounds with keystones were the sort of pompous detail the Victorians found irresistible. The rather distracting front porch was added later.

[9] 77 Havelock Street, 1876

An Italianate house that manages to be both elegant and utterly solid. The solidity comes from the repeated rectangular forms (not the rounded ones that typified the Italianate style), the elegance from their balance. The square shape and straight-topped windows are relieved by the smart double door, the rectangular bay windows, and the elaborate cornice and brackets (unusually distributed in twinned groups of four). The skinny paired windows above the door and the painted brick trim above the windows are characteristic local markings. The house was built as a wedding

11 *364 George Street*

13 *293 George Street*

present by the bride's parents when Ida Hayden married Alfred Reynar, a professor of English at Victoria College. The last surviving of the seven Reynar daughters lived here until 1980, which accounts in part for its mint condition.

10 **50 Havelock Street,** 1851

R.D. Chatterton was an English journalist who founded Cobourg's Tory newspaper, the *Cobourg Star* ("a friend and welcome guest at every fire side"). His Britishness extended to his house, an irregular, tightly knit version of a vernacular English house with Gothic details. The Tudor labels over the windows give it a churchy air that also accorded with Chatterton's politics. (The frame gable over the front door is a modern addition.)

11 **364 George Street,** 1857

Thomas Dumble came to Canada from the United States to settle the Maine–New Brunswick border dispute in the 1840s and stayed to live in Cobourg. From certain angles, Dromore, as he called his house, is almost dour; from others it's a cornucopia of mid-Victorian details: a steep mansard roof (one of the first in Ontario), wonderfully assertive brackets and bargeboard, heavy-lidded Gothic dormer windows. The bargeboard on the central gable, with trefoils separated by undulating forms, is particularly striking; the brackets underneath are marked with a D for Dumble.

12 **363 George Street,** 1857

John Cullingford's house and apothecary is a good example of the way a nineteenth-century carpenter could pick and choose from current styles, add some idiosyncratic details, and, in this case, achieve harmony. What has come to be called the Ontario cottage is essentially a low-slung Regency house with a central gable added to light the top storey. This one integrates Regency French doors, a simple pedimented porch, and a Gothic window in the gable into a crisp design of triangles and rectangles. The bargeboard, which evolves from a vaguely Chinese Chippendale effect along the front eaves to a flowery affair in the gable, prevents the whole arrangement from looking too geometrical.

13 **293 George Street,** ca. 1840s

A prim white stucco that retains its delicately pilastered neoclassical doorcase, an old-fashioned touch in larger centres by this date, but not in Cobourg. The modestly spooled and treillaged veranda is a later addition. The next-door neighbour, number 291, has a similar plan, although it's taller and its treillage and gable decoration are more folky. It dates from the mid-1870s.

14 **Victoria Hall, 55 King Street West,** 1860

When it came to public buildings, Ontarians in the mid-nineteenth century

14 *Victoria Hall,*
55 King Street West

16 *St. Peter's Anglican Church,*
King Street East at College Street

favoured a balanced Palladian style that had been popular in Britain and the United States a century earlier. Canada West – and Victoria Hall's architect, Kivas Tully – treated the style's classical elements freely, even floridly. Victoria Hall, with its yellow-brick walls covered on three sides with sand-coloured Cleveland free stone, is rich with every kind of decorative detail. But all its elements – from the projecting end wings that echo the central portico to the carved symbols of the three United Kingdoms (rose, thistle, and shamrock) around the main entrance – are beautifully controlled by the symmetry of its overall plan. As if to rest the eye, the elaborate window treatments on the first storey give way to increasingly plain treatments on the upper stories; their street-level fancyness is balanced by the columned cupola with its four clock faces. The interior, now handsomely restored, has an Old Bailey–style courtroom and a truly spectacular ballroom, both with *trompe-l'oeil* paintings by the German artist Joseph Moser. The courtroom and council chambers are in regular use, the local art gallery is on the third floor, and the ballroom is a fully equipped concert and banquet hall.

King Street West, from Second Street to Division Street

Well-preserved three-storey Victorian commercial buildings, many built in the 1870s, include ornate Italianate stores

(many on the south side) as well as older, simpler buildings (more on the north side). Beebe's Boot Shop, 15 **33 King Street West,** has kept its original pilasters and mouldings; the round-headed Italianate window surrounds on the second storey are decorated with leaves, and the whole building topped with iron cresting. Built in 1873, it was burned and rebuilt in 1881.

King Street East, from Division Street to McGill Street

This was the centre of early Cobourg, before the town began moving westward. Symmetrical, neoclassical buildings on the south side, some commercial, some domestic, some mixed-use, include number 35 (ca. 1837), number 37–39 (1844), number 41–43 (1844), number 45 (1844).

16 St. Peter's Anglican Church, King Street East at College Street, 1844, completed 1854

One of the oldest Anglican parishes in Upper Canada, St. Peter's opened for business on Christmas Day 1820 and made do with a wooden rectangle for almost a quarter-century. In 1843 the congregation engaged the young British-born architect Henry Bowyer Lane to design them a new church. By 1851, when the front façade and tower had been completed, Kivas Tully (not yet hired to design Victoria Hall) was commissioned to design the body and supervise its construction so as to enclose

17 *202 Church Street*

18 *139 Queen Street*

the existing one. Cobourg's elect, led by their long-time rector, the Reverend Alexander Neil Bethune, continued to pray in the old church while the new one was being built around them. Finally, in 1854, while the congregation worshipped briefly in the malt room of a nearby brewery, the old church was removed piece by piece. For all its Gothic trimmings – crenellations, drip moulds, side window tracery borrowed from the Perpendicular school – Lane and Tully's tidy church is a symmetrical, uncomplicated structure from the free-and-easy first stage of nineteenth-century Britain's infatuation with the medieval. (Lane's Little Trinity Church in Toronto, built in 1844, is a similar exercise in unacademic Gothic.) The hammerbeam roof inside is delightful.

17 202 Church Street, 1877
One of the finest Italianate houses in Ontario, in perfect condition. Built by a hardware merchant named Robert Mulholland, the house has the characteristic asymmetry, square Tuscan tower, and elaborate doorway of the Italianate villa. What it doesn't have are the decorative brackets that supported the deep cornice (a touch so representative that the mode was sometimes called the Bracketed style). Instead, the Mulholland house's horizontal emphasis comes from panelled and decorated cornices, and three jagged bands that cut boldly across windows, the tower, and the

first-floor bay. Subtle echoes abound: the boss at the centre of the bargeboard with a circle underneath and the semicircular arches with circles over the first-floor windows; the discreet drops hanging from the tower cornice that reappear in the main cornice and around the top of the bay window. The twisted little roll underneath the tower cornice is only one of many perfectly achieved small touches.

18 139 Queen Street, 1873
Katharine Cornell's aunt Lydia Cornell lived in this stucco Italianate house until 1958, and the actress was married to the director Guthrie McClintic in the double drawing room in 1921.

19 174 Green Street, 1842, second storey and rear wing added 1906
Looking credibly Anglican with its Tudor labels, this house was originally commissioned by the Reverend Alexander Bethune as an Anglican theological college and grammar school and designed by Henry Bowyer Lane. After Trinity College, Toronto, took over the training of priests, it was much enlarged and served as the "Corktown" public school (so nicknamed because of the Irish immigrants in this neighbourhood) and later as a summer home for American owners.

20 202 Green Street, 1879
The man most responsible for Cobourg's

20 *202 Green Street*   22 *221 Queen Street*

American colony, Colonel William Chambliss, built himself a brick mountain of a house in the fanciful late stage of the American Gothic Revival. Dormers, hooded balconies, and vaguely northern European–looking fretwork designs were all the rage in the prosperous American suburbs; this house looks very American and more than a touch sombre. Said to have been won in a poker game by another American, Colonel Douglas Cornell, the grandfather of Katharine, it was called Hadfield Hurst by the Cornells. Converted to a girls' school, Hatfield Hall, in 1919, it is now an apartment building.

21 195 Queen Street, 1854
A beguiling house built by Dr. James Auston on land owned by the Anglican Church. Auston named the house Glebe Lawn, and the grey stucco with black and white trim, the steep gables on the west side, the Gothic windows at the main door, and the demure white rickrack bargeboard do give it a faintly clerical air.

22 221 Queen Street, 1856
Purists beware: this immaculately pretty Ontario cottage is deceptive. The one-and-a-half-storey house acquired its door in the 1960s, when a King Street house to which the door belonged was demolished. And the door itself is a surprise. The elliptical fanlight and Ionic pilasters, which look at first like the early-nineteenth-century

Loyalist mode, actually date from the early 1920s, a decade fascinated with stylistic revivals. (The elaborately dainty details are a give-away.)

23 201 D'Arcy Street, ca. 1840
When D'Arcy Boulton Jr. built this house, called the Lawn, for his bride Emily Heath, it was a notably good example of the Regency villa. (A member of one of Ontario's most prominent families, Boulton was the son of D'Arcy Boulton, who built the Grange in Toronto.) Much enlarged to the north in a very sympathetic early-twentieth-century addition designed by Darling & Pearson of Toronto, the Lawn became a summer house and has now been converted to apartments. The house is difficult to visualize in its original elegant simplicity, but the finely pilastered east-facing door on the southern wing is a telling vestige.

24 272 King Street East, ca. 1840
The stylized bargeboard, drops, and finials are mostly original, although the house, called the Maples, has recently been covered with siding. Built by Mayor David Campbell, who gave his name to nearby Campbellford.

At the height of "Newport North," American-built mansions lined the fashionable end of King Street from the downtown to Coverdale Road. Most are now

26 *420 King Street East*

28 *308 Henry Street*

demolished, and this stretch is largely given over to motels and auto centres. But Sidbrook, Strathmore, and Midfield, three mansions where Pittsburgh steel magnates summered in neighbourly splendour, are still worth a look. They are about ten minutes' walk from King and D'Arcy Streets, or they can be skipped at this point and seen by car after the walk.

25 411 King Street East, 1857,
  remodelled 1902
Sidbrook was originally designed by Kivas Tully as a two-storey flat-roofed house topped by a balustrade. Remodelled first in the 1860s and then more drastically at the turn of the century by its new owner, William Abbott, the house had its roof raised while a third storey was added. Abbott was a former associate of Andrew Carnegie, and he redid the house in the style then fashionable with rich Americans, Beaux Arts Classical. Beaux Arts often teetered on the edge of pomposity, but Sidbrook today is not so much pompous as perfunctory. Its two-storey portico is its only easily visible interest, and even that is marred by a large private hospital sign.

26 420 King Street East, ca. 1870s,
  remodelled 1904
A rather cool beauty, but a beauty nonetheless, Strathmore is now part of a youth correctional centre. Charles Donnelly of

Pittsburgh commissioned Power and Son architects to build around an existing house when he bought it in 1904, and they created an asymmmetrical Beaux Arts mansion. The two-storey entrance portico with massive pediment and curved balcony is impressive, but hardly endearing. (Archival pictures show that the Donnellys warmed it up with striped awnings, rattan furniture, and huge potted plants.) By contrast, the square porch on the west façade and the rounded one to the east are genuinely inviting.

27 427 King Street East, 1877,
  enlarged 1905
Soft brick covered by stucco, this rambling, pleasant mansion doesn't have the knock-'em-dead pretensions of Sidbrook and Strathmore. Its rather indeterminate style was called French or Italianate villa, and it includes a Palladian window on the west façade, a relatively self-effacing west-facing main door, and a classical veranda facing the lake. The companionable cluster of three broad chimneys at the centre of the roof underscores the idea of hearth and home. When Roderick Pringle, a prominent Conservative and crony of Sir John A. Macdonald, built it, the property extended to the lake. When owned and enlarged by a Pittsburgh steel baron, George Howe, it was called Midfield.

29 *332 Henry Street*

32 *356 Walton Street*

Retrace your steps along King Street and turn right at Henry Street.

28 308 Henry Street, ca. 1855
The French doors on either side of the front door hark back to the Regency desire to be close to nature – in this case, a fine treed lot. The paning in the sidelights and transom is also a Regency design, but after that the ground-hugging Regency ideal is forgotten and the house, built by the Reverend Walton Beck, grows to a rather forbidding two and a half stories. The three gables were added in the 1870s.

29 332 Henry Street, 1859
A familiar Cobourg shape, this two-storey Loyalist cube with an Ontario peak tails off in a utility wing at the back that includes a winter kitchen, a summer kitchen, and a scullery. It was built by a merchant named Andrew Hewson and is owned today by his great-grandson and his wife; they are responsible for its careful restoration.

30 348 Henry Street, 1857–58
The Greek Revival door of this stucco-covered frame house bespeaks formality, but the bargeboard is downright folkloric.

31 349 Henry Street, 1864, 1897
A split personality. From the front, this outgoing house sports the requisite Queen Anne trappings: complicated massing, a busy roofline, balconies, a deep wraparound veranda, and fish-scale shingles in the large front gable. The front's facelift was the doing of Sarah Bothwell in 1897. The rear of the house, best seen through the opening in the hedge on your way down James Street to Walton Street or from the next house (356 Walton), is a very different story. The familiar Ontario peak and plain-spoken veranda are all that remain of the original 1864 farmhouse.

32 356 Walton Street, late 1880s
Nathaniel Burwash, the chancellor of Victoria University, built this welcoming clapboard house shortly before the college moved to Toronto. The potpourri of Queen Anne effects includes the enclosed balcony with half-timbering in the gable, the restrained bargeboard on the straight-topped side gable, and the graceful swooping roof over the "classical" veranda.

33 262 Walton Street, 1856
Regency cottages were ideally planned for a spectacular site, and builders de-emphasized the main door and constructed as many French doors as possible to open out onto the veranda. Spectacular sites were rare in Cobourg, and the original owners of this house made do with an extensive garden to the south, now gone. The veranda with its simple posts, three shuttered French doors, and recessed main door manages to conjure up a good deal of the informal Regency spirit. Locally known

37 *Coach house, 136 King Street East*　　38 *130 King Street East*

as the Vincent Cottage, after a colonel from New Orleans who summered here around the turn of the century.

34 Coach house of 236 Walton Street,
late nineteenth century

One of the humbler manifestations of what the architectural theorist Augustus Pugin called "Pointed or Christian Architecture," less reverently called Gothic Revival. This board-and-batten coach house has three pointed Gothic windows and a coordinating door. Each window had twelve small panes of glass separated by glazing bars.

35 170 King Street East, 1840s

The original central part of the house, with its hip-roof and symmetrical three-bay plan, embodies the Georgian virtues of simplicity, balance, and dignity. Loyalist builders typically aggrandized the front door with sidelights and fan-shaped transoms; the Georgian style, as here, kept it unadorned and in harmony with the windows.

36 144 King Street East, ca. 1905

A decorous restatement of classical values with a characteristic Cobourg window under the second-floor Ontario peak. Note the two stout chimneys set well in from the edge, and the unusually paned windows: twelve-over-two on the first floor, eight-over-two on the second.

37 136 King Street East, 1885

The stucco cottage, built to rent to summering Americans, is pleasing and unremarkable, but the board-and-batten coach house at the rear is a delight. Both exemplify the waning days of the bargeboard, which fancified many a mid-century Ontario house. The bargeboard on the house's main gable is solid (as opposed to lacy) and functional, with a design so reticent as to go unnoticed. That on the coach house confines its flourish to the apex of the peak, above what is called the collar-tie.

38 130 King Street East, 1875–76,
altered 1923

This stylish Georgian revival is a rarity in Cobourg, for its copper roof as well as for the front door's boldly panelled surround and the scrolled window above the porch. Forsey, Page & Steele did the 1923 make-over; from 1907 to 1921, when owned by Edward Osler, a cousin of Sir William, it was called Relso (Osler backwards) Villa.

College Street, which culminates in Victoria College, is one of Cobourg's most pleasant avenues and an anthology of housing styles from the mid-nineteenth century to the 1920s.

39 284 College Street, ca. 1850

First came a four-room cottage built by William York, a respected black merchant.

41 *354 College Street*

42 *Victoria College,*
100 University Avenue East

Whether the massive classical portico was original or dates from the 1870s is unknown; certainly the striated brick and cobblestones came from a 1920s make-over.

40 306 College Street, 1857

The merchant Lazarus Payne's house was a stolid rectangle built in stretcher bond. The fantasy is in the details: a dividing line of yellow brick decorated with crosses on the side and inverted pyramids on the front, and the Gothic doorway with an ogee-shaped transom.

41 354 College Street, ca. 1840

Take away the two bracketed bays, and this is the quintessential Ontario cottage, built for people who saw little need to light their bedrooms. With the bays, which were probably added in the 1860s, the charm is irresistible. The downward diagonal lines of the peak, the roofs of the bays, and the shed roof over the door plant the little structure firmly on its site, while the graceful bays assert that there is more to life than thrift and function. Built by Henry Hough, the founder of the liberal *Cobourg-World* newspaper.

42 Victoria College, 100 University Avenue East, 1836

Canadian Methodists had strong American connections, and Victoria's Methodist founders sent to Cazenovia College in New York State asking for its "plans and specifications." Cazenovia was built in the Greek Revival style fashionable for colleges in the United States in the 1830s; with that as an inspiration, Edward Crane, Victoria's architect and builder, designed a movingly pure building with a three-storey Doric portico and two flanking pediments, an elongated cupola, and a solitary line of dentils for decoration. Although an advertisement in the *Cobourg Star* called for sealed tenders for 300,000 bricks in 1831, the building's formidable cost ($40,000) meant that it was not completed until five years later. Crane engaged local craftsmen to outfit each of twenty student studies with a French bedstead, two chairs, and a table, all in pine. (Only mahogany was good enough for the principal's study, which also included a sideboard, sofa, and candle stand.) Since Victoria College moved to Toronto in 1892, the building has served as an asylum, a hospital, and a training centre.

43 411 John Street, 1857

William Hitchins made a small fortune selling candles and groceries, and built this smart Regency cottage. The house's composition, with French doors flanking a similar-sized main door and dormer windows balanced on a hip-roof, is harmonious but perhaps a touch too calculated. The florid wrought-and-cast-iron fence, transplanted in the 1920s from a Kentucky plantation, is a welcome addition.

44 *18 Spencer Street East*

45 *420 Division Street*

44 18 Spencer Street East, 1827

The Poplars is not only Cobourg's oldest house, but one of Ontario's most thoroughgoing exercises in the Regency style. When John Spencer, Northumberland County's first sheriff, built the house, it was north of the infant village; Regency villas were ideally built out of town with a view. The relatively simple, horizontal house has recently been restored; shorn of the shutters and vines seen in an archival photograph, it looks neat but somewhat bereft. The bowed bays are rare in Upper Canada, but very characteristic of the Regency style.

45 420 Division Street, 1835

Cobourg tradition says that Ebenezer Perry, a Loyalist cousin to Commodore Oliver Perry, the American naval hero of the War of 1812, settled in the tiny village of Hamilton, soon to be renamed Cobourg, and built this Regency house. The less romantic truth seems to be that Perry's son George built a one-storey, five-bay house with a magnificent pillared doorway. (Two side wings and a second storey were added later in the nineteenth century.) The veranda – with its six Doric columns, twelve-over-twelve-paned windows with stone voussoirs, and the superb doorway – remains one of Cobourg's most beautiful "rooms." Woodlawn, as the house was called, is now a restaurant and inn.

This ends the main Cobourg tour. For keen walkers, an additional shorter walk in the west end of town is recommended.

46 212 King Street West, 1840s

A four-room Ontario cottage with the locally familiar deep eaves; its elliptical fanlight looks rather like an afterthought above the moulded architrave. A relatively recent local tradition connects this house with Charles von Koerber, the organist at St. Peter's Church and the father of Leila von Koerber, who became the silent movie star Marie Dressler. Von Koerber is said to have rented this house, where his daughter was born in 1868. The Dressler-in-Cobourg legend (to which Dressler herself contributed) includes appearances in Victoria Hall in her father's *tableaux vivants* and departure at the age of fourteen to join a light opera troupe. In fact, there are a number of candidates for the house where Dressler was born, and she left Cobourg at the age of three months. This house is now the Chamber of Commerce and a small museum of Dressler memorabilia.

47 250 Mathew Street, ca. 1835

Mathew Williams, for whom this street is named, was a carpenter and landowner who built himself a "house with a hat," as this local specialty was called. Its exaggerated eaves project at least three feet.

48 *258 Mathew Street*

51 *326 King Street West*

48 258 Mathew Street, ca. 1840

This clapboard house looks very American, mostly because of its saltbox shape with a short front roof and a long back one, best seen from the north side. Its stylish eared door and window trim, the deep returning eaves, and the cornerboards that end in simplified capitals derive from the Greek Revival style, also a favourite with Americans.

King Street West between Ontario Street and Forth Street has a variety of houses from the 1840s and '50s.

49 317 King Street West, 1851

A one-and-a-half-storey stucco cottage with two sorts of bargeboard and exclamatory finials. The many-paned transom and sidelights around the main door are not original but handsome. Note the longish windows on either side of the door, with their Regency paning (half-panes, surrounding two full panes).

50 323 King Street West, 1847

A more citified version of 317 King. Its urbanity is partly due to the Flemish-bond brick with so-called soldier lintels standing smartly at attention over doors and windows. It's also that it takes its Regency model a little more seriously, with proper French doors, Regency paning throughout, and a relatively unusual front door with the sidelights reaching up and framing the transom.

51 326 King Street West, ca. 1870s

Not a house to make the heart sing, but a solid, successful amalgamation of Italianate and vernacular elements. The rectangular shape, wide eaves, and generous round-headed windows derive from the Italianate style that became popular in mid-century. Note the swooping bell-cast roof on the veranda; the squared pillars and brackets succeeded the elaborate veranda decoration called treillage that had been fashionable since the 1830s.

Retrace your steps to Ontario Street and head south.

52 184 Ontario Street, ca. 1940

Two brick houses face each other across Ontario Street, one dating from the mid-nineteenth century, the other a twentieth-century revival style. The latter, number 184, gives the game away almost immediately with the darkish brown of its bricks, a popular colour in the first half of this century. The very thick surround on the fanlight is another twentieth-century revival touch. The Georgian or Loyalist elements – the oculus or round window on the third floor, the petal-shaped dividers in the fanlight, the quoins and string courses, the arrangement of openings – are credible albeit used freely.

57 *121 Bagot Street*

58 *106 Bagot Street*

53 181 Ontario Street, 1844,
   addition ca. 1874

The Burnets were a family of builders who were responsible for Victoria Hall's construction; they built four houses for themselves on Ontario Street, of which this one and number 163 survive. Note the orange nineteenth-century bricks on this house, in contrast to number 184. The 1874 addition included the graceful second-floor window under the peak, its four slim lights topped with an ellipse.

54 163 Ontario Street, 1844

This house, built by Francis Burnet Jr., requires a bit of imagination. Erase the unwieldy dormer and the additions to the rear on the north side, and the familiar heavy-lidded cottage emerges. The storm porch, conveniently dated 1862 above the door, is a mid-Victorian piece of confectionery.

55 110 Ontario Street, ca. 1871,
   remodelled ca. 1900

Corinthian columns, dentilled bays, and a deep bracketed cornice notwithstanding, this is still a puffed-up Ontario cottage with a central peak. The first owners were William Riddell, a justice of the Supreme Court of Ontario, and his wife, Anna Crossen, of the Crossen Car Works family. Later owners named it Illahee, and the classical accessories were added by a third owner, Madame Soria. The board-and-batten coach house and cottage to the north of the mansion have a similar shape but more appeal; they are older than the house.

56 132 Ontario Street, 1862

Cobourg has plenty of two-storey, three-bay houses with a central peak, and they often look forbidding. This one avoids that fate with three simple variations: the projecting central bay, the rounded tracery in the long window in the peak, and a portico that echoes the peak and is trimmed with eyelet fretwork. (The portico and the side wing came later.)

57 121 Bagot Street, ca. 1855

Part of the charm of this vernacular style lies in its familiarity. There are hundreds of unassuming houses very like it all across Ontario, too unimportant and out of the way to ruin by renovation. This modest example in painted brick was housing a family of ten by the mid-1880s. The rectangles in the "Chinese" veranda railing, the spools in the treillage, even the mass-produced diamond-patterned trellis at the basement level make a particularly pleasing composition. Note the seven-paned Gothic window in the central peak, and a typical late-century bargeboard so discreet it has almost refined itself out of existence.

58 106 Bagot Street, 1850s

One of Cobourg's finest Greek Revival

Barracks, 128 Durham Street

Fire Hall, 213 Second Street

houses. The pilastered and recessed door may look in need of a larger house, but its massiveness was a calculated part of the Greek Revival style. The wing to the south is a later addition.

59 138 Bagot Street, 1875
P.J. Lightburne's villa was assessed at $3,500 when he built it. Its chief ornament is the veranda-cum-balcony; the anonymous builder combined the Gothic trefoil balcony railing, the classical dentils in the frieze below it, and the bold treillage into a deft, idiosyncratic whole.

60 166 Sydenham Street, ca. 1875
An unpretentious example of Cobourg's favourite marriage of the classic and romantic. The classic is the door with pilasters and deep frieze; the romantic is the Gothic window crammed into the peak trimmed with undulating bargeboard.

61 Lakehurst, 128 Durham Street, 1832
Lakehurst began life as a Loyalist house with a fine fan transom doorway. Behind the cumbersome balconies and fire escape, it's still there, along with a graceful veranda added in the 1870s.

62 128 Durham Street (behind Lakehurst), 1812 or earlier
The low rubblestone building at the north end of the property, a barracks during the

War of 1812, is probably Cobourg's oldest surviving structure.

Return to the Victoria Hall complex along Orr, Hibernia, and Albert Streets, looking out for Cobourg's characteristic neoclassical doorways on early houses, some now covered with siding.

63 205 Third Street, ca. 1845, second floor and south wing added ca. 1870
This solid, hip-roofed building was built as a private house, and probably acquired its double-decker veranda when it became a hotel.

64 Market Building, Albert and Third Streets, ca. 1856–60
Kivas Tully's plans for a market building specified a brick building 15 feet tall, 60 by 35 feet, "with ten Butchers' stalls, with cellars underneath 8 feet in height and a covered walk 10 feet wide all around." The result is a most attractive combination of the domestic (it resembles the local wide-eaved cottage) and the commercial (the twelve-over-eight windows are original).

65 Fire Hall, 213 Second Street, ca. 1882–83
Cobourg's stylish Second Empire fire station is now in use as a community theatre.

St. George's Anglican Church

Goderich

"Most Peculiar and Admirable"

Much about Goderich is improbable. It is a town at the edge of nowhere founded by a Scottish novelist and a doctor-adventurer as part of a complicated scheme to recompense British North Americans who had suffered losses in the War of 1812. Perched on a bluff overlooking Lake Huron, it was planned around a rational, urbane octagon more suited to eighteenth-century Edinburgh than to a wilderness settlement. Days and days over bone-shaking corduroy roads from Toronto and London, it attracted an extraordinary number of educated settlers as well as more than its share of intrigue.

Its beginnings were shaped by two larger-than-life figures. The first was John Galt, a gangling Ayrshire-born novelist who in 1824 conceived a land and colonization enterprise that would compensate Canadians for their war losses, resettle interested Britons, and make some money for its shareholders. Called the Canada Company, it delivered on the second and third goals but not the first. It also became closely associated with Ontario's Tory elite, the Family Compact, and frustrated uncounted settlers with rosy-coloured advertising and unfulfilled promises. But while hopes still ran high, the company acquired the Huron Tract, a million-acre triangle in western Ontario with what would become Goderich at its northwestern edge. Galt served as the Canadian supervisor, and his collaborator Dr. William "Tiger" Dunlop probably bestowed the grand sylvan title "Warden of the Woods and Forests" on himself.

A shambling redheaded exhibitionist whose exploits have a Paul Bunyanesque quality, Dunlop had many talents. One was the ability to produce a celebratory bottle in the unlikeliest circumstances. On June 29, 1827, in a log cabin overlooking Lake Huron that he called the Castle, he and Galt toasted the newborn town of Goderich with a near-miraculous bottle of champagne. With a party of seven, the Warden of the Woods and Forests had hacked and surveyed his way through the Huron Tract, looking for a likely harbour. Congratulating themselves on the paradisical fertility of the land and the fish-choked waters, Galt and Dunlop renamed the River Red the Maitland in honour of the lieutenant-governor and called the harbour settlement Goderich, for the colonial secretary. (It was a name the Canada Company had intended for Guelph, but Galt had insisted on his own choice.)

The two founding fathers' public life in Goderich was remarkably brief. Galt was fired by the company in 1829 and returned to Britain; Dunlop resigned from the company in a dispute with the commissioner in 1838, and constituted a kind of government in exile until his death ten years later. The relative brevity of their involvement has increased their legendary status; their indisputable achievement was to make Goderich second only to Guelph in the company's estimation.

Other Canada Company towns, Stratford for example, complained bitterly about the lack of roads and services; Goderich had little to complain of. Roads were planned around Goderich, the company offices were located there, advertisements and optimistic accounts of pioneer life that emphasized the town's prestige drew an unusually high number of affluent settlers to Goderich and the vicinity. In the 1830s the average settler in the area was worth five to six times as much as settlers in the neighbouring townships.

Some of the society that these genteel types created had an unreal quality: the son of one of them, a scholar named John Haldane, complained, "Our fathers sacrificed their children to satisfy their whim to farm." The West Street house of Thomas Mercer Jones, the Canada Company commissioner, and his wife, the daughter of Bishop Strachan and significantly nicknamed "the Ranee," became a tiny court, all the more rigid because it existed in a stump-filled, dusty village.

As it turned out, the company's choice of its fair-haired child was misguided. Goderich was chosen because the directors imagined that water transport was primary; they did not realize that Goderich's harbour persistently silted up and that the best way around the Huron Tract was by land. It took the company more than twenty years to understand that Goderich was destined to remain remote: as the historian Hugh Johnston put it, "the end of a line rather than the beginning." Once they realized that, beginning around mid-century, support was gradually but inexorably withdrawn. In the stone-cold but inarguable words of Jones's co-commissioner Frederick Widder, the company had created "a fictitious community which fell off when the Company ceased spending money."

Which is not as negative as it first sounds. When the fictitious image fell off, a real town emerged. Less glamorous, less "important," Goderich remained the market town for a prosperous agricultural region. Like scores of other small

Ontario centres, it went on to have its share of booms and recessions, some purely local, others connected to the larger economy. The half-pay officers and literati – people like the Haldanes and Lizarses, "who should never have tried farming," in the tart words of the local history *Memories of Goderich* – either left or, more often, learned how to survive in Huron County.

Goderich's famous octagon-in-the-square is a case in point. It was conceived when the town was bound for glory and now suffers the slings and arrows of everyday commerce. The world is divided between those who, like the restoration architect Peter John Stokes, consider it "Ontario's grandest square," and those who find it awkward and confusing. In *A Century of Goderich*, Victor Lauriston tells the story of a traveller who set out from the Hotel Bedford on the Square and walked a long time before he realized he was going over and over the same ground. He complained, "It's a lang street, an' I ne'er kenned a toon wi' sae mony Charley Nairns in it." (Charley Nairn ran a grocery shop on the Square.)

Although no one is quite sure who designed the eight streets that radiate out from a central marketplace and are then enclosed in a square, it was clearly part and parcel of Goderich's grandiose beginnings. John Galt favoured such a plan, although other accounts credit Tiger Dunlop. Many Europeans had admired the Roman architect Vitruvius's radial plans since *De Architectura* became fashionable in the Renaissance, and North America offered the new towns on which they could be tried. Even in the New World, though, such designs were proposed but few were realized: only Galt's Goderich and Pierre L'Enfant's Washington, D.C., are thoroughgoing exercises in radial planning.

And in Goderich, the rational European model was frustrated by the vagaries of North American individualism. The Square began to be built up around 1840, when most businesses were still located around the harbour. The building of the Court House in the centre of the octagon, begun in the mid-'50s, encouraged businesses to make the trek uphill, but construction was sporadic and piecemeal. As the restoration architect Nicholas Hill conceded in the 1970s in a conservation proposal for the Square, the "bold and magnificent architectural composition" required by the radial plan never happened. Its best days were the 1880s and '90s, when it was ringed with more or less homogeneous buildings, but then and now the Square has faithfully mirrored the real world of business, where buildings rose, fell, and not infrequently burned down according to their luck with commerce and nature.

By the 1970s, not even the business community could defend the Square's mishmash of building styles, signage, colours, and materials as healthy signs of free enterprise. (The presence of two rival malls siphoning business from the downtown core helped to focus their aesthetic objections.) After several energetic campaigns to restore and unify the Square, led by Goderich's well-informed conservationists, the situation has improved. For purists, the Square today is like the curate's egg: excellent in parts, but with remaining eyesores. For others, occasional modern storefronts and clashing signage simply mean that Goderich is a living country town, neither a contrived theme park nor part of the Canada Company's master plan.

Goderich's most go-ahead decade, as the Victorians would have put it, was the 1860s. It began two years prematurely, on June 28, 1858, when the first train of the Buffalo and Lake Huron Railway arrived in town. The welcoming party in the Square, with champagne, evergreen triumphal arches, and a brand-new Court House to boot, was so splendid that the *Illustrated London News* published an engraving.

The railway was long awaited and planned for, but the major source of prosperity in the 1860s was surprising and serendipitous. In 1866, while drilling for oil, Samuel Platt and Peter MacEwan struck the first salt well discovered in North America. Within a few years, there were a dozen salt wells around the harbour and the Maitland valley, speculators were buying up likely land, vacancies were a thing of the past, and cooperages and other ancillary businesses flourished. Roads were graded and gravelled for the sake of the well-owners; the town acquired its first drain.

The amenities and improvements that came with the salt boom were overdue, perhaps because Goderich was still outgrowing the notion that the Canada Company would provide. Forty years after its founding, the town had no sidewalks, and wandering cows, pigs, and horses were a constant nuisance, even a danger at night. The Court House Park, surrounding the elegant Palladian Court House, served as a cow pasture.

As late as 1879, Belden's *Historical Atlas of Huron County* found Goderich distinctly lacking in enterprise. Noting that the streets and buildings were still lit with coal oil, long after gas had become current, and that thirty years after incorporation there was no town hall or "any public hall worth the name," Belden sighed that the locals were "a decidedly conservative class of people." Even the salt mines now looked disappointing.

The mines' failure could not be laid entirely at the townspeople's feet. As the local forests were depleted, the wood needed to heat the evaporator pans grew prohibitively costly. The Americans began producing their own salt and imposed a protective tariff. The boom ended as quickly as it had begun, in 1872. One by one the wells closed, all but two. Thirty years after the boom's unexpected beginning, the river flats were littered with derelict wells.

The picture was not all bleak, even during the recession that gripped most of North America during the 1870s and '80s. The Dominion government declared Goderich a "harbour of refuge" and invested generously in its improvement. Important local industries, such as Ogilvie Milling Company and the Goderich Organ Company, flourished. Even the "decidedly conservative" Goderichians had had enough of some inconveniences: they replaced the unreliable town bell-ringer with a clock on the Court House, and hired a water wagon to hose down the dusty streets.

Like so many lakeside towns, Goderich benefitted from the late-century North American craze for long summers at resort hotels. The first man to build a resort in the area, the original Point Farm Hotel in Colborne Township, was significantly nicknamed "Crazy" Davis by the locals. Its successor, the second Point Farm Hotel, slept 200 and was an international success for thirty years, inspiring imitators, royal visitors, and a new sense of Goderich as a summer resort. A.M. Polley, the owner of a Goderich livery, ran a coach between the hotel and the town, which he described as "swarming with living freight who were waving stars and stripes."

With Americans proclaiming the town as "the principal watering-place of Western Ontario," even Tiger Dunlop's log Castle in Harbour Park was reportedly sacrificed around 1879 to make way for more hotel rooms in what is now the Park House. In 1889, citing a town plan "most peculiar and admirable," vistas that appealed to the artistic eye, and summer breezes "that come over the broad breast of the blue Lake Huron [as] the messengers of health," *Canada: A Memorial Volume* claimed, "No place offers a more attractive claim for summer rest and healthful sojourn than this beautiful town."

Today smaller Lake Huron towns such as Grand Bend, Bayfield, and Kincardine look more purely like summer places than Goderich does, although it claims its share of the summer revenues. With a population of about 7,500, it is by far the biggest centre in Huron County, with the county's two major industries, the Champion Road Grader plant and Sifto Salt Mine, one of the largest salt mines in North America. Visually, there are very few vestiges of the "fictitious community" that began it all. The Square, the Gaol, the number of late-blooming Georgian houses made of soft local brick and prefaced by shapely iron fences hint that this is not your average country town. But they are as firmly woven into the everyday life of Goderich as its celebrated sunsets, its huge pipe organ of a grain elevator, and the endless aquamarine of Lake Huron.

16 16 Wellington Street South

Lighthouse

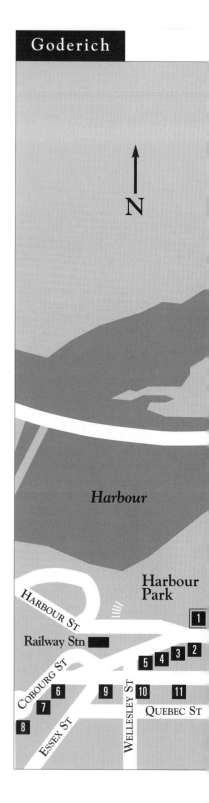

N

Harbour

Harbour Park

HARBOUR ST

Railway Stn

1

5 4 3 2

COBOURG ST

6 9 10 11

7

WELLESLEY ST

QUEBEC ST

8

ESSEX ST

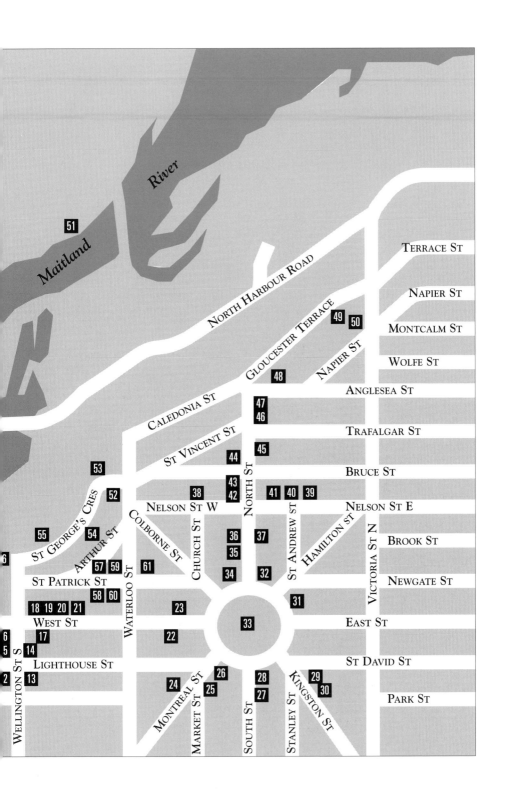

CPR Station

2 169 West Street

The ideal way to walk Goderich is to begin where the first settlers did, down at the still busy harbour and river flats. The harbour was Goderich's *raison d'être*, and the first houses, tavern, store, and tannery were located here. With the spectacular Goderich Elevators Ltd. to your left and the jolly Queen Anne CPR train station to your right (in use from 1907 to 1955), you can climb Harbour Street to West Street or take the wooden steps to your left to Harbour Park. The park was the location of Tiger Dunlop's Castle, close to the cairn that commemorates the founding of Goderich. Bear left as you pass under the Harbour Park portal.

1 The Park House, 168 West Street, ca. 1839

What is now a flat-roofed stucco hotel was one of Goderich's first buildings above the bluffs and the glittering centre of its social and administrative life. Built for the Canada Company commissioner Thomas Mercer Jones and his bride, Elizabeth Mary Strachan (the daughter of the ubiquitous Bishop Strachan), by the company engineer, John Longworth, it began life as a pine building whose third storey had dormer windows in a sharply inclined roof. The twenty-one wagons that transported the couple's luxury goods over corduroy roads from Toronto, the garden where grapes, melons, peaches, and apricots grew, the standoffish mistress who reversed the

staircase so that the house faced onto the garden and rarely left her little palace are all the stuff of local legend. Jones used the building as home and office until 1855, when the Canada Company fired him; he managed the Bank of Upper Canada here for a few years, and the building then became a hotel. The symmetrical proportions and original windows remain; the flat roof and stucco covering are the results of a 1945 fire.

2 169 West Street, early 1840s

This gaunt survivor is another of the first substantial houses built above the harbour. Probably inspired by an American pattern book, the façade of this house is Goderich's most wholehearted example of the Greek Revival style. The asymmetrically placed, massive door, with its paired Doric columns topped by an elaborate entablature and bordered by pilasters, illustrates both the gaucheness and the odd impressiveness of this branch of the Greek Revival family. The flushboard front and the original all-white colour were designed to concentrate the eye on the doorcase and the heavily dentilled pediment; with the original veranda peeled off, they are even more prominent than the builder intended. The house was built by D.B.O. Ford soon after he bought the land in 1839; it became a bakery in the 1850s and is still known locally as Hands' Bakery.

 3 *181 West Street*　　　**5** *5 Cobourg Street*

3 181 West Street, 1880s

The first of two companionable houses set back on deep lawns, 181 West Street is the busier. The elaborate treillage on the portico can be seen on other late-century Goderich houses and probably was made at Buchanan's Mill, a local planing shop.

4 1 Cobourg Street, 1880s

Built in the same decade as its next-door neighbour, this house eschews daintiness for the masculine power of its geometric bargeboard, echoed in the unusual shape of the second-floor windows.

5 5 Cobourg Street, 1858

Built by the Bank of Upper Canada to house its business as well as its staff, this Georgian/Regency amalgam is a model of relaxed composure. The composure derives from the Georgian symmetry, the brick string course that tactfully bisects the stories, the characteristic chimneys close to the roof edge; the relaxation comes from the gently hipped roof and the tweedy early brick. (The original house, without the modern side wings, had a veranda.) The bank manager who lived and worked here was John McDonald, the Scottish-born engineer who planned Guelph and Goderich and helped carve the Huron Road (Highway 8) and Highway 4. The nubbled cast-iron contraption in front of the house is a carriage step.

6 257 Cobourg Street, 1922

Early in the nineteenth century, British officers stationed in hot countries brought back the idea of a simple, low house with deep verandas. The Regency cottage, as it was called, found favour even in the Empire's colder climes, but it was ideally suited to views and open-air living. Looking appropriately like a beach hat on poles, this is a stripped-down twentieth-century Regency cottage perfectly at home overlooking Lake Huron.

7 263 Cobourg Street, ca. 1860

Looking very urban on this lakeside strip, this broad-eaved Georgian was built for a Lake Huron shipping agent named William Seymour with locally fired salmon-and-greyish brick. The veranda is a newish replica of a nineteenth-century version; the six-over-six windows are original.

Go around the turning circle, passing the stocky 1847 lighthouse with its unusual square shape. The light from its mercury vapour bulb is reflected in a rotating aluminum sheet.

8 281 Cobourg Street, 1911–19

Another descendant of the Regency cottage, called Snug Harbour. This one is embellished with an eyebrow dormer and lattice-work treillage on its two-sided veranda.

Go back up Cobourg Street and along Lighthouse Street to the next block.

11 *165 Lighthouse Street*

12 *34 Wellington Street South*

9 37 Essex Street, ca. 1857

A clapboarded neoclassical house whose high narrow proportions are emphasized by the shorter second-floor windows and the nearly windowless side walls. The civil engineer Sir Casimir Gzowski lived here while superintending the building of Goderich's first railway line.

10 203 Lighthouse Street, ca. 1845

One of Goderich's most glamorous forefathers, William Bennett Rich was a Grenadier Guard who fought at Waterloo under Wellington and then found civilian life in London beyond his means. He emigrated to Goderich in 1833 and mastered pioneer life the hard way. Finding his land "all trees and close underwood," he built five houses of wood so green "they fell to pieces." Finally he built this square brick residence he called Wellesley House, probably a salute to the Duke of Wellington's family name. The front door, on Wellesley Street, is now obscured by a storm porch, but even in its altered state the house breathes a leisured, gentlemanly air: the French windows, the muted brick, the stone sills and base course, the fine garden that extends to Quebec Street were all marks of Old Country quality. Rich, who gradually acclimated himself to the New World, was locally famous as the father of seven beauteous daughters, several of whom married other prominent men.

11 165 Lighthouse Street, 1845

Believed to be the oldest red-brick house in Goderich, this was built by John Lancaster, a hotelkeeper who decamped for the Gold Rush in 1849. Its position close to the street, the parapet walls, the sawn-stone string course, and the stone window treatments give it a formal, early-nineteenth-century aspect unusual in Goderich. The Huron Rifles were billeted here during the Fenian Raids.

12 34 Wellington Street South, 1870s

Goderich has several houses in which wood, usually pine, imitates ashlar or squared stone. This one, an Ontario cottage putting on airs in the nicest possible way, emphasizes its deep eaves with plainish brackets and a wide cornice (the dormer is a Johnny-come-lately). The heavy window trim is original, as is the soft grey-and-white colour scheme.

13 35 Wellington Street South,
    ca. 1897

A typically eclectic turn-of-the-century side-plan house. Its most attractive feature is the deep, curving cornice, with a special Eastlake flourish in the way the spooled, rickrack-edged brackets meet in the centre of the bays to form angled supports for the cornice. The side garden, planted to a Victorian design, has an ironwork fence resurrected from several local buildings. Built for an Orkney immigrant named

15 *20 Wellington Street South*

16 *16 Wellington Street South*

William Wallace, it is still inhabited by Wallaces.

14 19 Wellington Street South, 1886
Like Stephen Leacock's knight, this idiosyncratic house looks as if it might just ride off in all directions. Below the steeply pitched roof, three different protrusions – a polygonal porch, a truncated tower, and a gabled bay – achieve an odd but likeable harmony. The strangely set chimney and the lead screen windows add to the fanciful mood; things get less playful and more rectangular at the sides and back. Built for a lawyer named Ira Lewis.

15 20 Wellington Street South, 1880
Nothing but the best for Donald Strachan, who owned two stores on the Square and did a brisk business in ship supplies. (Born in Scotland, he had arrived in Goderich at age sixteen, to be head clerk of a grocery.) He engaged one of Goderich's master builders, Adam MacVicar, imported 40,000 bricks by schooner, and ordered up a house in the luxurious Second Empire style. The Goderich *Signal* pronounced the result "one of the most elegant and substantial in our town," and it was, from the iron cresting on the bombé tower down to the leafy brackets and fretted-wood window surrounds. Far too fastidious to sprawl, Strachan's tall house leaves room for a generous swath of garden on its corner lot.

16 16 Wellington Street South, 1873
Stripped of its several verandas, this buff-brick house looks more daunting than its builder intended. The triangular dormers that mimic the gables, the narrow windows whose length is emphasized by the cast-stone surrounds, the twin sets of no-nonsense brackets add up to something picturesque, but perhaps also a touch forbidding. Built for Archibald Dickson, an early postmaster.

17 117 West Street, 1883
The rather poignant grey stucco skin of this modest L-shaped house makes it easy to see quite a lot of simplified style: the grave classical doorcase complete with triglyphs above and pilasters to the side, the Gothic peaks and rounded windows, and the robust Eastlake porch supports.

18 122 West Street, ca. 1840
Behind the aluminum siding (and the porch, which was probably built after the house) is a countrified pine Georgian built for Goderich's first mayor, a druggist named Benjamin Parsons who triumphed over Tory forces in 1850. Parsons was also Goderich's sole agent for Dr. Moffat's Vegetable Life Pills and Phoenix Bitters, both cures for an astonishing range of complaints; early historians suspected Parsons was taking both medications and that they were the source of his extraordinary calm during the heated mayoral struggles.

19 *116 West Street*

22 Town Hall, 57 West Street

19 116 West Street, ca. 1857
Goderich builders were partial to vernacular versions of the Georgian, but the Honourable Gillespie Moffat's house owes more to the style's finer-featured descendant, called Loyalist in Canada. Symmetrical and restrained like the Georgian model, the Loyalist house has a more vertical emphasis and makes much of its front door. In this case, the recessed door is topped with the typical Loyalist fan-shaped transom, then encased in pilasters and an elegant broken pediment.

20 110 West Street, 1893,
21 106 West Street, 1892–93
Two modest, pleasing houses that combine a very vernacular Greek Revival (the front-facing gable, door at the side, and returning eaves) with the picturesque (the wavy bargeboard and modified Gothic second-floor window). Note the flushboard construction on number 110, which is closer to its original state.

22 Town Hall, 57 West Street, 1890
For about $20,000, Goderich got itself a post office and customs house (since 1961 the town hall) and a wonderfully absorbing building. It was designed by Thomas Fuller, the architect (with Chilion Jones) of the original Centre Block of Parliament, later the Dominion Architect, and definitely a man who knew his way around Guelph stone. Both compact and monumental, the

building melds Romanesque arches, a deep hip-roof, a romantic gable, and a clutch of stone embellishments in a typical display of *fin-de-siècle* eclecticism. What isn't typical, especially in an era where picturesque too often spelled over-the-top, is the taste with which all the details are firmly knitted into the larger picture. Note especially the remarkably deep-set windows, the way the lines of the hip-roof are repeated in the flaring string course, the cunning row of carved stone circles underneath the voussoirs in the rounded windows, and the rounded bars of stone underneath the corbels and in the central gable.

23 44–48 West Street, 1863
The Bank of Upper Canada and its manager moved into this Georgian box a mere three years before the bank went bankrupt in 1866. The expensive Flemish-bond brick at the front and the common bond at the side suggested a bankerly balance of respectability and thrift. The boxed-in side entrance and the large rounded window look like alterations from the end of the century, when the Bank of Montreal did business here.

Enter Court House Square from West Street, and turn right. The next dozen buildings are on a counter-clockwise circuit of the Square and its near vicinity.

24 *Public Library, 52 Montreal Street*

27 *Polley's Livery, 35 South Street*

24 Public Library, 52 Montreal Street, 1903–04

Andrew Carnegie made his standard offer to Goderich in 1902: $10,000 for a library building, with the town providing books, site, staff, and upkeep. After some wrangling about the site, which was then the marketplace, the Goderich Public Library Board engaged Joseph A. Fowler to design a doughty but compact Richardsonian Romanesque building in brick and rusticated stone. The style's characteristic tower capitalized on the triangular lot, but the Carnegie people fretted that the building's idiosyncratic layout made the reading room difficult to supervise from the checkout desk. After 1908, James Bertram, Carnegie's private secretary and library overseer, insisted on approving library designs, most of which were more manageable revivals of classical styles. All five Huron County libraries were Carnegie gifts, and more than buildings resulted from Bertram's close involvement: he married Janet Ewing of Seaforth in 1904.

25 First Baptist Church, Montreal and Market Streets, 1905

Goderich's churches tend to be sprawlers (North Street United) or Gothic climbers (St. George's, St. Peter's), so one that is neither, but takes tidy possession of its corner site, has a special appeal. Student minister C.R. Jones was sent to Goderich in 1902 to found a Baptist church. The result, a forthright red-brick meeting of Romanesque and Gothic, nods companionably to its more thoroughgoing Romanesque neighbour, the library.

26 33 Montreal Street, 1842

Settling in Goderich with almost no money but "two toil hardened hands," according to the *Huron Signal*, Robert Gibbons opted for civility as soon as possible. The butcher and cattle merchant hired one of the best local masons, Thomas Kneeshaw, to make him a five-bay Georgian townhouse that emphasizes its breadth by spacing the windows closest to the edge further apart. The plain doorcase with its deep reveals is another Georgian touch.

27 Polley's Livery, 35 South Street, begun mid-1840s, completed 1878

How fitting that Polley's Livery has become the home of Goderich's Little Theatre: the flamboyant shaped gable and the rather stagy polygonal windows with their cut-stone voussoirs are rare, not just for Goderich but for small-town commercial buildings in general. New Hampshire–born A.M. Polley, who settled in Goderich in 1862, bought a building that dated from the 1840s for his livery and stagecoach business. The oldest section is at the rear; Polley added the middle section in the 1860s, and the front in 1878. "Polley's Spots," as his pair of dappled greys were called, were a Goderich fixture for

30 *29 Kingston Street*

32 *158 Court House Square*

years. A more problematic part of the business – a black coachman – was put in a barrel by locals and rolled down the hill to the harbour.

28 Hotel Bedford, 92 Court House Square, 1896
The third hotel on this site owned by the Bedford family makes much of its corner with a three-sided bay and a cupola, but by and large the Bedford is a workaday affair.

29 112 Court House Square, 1839
Unadorned except for its corbelled cornice and piers, at first this three-storey building on the Square at Kingston Street looks like a stripped-down 1920s or '30s structure. In fact it's the oldest building on the Square, built when Goderich was still making its way up from the harbour but when Kingston Street was the farmers' access road from the countryside. The owner, Christopher Crabb, was an English immigrant who was in turn merchant, magistrate, mayor, and Goderich's busiest builder of commercial structures; in 1889 the local newspapers proclaimed him "among our largest taxpayers." His store, which sold "everything from a needle to an anchor," continued in business for more than fifty years.

30 29 Kingston Street, 1849
Above the modern storefronts is the most glorious remnant of Christopher Crabb's business empire, the richly textured Victoria

Opera House. The golden patina of its yellow brick and its parade of round-headed windows (taller on the third floor) framed by arcades give it the look of a Roman amphitheatre in a far-flung provincial town. "One of the neatest opera halls in the west," as the proud local paper called it, held 750 people and was Goderich's best venue for road shows, musical evenings, and the like until the 1930s.

31 140–142 Court House Square, 1900, 146 Court House Square, 1906
Lift your eyes to the textured tops of these early-twentieth-century buildings to admire the versatility of the humble brick. Number 146's relatively modern look comes from its flattish façade and large windows.

32 158–164 Court House Square, ca. 1879, 166–168 Court House Square, ca. 1865
There's a fair sampling of High Victorian decorative motifs along this little stretch – from the Gothic-inspired pointed arches on the cornice of number 158 and its innovative cast-stone window surrounds, through the charmingly pompous vermiculated window surrounds of number 164, to the graceful flourishes of number 166's windows.

33 Huron County Court House, 1954–56
Just as Goderich was seriously outgrowing

33 *Huron County Court House*

34 *2–18 Court House Square*

its elaborate 1856 courthouse, it burned to the ground in February 1954. L.G. Bridgeman's fireproof replacement, made of reinforced concrete but sheathed with Indiana and Queenston limestone, looks like an Art Deco throwback in its flatness and angularity. The row of corbel- or dentil-like forms near the top of the building is the sort of stylized classical touch that Deco builders favoured, particularly in a public building. The Court House might well be a creditable component on a city street, but it seems to have landed on this verdant octagon without much thought for its surroundings.

34 2–18 Court House Square between North and Colborne Streets, 1873, 1889
This unusually harmonious and well-preserved row was the work of three owners over a span of sixteen years. William Savage, a fur merchant, built the three-storey building at the North Street corner in 1873; its double row of decorative brickwork at the top suggests medieval arches and crenellation. Horace Horton, a harness-maker and later banker, built the matching building at the Colborne Street end of the row in the same year. In 1889, a Dr. McDougall added the middle six stores, adapting the decorative brickwork and the rounded windows of the corner stores to his two-storey row.

Return to North Street.

35 41 North Street, 1916,
36 43 North Street, 1870s
Two houses built by A.M. Polley of Polley's Livery Stable suggest that Ontario's conservative ways also created a measure of timelessness and freedom. When being out of date entailed no shame, a man could choose whatever style pleased him. Number 41 is a simplified version, built during World War I, of the Greek Revival houses that made their first appearance in the 1830s. Polley's first house, number 43, is a neoclassical townhouse that would have been credible half a century before it was built in the 1870s; note the frieze of brick diaperwork and the very show-offy keystones above the second-floor windows.

37 North Street Methodist (now United) Church, 56 North Street, 1902–03; porch added 1925
Wesleyan Methodists had been worshipping on this site since 1841, and at the turn of the century they replaced their frame church with a Richardsonian Romanesque building. The architect was Joseph A. Fowler, who also designed the library. In addition to being fashionable (well, only a decade past its peak), the Romanesque style appealed to low-church congregations simply because the Anglicans and Catholics monopolized the Gothic.

38 *28 Nelson Street West*

39 *35 Nelson Street East*

Turn left on Nelson Street; go past St. George's Anglican Church for the moment.

38 28 Nelson Street West, ca. 1870
Best admired from Church Street, this accomplished Italianate house is planned along lines more vertical than usual for this style. Its long thin windows are paired, then framed in arcades that tie the two stories together. Instead of the usual pointed pediment, the rounded forms continue above the cornice, with the gable and the oval window. Built for a lawyer named Sinclair, it has one of Goderich's fine iron fences.

Retrace your steps, crossing North Street, and go to the end of Nelson Street East's first block, which has three interesting houses in three distinct styles.

39 35 Nelson Street East, ca. 1855
Once called Heartsease, this house originally had gardens that stretched to Victoria Street, on land now occupied by three houses. In style it's a Georgian that tolerates some informal Regency attitudes – the importance of the garden, the gently pitched roof, the French doors, the two-storey veranda, the chimneys set in from the edges of the roof (where Georgian builders placed them). The soft red bricks under the paint were probably made on the building site; this is one of a few candidates for the town's first red-brick house. Built as

the Church of Scotland manse, it was owned for many years by John Galt VI, the grandson of Goderich's founder.

40 27 Nelson Street East, 1911
A red-brick villa with the usual Queen Anne bundle of tricks: the half-timbering and tiny-paned windows borrowed from the Tudor, the classical porch, the rocky foundations, the gable that looks too big for the shingled half-tower. And as usual, it doesn't quite add up, but the result is both happy-go-lucky and reassuring.

41 21 Nelson Street East, 1923
A California Bungalow (see page 146) with the downward-swooping roof and heavy pillars that spelled Home in the 1920s and '30s. To add to the sheltering, "natural" effect, this one has a carapace of uncoursed pebbles.

**42 St. George's Anglican Church,
16 Nelson Street West,** 1880,
**43 St. George's Rectory,
87 North Street,** 1862
St. George's, as you approach it on North Street, is a well-groomed yellow-brick church with its spire placed at the intersection of North and Nelson Streets for greatest visibility. (Forced onto tight, rectangular town lots, many Ontario Gothic Revival churches adopted this arrangement.) The silvery monochromatic sheen of its slate roof, the painstaking brick

43 *St. George's Rectory,*
87 North Street

45 *Huron County Museum, 110 North Street*

ornamentation, and the 168-foot spire are admirable but not exceptional.

For a far prettier view, slip between the church and the rectory on North Street: with St. George's growing a tail that includes the church office and parish hall and the vaguely Tudor Gothic rectory facing it across a strip of green, it has the feeling of an English ecclesiastical compound where Trollope characters might appear at any moment. The rectory originally had this plot to itself; the Anglican church was built on St. George's Crescent in 1843. When that church burned in 1879, the replacement was built on the rectory's front lawn; it is said that the incumbent, Archdeacon Edward Lindsay, drew the rectory blinds in mourning for the trees sacrificed for the new church.

St. George's interior, which can often be seen by going through the church office on Nelson Street, has an unusual aspect for an Anglican church: a sloping floor. The Methodists often used a sloping floor to concentrate attention on the pulpit, but the Anglicans almost always opted for a level surface; the difference in perspective is small but significant.

44 105 North Street, 1865

Another example of the Goderich penchant for wood aspiring to the look of ashlar, this pleasant near-square was built for a banker and politician named Alexander Ross. The dentilled pediment, Ionic pillars, and carved voussoirs, all pine, make for a house that is countrified but not naive, framed by the deep garden and handsome iron fence. The Ionic pillars are original but the first, more graceful veranda has disappeared.

45 Huron County Museum, 110 North Street, 1856–58

The museological gods smiled on Goderich: not only did the Huron County Museum inherit Herbert Neill's impressive collection of pioneer artifacts, it houses them in a building that much larger towns might envy. Designed as a school by one of nineteenth-century Ontario's most sought-after architects, William Thomas, and built by a local master builder, Thomas Kneeshaw, Goderich's first public house of learning was a surprisingly sophisticated structure for a town of about 1,300. Perhaps it was hoped that the very upright character of Tudor Gothic (unusual in Ontario) would inspire good behaviour: from the deep stone baseline to the perky Tudor gable at the top, this is a highly disciplined building, decisively sectioned off by string courses, vermiculated quoins, and stone corbels, its side walls comprising two gables with a recessed panel between. The sympathetic modern extension was added in 1990 to designs by the local architect Christopher Borgal. Along with Herbert Neill's log cabin, which now houses the Genealogical Archives, the museum's three largest artifacts are

47 *138 North Street*   49 *Huron Historic Gaol*

buildings from three distinct periods of Ontario building history.

46 126 North Street, 1881 or 1882
Another blowsy Queen Anne house whose proportions may disconcert modern eyes. The handsomely banded tower looks too slim for the rounded porch that skirts it; perhaps to compensate, the gable that tops the bay on the other side is oversized. Built for a druggist named James Wilson.

47 138 North Street, 1887
The chimney set slantwise on the roof slope suggests that *gravitas* was not the operating principle here, as does the diagonally set bay. The steep downward sweep of the roof over the main door and the oriel window to the side are pleasant Queen Anne touches, but the builder's light touch deserted him when it came to the stone window and door surrounds: they are *de trop*, especially on top of the classical door's triglyphs.

**48 St. Peter's Roman Catholic Church,
156 North Street,** 1896
At a cost of $17,000, St. Peter's parishioners replaced their 1834 church with one made from stone quarried from the Maitland River. The pastor, Father West, was so well liked that the Orangemen from Goderich Township each contributed one ecumenical day's work to the papists' church. Relying on the fashionable rock-faced stone and a

pure Gothic outline, the architects, Post & Holmes, left the walls relatively unadorned; unfortunately, compared with the intricate brick and stone effects knitted into St. George's, it ends up looking rather featureless.

Turn right on Gloucester Terrace.

49 Huron Historic Gaol, 1839–42
The octagonal wall with the classical pediment and the cupolaed octagonal building within look so ancient that it's difficult to believe they functioned as a jail as recently as 1968. Even more surprising, Goderich's "other" octagon is a rare and well-preserved version of the British philosopher Jeremy Bentham's ideal prison. The essence of Bentham's plan, described in *Panopticon: or, The Inspection House* (1791), was a circular building with cells around the perimeter and an all-seeing jailer or guardian in a central tower. Bentham promised, "Morals reformed, health preserved, industry invigorated, instruction diffused, public burthens lightened...all by a simple idea of Architecture!"

Bentham's scheme, modified over time, was a mixture of lenity and severity; the Goderich supervisors tended to the milder end of the spectrum. Prisoners (and debtors, the aged, and the insane, who were also housed here) were segregated according to age, offence, and condition; the cells for "lunatics and vagrants," on

[50] *Governor's House, 181 Victoria Street North*   [51] *Baron de Tuyle house*

the third floor, were the nicest. Communal rooms and exercise yards were provided, although prisoners cutting the grass had to wear ball-and-chain. Training and useful employment were attempted, at least sporadically.

Radiating out from the octagonal block of cells are eighteen-foot-high walls separating the various exercise yards and gardens. Those in turn are enclosed by the outer octagon, made of two-foot-thick stone walls. The chapel on the top floor, an essential part of Bentham's plan, was seconded for the Huron District Court House. But the councillors complained of bad smells, the distance from town, and the unpleasantness of passing by the prisoners' cells; they usually met in local hotels, until the Court House was built on the Square in 1858.

A fair amount is known about the building of the Gaol, from the two-foot blocks of stone quarried from the Maitland River to the final price (£4,868) to the builder, William Day of Goderich, and the troubled arrangements with the Gaol's architect, Thomas Young of Toronto. What remains a mystery is the more interesting question of how Bentham's ideas, generally reviled in Britain, got to Huron County. The Gaol has been a museum since 1974.

[50] Governor's House, 181 Victoria Street North, ca. 1900

In the Gaol complex but deliberately quite different, the Governor's House combines the domesticity of many a hip-roofed and peaked Ontario farmhouse with the dour stone building blocks of the Gaol. The first jailer had lived in what is now the Gaol's kitchen. His discontented successors lived first in a damp cottage built within the walls, then in a house on Anglesea Street. At the turn of the century, the jailer was upgraded to "governor," and one of the exercise yard walls was sacrificed to provide stone and space for his house.

[51] Return to Caledonia Street via Napier and Anglesea Streets. Past 44 Caledonia and the small park, look across the Maitland River to the large white house with two tall chimneys. Too altered to require a closer visit, it still bears the marks of three generations of foreigners who repaired to the wilds of Huron County. Originally the property of Baron de Tuyle, whose son built a log hunting lodge there in 1829, it was later the home of John Galt's son. Although it was much enlarged in the 1870s by an American named H.Y. Attrill (who planted a vineyard down the hill and tried unsuccessfully to mine salt), the shape of the original lodge can still be seen at the front of the house.

At the corner of St. George's Crescent and Waterloo Street, go first to the tall yellow-brick house on the left.

52 *103 St. George's Crescent*

53 *92 St. George's Crescent*

52 103 St. George's Crescent, 1877
(best viewed from Waterloo Street)
A "conspicuous object from the harbor"
and "one of the finest residences in town,"
as a promotional booklet from 1897 called
it, was the home of a developer, banker,
town councillor, and mayor named Horace
Horton. Today its restrained opulence is
better seen from the rear; the front has
been disfigured by a rounded two-storey
porch and a sunroom. Built by one of
Goderich's master contractors, Walter
Sharman, in the Second Empire style, its
concave and convex rooflines, broken by
dormers, are balanced on the lower stories
by the arcading, quoin-like banding and
elaborate window treatments that complement the dormers. Note the grapes in the
cast-stone keystones.

53 92 St. George's Crescent, 1861–62,
finished 1903–04
Many small towns have a Castle, as this
house is known, or the equivalent – a locally
famous "great house" that strikes a romantic chord. In this case, the romance derives
from the baronial tower, the magnificent
site, and the fact that the house remained
unfinished for decades. It reportedly began
with Henry MacDermott's desire to re-
create a castle from his native County
Antrim in Ireland. MacDermott, a deputy
master in Chancery, had built two floors
and most of the tower when he ran out
of money. After almost forty years as a

picturesque beginning, the house was
bought for $2,500 by a widow named Jessie
Cameron; she finished the tower, added the
third floor, and created a steep, very busy
roofline that suggests two currently fashionable period revivals, Château and Tudor.
The blocky tower contained an elevator
powered by water from a cistern at its top.

St. George's Crescent offers the best views
of the working side of Goderich's port,
with, from this point, Goderich Elevators
Ltd. to the left and piers and breakwaters
to the right. Straight ahead is Snug Marina
and behind that the Sifto Salt Mine.

54 133 St. George's Crescent, ca. 1863
A tasty local stew of Gothic Revival gables
and bargeboard, classical-inspired pedimented windows and cornerboards, and
one utterly Goderich touch: pine imitating
ashlar. Built for a stagecoach manager and
contractor named William Geary.

55 150 St. George's Crescent, 1881
Lumber king and shipowner Joseph
Williams's yellow-brick box drips with
luxurious touches: the balustraded bays
that face the street, the curtailed gable
above the front door, the decorative
woodwork between the cornice brackets. If
some of the details, the cast-stone window
surrounds for instance, are reminiscent
of 103 St. George's Crescent (**52** above),
that's because the same fine mason, Walter

55 *150 St. George's Crescent*

59 *90 St. Patrick Street*

Sharman, was responsible for both houses. (The circular portico dates from this century.) Williams was the owner of the *Sephie*, the fastest schooner on the Great Lakes; the original Sephie was Williams's daughter Josephine, a painter who used the gazebo in the garden as a studio.

56 27 Wellington Street North, 1853
A much-altered house whose front door may originally have been on the north side: the French windows with their Regency-style panes and a view of the lake suggest as much. It was built as home and office for Charles Widder, a Canada Company agent and later agent for the Queen's Bush, Crown lands north of the Huron Tract.

St. Patrick Street, no doubt an Irish neighbourhood originally, is a street of simple early houses, many now encumbered by boxy storm porches as well as siding.

57 98 St. Patrick Street, ca. 1852–54
This house is thought to have been both a bakery and a dwelling, and a bricked-in second door is still visible. The shed roof and heavy columns were afterthoughts but attractive ones.

58 97 St. Patrick Street, ca. 1850
Andrew Garvie, a cooper who specialized in barrels for salted fish and hides, was the first owner of this Ontario cottage. The concrete veneer, scored to look like over-

sized brick, probably covered the original red brick soon after construction. Until 1890, this was Goderich's post office.

59 90 St. Patrick Street, 1904
Like an Amish quilt where the design is mostly in the patterned stitching, this beguiling Queen Anne house makes the most of clapboard, two kinds of shingles, patterned pressed wood at the apex of the gable, brackets, and simple treillage. The asymmetric gable is a bold move, and the green-and-yellow colour scheme is just right, especially when the sun lights up the butter yellow.

60 87 St. Patrick Street, ca. 1857
In the 1830s a German immigrant named Jacob Seegmiller began trading pork, whiskey, and flour from Waterloo for hides and salted fish from Goderich. He settled in Goderich in 1841 and made a fortune from a tannery and real estate. His symmetrical house, built in the muted local brick, began as a Georgian rectangle and soon developed into a saltbox; it may well have been built by Adam MacVicar, one of Goderich's premier masons. The longer first-floor windows were a favourite local way to give a house the illusion of height.

61 56 St. Patrick Street, ca. 1857
Also built by Jacob Seegmiller, this mock-ashlar house has distinctive labels over the windows.

Public Library

Merrickville

"A Good Point for Capitalists"

O n a Sunday afternoon in fine weather, daytrippers throng Merrickville, pricing old china and Inuit prints, taking tea, inspecting the blockhouse or the Rideau Canal's flight of locks. Shortly after 5 p.m., it is as if the trippers have been vacuumed away. The shops look not so much closed as boarded up, and the streets, roughly seven up and seven across in the main part of the town, are startlingly empty.

Merrickville is by no means a deserted village – its population of 1,000 is roughly what it was 150 years ago – but its company face is very different from its at-home face. For company, its tininess is quaint, its limestone buildings nostalgic. At home alone, its tininess and its stone buildings are movingly real, even vulnerable. A cut-stone neoclassical house is only steps away from pedestrian modern stores. Bucolic Elgin Street, where Queen Anne's lace and chicory strain at split-rail fences and clotheslines full of shirts flap against sagging silvery barns, is one block from the souvenir stores on St. Lawrence Street. Filled with tourists, Merrickville can look oppressively cute. On its own, it suggests Gerard Manley Hopkins's "sweet especial rural scene" with some fine stone buildings as a bonus.

For such a village, a coat of arms sounds grandiose, particularly one designed in 1993 for its 200th anniversary. But Merrickville's coat of arms is an apt little summary of its history. The coronets worn by the animals flanking the central shield symbolize the United Empire Loyalists who founded the village. The broken limestone beneath the animals represents the Precambrian Shield that underlies Merrickville and supplied its building stone; the mason's hammer brandished by the demi-lion at the top refers to the masons who worked the stone, many of whom were imported from Britain to build the Rideau Canal. The pictures in the shield of the blockhouse and a mill point respectively to the canal and to Merrickville's considerable industrial activity in the nineteenth century. Underneath it all are the wavy lines of the Rideau River with the village motto *Ad Aquas Florens* ("flourishing by the water").

The United Empire Loyalist who flourished by the water in question most prominently was William Mirick (1760–1841), or Merrick as it was later spelled. The Upper Canadian distaste for self-aggrandizement has ensured that few Ontario towns commemorate their founders by name. As Bytown, Smith's Creek, and Meyers' Creek grew in population and consequence, they became, respectively, Ottawa, Port Hope, and Belleville. A cluster of early, much smaller settlements in the so-called Rideau Corridor around the Rideau River and Lakes, perhaps significantly founded by immodest United Empire Loyalists, is an exception to the general rule: Burritts Rapids, Smiths Falls, Eastons Corners, and Merrickville keep their founders' memories green some two centuries after their beginnings.

In fact, as Larry Turner writes in *Merrickville: Jewel on the Rideau*, it was another Loyalist, a Vermonter named Roger Stephens, who built the first sawmill in what is now Merrickville sometime before his death by drowning in 1793. Stephens had sold the mill to Merrick, a Massachusetts-born millwright, and it was around Merrick that legends accumulated almost from the start. Reportedly guided by Indians to the "Great Falls" where the Rideau dropped fourteen feet, Merrick fixed on the location in the early 1790s and settled there with his wife, Sylvia. Another story has it that Indians cured the fever-stricken Merricks with herbs soon after they arrived; in gratitude for that and/or the location, they kept four bunks for Indians in their woodshed. According to Ruth MacKenzie in *Leeds and Grenville*, after the patriarch died, Indians passing through town would tell his sons, "This is old Merrick's house and we have a right."

By 1800, Merrick was joined by other Loyalists – among them John Chester, who built a store, and Samuel Dow, who started a smithy. The little clearing, which soon included a gristmill and carding mill, was called Mirick's Mills. Institutions followed, in an order that says something about priorities: a school was built in 1813, a Presbyterian church in 1821, a post office in 1829, a temperance society in 1830, a Roman Catholic church in 1832, an Anglican church in 1837.

In 1826, when Colonel John By's sappers and engineers began connecting 123 miles of lakes and rivers into the Rideau Canal, Merrickville was one of the most important settlements along the canal route. Worryingly exposed to American invasion by virtue of its position on both the Brockville and the Prescott roads, the village of 300 had three significant advantages. There was abundant water power for industry, fertile clay soil lining the river for farming, and the so-called Smiths Falls Limestone Plain (part of the Precambrian

Shield) for buildings and masonry locks. Planned primarily as a defensive highway, the canal would protect Merrickville from invading Americans; to this end, the canal's first and biggest blockhouse was erected there. At the same time, and as an almost unlooked-for side effect, a viable transportation system could only enhance Merrickville's other assets.

John By is remembered for the enormousness of his cost overruns and the ingenuity of his engineering feats. Both were unprecedented: no military building project in the British Empire had cost as much (more than £820,000, almost five times the budget approved by the Ordnance Office) and no one had built locks and dams on such a scale in such demanding terrain.

In spite of By's reputation for extravagance, the flight of three locks he designed for Merrickville shows a sensitivity to existing structures as well as thrift. Built "in the dry" on the river's east bank, the canal cut left the village's complex of mills more or less intact. Although the overflow dam was built of timber rather than masonry to cut costs, the limestone for the locks was quarried at nearby Clowes Lock. The basins between the locks allowed the builders to follow a natural depression, minimizing excavation. The resulting flight, with a cumulative lift of twenty-five feet, is far from mundane: for a Rideau aficionado such as Robert Legget (*Rideau Waterway*), it is the most graceful of the canal's groups of locks.

Although William Merrick was a primary beneficiary of Merrickville's place on the canal, it took a reprimand from the Ordnance Office before he stopped treating the river as his own. Colonel By had optimistically ordered four silver presentation cups engraved with the completion date of 1831 for the principal contractors, but Merrick had other plans. In the autumn of 1831, he dammed the river in the course of repairing his mills, which so lowered the water level that the official opening had to be postponed until spring 1832. Asking the Ordnance to intervene, an exasperated By complained that if individuals were allowed to control the water level, "the great expenditure" would be seriously impaired.

During the middle decades of the nineteenth century, it looked as if the canal was the making of Merrickville. The services attendant on its building alone had galvanized the village economy, and within a few months of the start of construction, Merrickville reported fifty-six new houses. The canal's effect on Merrickville's little industrial sector was more lasting. The village was already a mini-hive of industrial activity by 1826, but the frustrations of water and land transportation had limited production to purely local needs. The canal changed all that: Montreal was now a five-day rather than a twenty-day journey, and flour, potash, wheat, and lumber from Merrickville's mills found ready markets.

By 1840, the industrial island northeast of the Blockhouse housed two gristmills, a carding mill, a distillery, an axe factory, and a sawmill. When the Reverend Adam Lillie addressed the Toronto Mechanics' Institute in 1852, he reported that Merrickville had a population of 700, cloth and shingle factories, and "most excellent water power." He concluded, "This is an improving town, and a good point for capitalists to invest in."

The father of all Merrickville capitalists, William Merrick, had died in 1841 at the age of eighty-one. (His above-ground tomb, along with those of his wife and other family members, can be seen in the Collar Hill cemetery, near Brock and Charlotte Streets.) Merricks, or Miricks as they were still called, in the shape of four sons, continued to dominate the village for most of the century. In the *Mirickville Chronicle* for 1858, Stephen Hedger Mirick invited purchasers for his "woollen, satinetts, Tweeds, flannels etc.," while his brother William advertised the products of his shingle factory and machine shop; Terence H. Mirick was half-owner of Mirickville New Mills as well as a barrister-at-law. Aaron Mirick, who founded the public library, ran a general store and served as the village reeve. Mirickville officially became Merrickville in 1862, two years after the village was incorporated; the Miricks presumably became Merricks about the same time.

Merrickville's best days lasted only about a decade and a half after the canal was built, but its decline was as attenuated as its pre-canal growth. The canal's commercial heyday ended early, with the opening of the St. Lawrence Canals in 1847, although immigrants and local merchants continued to use the Rideau Canal. With his usual attention to detail, By had drawn up a list of transport rates, ranging from passengers to pigs, from salted fish to spirits. Although the numbers went steadily downward and the rates changed, the kinds of canal traffic, human and non-human, remained constant for half a century.

From the 1870s until 1935, when the last steamer made her final voyage, commercial pleasure boats gave the canal and the settlements along it a new, limited lease on life. But pleasure on the Sabbath was a concept Ontario resisted, and once again a Merrick made life difficult. On Sunday, May 14, 1871, Henry Merrick, acting as village reeve, held up the steamers *Carlyle* and *Alice* for ten hours, until 1 a.m. Monday, in spite of the lockmaster's protest that the *Alice* was a passenger boat. The Lord's Day Act would forbid unrestricted Sunday hours on the canal until 1913.

By 1932, the Rideau Canal was considered such a white elephant that Parliament commemorated its centenary by seriously discussing filling in the canals. Even before that humiliating (and unworkable) idea surfaced, Merrickville had become a place where, as the mock-historical plaques say, "Absolutely Nothing Happened." The flamboyant and eccentric contractor Harry McLean roused the village from its slumbers from about 1920 to 1960, but only in a partial and personal way. A builder of railroads, harbours, and tunnels, a great drinker, and a thrower of dollar bills out of hotel windows, McLean supplied the ballast for the CPR from Winnipeg to Quebec City. To that end, he employed 200 people at nearby Deeks' Quarry, while he ran his international contracting business from the Jakes Block at the corner of Main and St. Lawrence Streets and renovated the grandest of the Merrick sons' houses. His parties, his airport, his private zoo became part of the legend of Mr. X, as he was called, but when he died in 1960, Merrickville was in decline.

Today there are no Merricks left in the village, and the nearly sixty industries that have operated here over the last two centuries have been reduced to one, the Alloy Foundry on Mill Street just north of the bridge. But Merrickville is no longer in decline, although the village has been not so much revived as stabilized. Its proximity to Ottawa, the canal's latter-day recreational appeal, and the growth of the heritage movement have led to the restoration of the Blockhouse and other important local buildings. With thirty-three buildings designated by the Ontario Heritage Act, as Larry Turner notes, the village has one of Ontario's richest architectural caches for its size. As with many Ontario towns, too unimportant to have undergone extensive modernization, returning Merrickville to its nineteenth-century looks has required will but no superhuman efforts.

Cynics, pointing to the Sunday shoppers and tea drinkers, may say that Merrickville is more than ever "a good point for capitalists." It's a remark addressed only to the company face of the village. On the other hand, it would make William Merrick smile with pleasure.

4 *Rideau Canal Industrial Heritage Complex*

26 *105 Lewis Street West*

Lockmaster's house

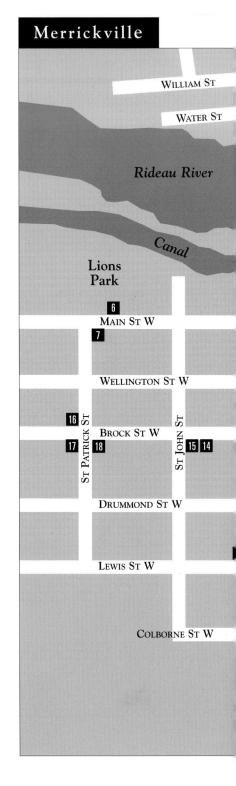

1 *129 Mill Street* 2 *106 Mill Street*

1 129 Mill Street, ca. 1821

William Merrick's first house was a log cabin close to the falls; the second, a stone house, was built sometime between 1800 and 1820. This is his third, a rubblestone Georgian considerably altered by William Pearson, who bought the house in 1869. Pearson, the co-owner of the nearby Magee and Pearson Foundry, covered the stone with a stucco wash and added the barge-boards. The view from the road shows an eclectic but compatible ensemble that includes a veranda and two magisterial triple chimney-stacks on the main stuccoed house, an attached stone carriage house beyond that, and a red-brick outbuilding.

Merrick's second house, much altered, is not far away, at 106 Amelia Street. Walkers who wish to can see it by turning right at the end of Rideau Street and walking down the dirt road.

2 106 Mill Street, ca. 1830

Like many eastern Upper Canadian communities, Merrickville's citizens grew exercised about alcohol in the 1830s and '40s; Merrickville was in the vanguard with a temperance society founded in 1830. Not everyone shared their distaste: about the same time, according to village legend, this asymmetrical, primeval-looking rubble-stone house was built as a tavern and inn by two of William Merrick's sons, Aaron and Terence. The deep chunky chimneys and the secretive look that comes from few

and small windows and a recessed door are typical of the period.

3 Peter Ayling Boat Works, Mill Street, behind the Alloy Foundry, ca. 1895

Probably Merrickville's most successful business, Magee and Pearson was nationally known for its farm machines and stoves. Under its second owner, Roger Percival, who took over the company in 1887 and renamed it Percival Plow and Stove in 1906, it was even more prosperous, turning out best-selling stoves named Fairy Queen and Prince of Wales. The handsome five-bay finishing shop and plough department (now Peter Ayling Boat Works) sets off its broken-coursed rubble with large, dark rusticated quoins.

4 Rideau Canal Industrial Heritage Complex

Parks Canada's straightforward name for this industrial island doesn't do justice to the poetry here. Looking like the ruins of Crusader castles or a hoard of dinosaur skeletons, these uncoursed or roughly coursed rubble buildings once housed gristmills, an axe factory, a cooper's shop, a furniture factory, a potashery, and a woollen mill. The first mills on the island date from the 1830s; the disruption involved in the building of the Rideau Canal may well have caused the emergence of the island. Chief among the

 Rideau Canal Industrial
Heritage Complex

5 Blockhouse, Mill and Main Streets

businesses here, and still inscribed in the keystone over the main door of the large ruin to the left, was Stephen Hedger Mirick's woollen mill, built in 1848 and thought to be the first woollen mill in Ontario. It operated under various proprietors and finally expired as Watchorn and Company in 1954. As the exhibit in the main building in the complex indicates, Merrickville's abundant water power called into being a full range of mills and factories that produced everything from oatmeal to coffins. But it was never able to compensate for a small population, awkward transportation, the decline of raw materials, and competition from large urban centres.

5 Blockhouse, Mill and Main Streets, 1832

Merrickville's doughty blockhouse owes its existence to a bureaucratic oversight. In 1830, Colonel By considered it "absolutely necessary" that blockhouses or other defensive structures be built at all the canal locks. Unwilling to add £69,000 to a budget already spinning out of control, the Ordnance withheld approval but only notified the colonel two years later. By that time, four blockhouses were under way. All are two-storey squares with massive limestone first stories (walls four feet thick in the case of Merrickville), overhanging second stories, and tin roofs (recommended by By because "tin remains free from rust in

this climate for upwards of 60 years").

The first, largest, and closest to By's design, Merrickville's blockhouse was intended to shelter up to fifty soldiers, their arms, and ammunition. The four gun ports on the first storey were for mounting cannons, with small-arms openings and rifle slits (called machicolations) on the second storey. The interior staircase rotates to the right so as to constrain the rifle-arms of mounting attackers while freeing up those of the descending defenders. With a powder magazine in the basement and the second-floor rotunda bomb-proofed with rubblestone two feet thick, the blockhouse was ready for defensive business that never quite arrived.

During the 1837 rebellion and the Fenian troubles in the 1860s, militiamen did occupy the building and displace the lockmaster, John Johnston, and his family. But in general, the Johnstons lived undisturbed in the blockhouse, and Johnston, a sergeant in the Royal Sappers and Miners, earned four shillings a day for maintaining the locks. (When he died in 1869, his son Matthew replaced him as lockmaster.) Early in its life the blockhouse served for church services; after the lockmaster moved out at the turn of this century, the building became a village meeting place. In 1908–09, when the roof was in imminent danger of collapse, much of the second storey and the staircase were removed; the roof was restored and the

229 Main Street West

8 *106–112 Main Street East;*
105–129 St. Lawrence Street

blockhouse turned into a museum in the 1960s.

The Museum Annex upstream, covered with puckered metal siding that mimics coursed stone, is a canal storage depot, built about 1870.

6 229 Main Street West, ca. 1852–60
Merrickville's former town hall, which also served in its day as jail, school, firehall, and theatre, now houses Ste. Marguerite Bourgeoys School. Designed by Samuel Langford, one of the town's master masons, the hall inspired persistent complaints ("a disgrace" as a theatre, "utterly unfit" as a jail) until the municipal offices were moved to what is now the library in 1938. Nevertheless, the flaring compound headers over the windows, the cut-stone quoins, and the recessed double doors were signs that the mid-nineteenth-century village of 1,000 souls was taking itself with due seriousness. (The stone portion of the Canadian Legion building next door at 223 Main Street is what remains of a township school built in 1840.)

**7 St. Ann's Roman Catholic Church,
230 Main Street West,** 1902
The statue niche and the tin roof and turrets may suggest the churches of nearby Quebec, but a Westport architect named Speigle designed St. Ann's, which replaced an earlier church built in 1842. The quarry-faced stone was chic for turn-of-the-

century churches, but the elegant Italianate brick rectory next door has more staying power.

Return to the corner of Main and Mill Streets.

**8 106–112 Main Street East; 105–129
St. Lawrence Street,** ca. 1861
Three stories high, wrapping around the village's main intersection, its front made of woolly-looking rough-cut stone overlaid by a rusticated gridlock of string courses and piers, the Jakes Block was a very up-to-the-minute piece of commercial architecture when it was built.

Begun by Eleazar Whitmarsh and bought by an Irish immigrant named Samuel Jakes in 1871, the building under Jakes's aegis housed a department store said to be the largest between Montreal and Chicago. In the 1940s the building was owned by the contractor and philanthropist Harry McLean. McLean used the first floor for offices and the second for employees' living quarters; he made the third a village badminton court.

9 106–108 St. Lawrence Street,
ca. 1859
A three-storey commercial structure built by Aaron Merrick, a son of Merrickville's founder. Stand across the street to admire the contrasting textures of the ashlar quoins and window sills and the panelled first-

9 *106–108 St. Lawrence Street*

15 *136 Brock Street West*

floor storefronts with the rougher masonry of the upper floors.

10 118 St. Lawrence Street, 1830–40
An early commercial building used by the Mechanics' Institute as its library. Note how the rubble courses on the front are tidied with a line of mortar, unlike the side.

11 206 St. Lawrence Street, 1861
The upper stories of this commercial building are a tweedy local specialty, a basketweave pattern of red and yellow bricks laid in Flemish bond, with the yellow bricks used as headers throughout.

12 212–224 St. Lawrence Street,
ca. 1835
A rubblestone commercial building with lodgings above, possibly built by William Merrick. Like many early stone business blocks in the area, it would look at home in Scotland, Ireland, or the north of England; except for the commercial size of its first-floor windows, it could be a six-bay rowhouse.

13 236–242 St. Lawrence Street,
1870s or 1880s
Brick buildings were relatively rare in the Rideau Corridor, although Merrickville had several brickyards by mid-century. This unusually shaped commercial building with smart contrasting brick trim served as John Mills's furniture shop (supplying "Plain and

Fancy Furniture, Broom Handles etc.") from the mid-1880s until the 1930s.

Turn right on Brock Street.

14 130 Brock Street West, ca. 1860
Looking both citified and timeless, the stony, parapeted western half of this house began life as cabinetmaker John Mills's furniture store. As tiny Merrickville separated itself into industrial, commercial, and residential streets, the shop moved to 236–242 St. Lawrence Street, the factory (which had been at the rear) moved to the industrial island in the river, and the Mills family moved into the former store and added the eastern section in 1885. The porch on the original building probably dates from the beginning of this century, when Ionic columns and other classical accessories were popular.

15 136 Brock Street West, ca. 1855
The hip-roofed house has been neutered with siding, but the porch throbs with life. Someone who understood just how delightful overstatement could be combined the standard shapes and forms – quatrefoils, husks, rosettes – with great brio. Note the spindles at the top that mimic a beaded fringe, the busy sculpted posts, and the cheap but bold railing and foundation support.

21 *412 St. Lawrence Street*

26 *105 Lewis Street West*

16 **305,** **17** **306,** **18** **230 Brock Street West,** 1850s and 1860s
A trio of early one-and-a-half-storey frame houses keep company at the corner of Brock and St. Patrick Streets. Beyond their handsome simplicity, they share some stripped-down, countrified Greek Revival touches: returning eaves, deep cornices, and cornerboards like vestigial pilasters. Number 305 has a finely moulded cornice, and numbers 230 and 306 have early doorcases with highish architraves.

Retrace your steps to St. Lawrence and turn right.

19 **317 St. Lawrence Street,** 1858
The original hotel, built by James Armstrong during the village's boom, had five bays centred on the tony pedimented door. In 1902, four bays to the north were added, as well as a mansard roof that allowed more bedrooms.

20 **323 St. Lawrence Street,** ca. 1830
A very early house of broken-coursed rubble with cut-stone lintels and minimal treillage on its veranda. The stuccoed portion may have come later.

21 **412 St. Lawrence Street,** ca. 1860
Boomtown façades are rare in well-settled southern Ontario. This charmer, with appliqués across its frieze and the trim little shelves atop its windows and door,

served as a bakery for its first four decades, later as the telephone exchange, and is now home to the Merrickville Bible Chapel. It was the model for the tinsmith shop in Upper Canada Village.

22 **418,** **23** **424–430,** **24** **505,** **25** **511 St. Lawrence Street,** ca. 1880–1900
By their knobs ye shall know them, when it comes to Eastlake porches. St. Lawrence Street between Drummond and Colborne has a quintet of modest houses, all of whose porches are touched by the Eastlake fondness for knobs, spindles, and other rounded forms produced by lathe, gouge, and chisel.

26 **105 Lewis Street West,** ca. 1855
The house is plainness itself, like a rectangular boulder heaved up by a field. There are no quoins or window headers to delineate walls or windows, and only the most rudimentary pairs of brackets; the front is rubble-stone laid in courses and the side uncoursed. All of which makes the sophisticated, deeply set elliptical doorway – one of three in Merrickville – even more remarkable.

27 **512 St. Lawrence Street,** ca. 1855
A "second generation" Rideau Corridor stone house with the signature spreading central gable. The rectangular Greek Revival transom and sidelights that superseded the semicircular and elliptical fanlights on the earliest houses are recessed

29 *518 St. Lawrence Street*

30 *606–612 St. Lawrence Street*

here; the mutules in the cornice provided attic ventilation as well as another classical touch. Traces of an entrance porch with balcony are still visible. John Johnston, Merrickville's long-serving first lockmaster, was the first owner, and he may have used this as a summer house.

28 605 St. Lawrence Street, 1861

A stone house with a particularly handsomely moulded cornice, built for a shoemaker named Daniel McIntyre. Note how generously the mason applied the mortar; even the quoins are surrounded by mortar and the "grouting" is painted on.

Best seen from 605 St. Lawrence, two tall, proud houses lined with cut-stone quoins share the corner of Colborne and St. Lawrence Streets.

29 518 St. Lawrence Street, ca. 1861

A dashing blend of the vernacular and the formal, built for a prosperous land surveyor named John Burchill. The formal is the Georgian symmetry, the cut-stone elliptical door surround, the lintels made from a single piece of stone (rather unusual in this village). The vernacular is the red-and-buff-brick basketweave pattern. One of Merrickville's first brick houses, this was clearly a building of substance: Flemish bond is used on all four sides (the usual method involved less time-consuming common bond on the sides and back).

30 606–612 St. Lawrence Street, ca. 1866

A double stone house, its doors set high above the first of two string courses. The splendid cornice is Merrickville's most elaborate, with two rows of rolled dentil-like forms, idiosyncratic brackets, and deep returning eaves. Seen in demi-profile from the south, when the sun lights up the rough uncoursed rubblestone side, the coursed rubble front, and the cut-stone details as well as the flossy cornice, it's a cornucopia of forms and materials.

31 618 St. Lawrence Street, 1861

Looking like the paradigm country church, what was Knox Presbyterian now functions as a day nursery. The long Gothic windows have a genially civilized aspect; the square tower, with its abrupt spire and threatening wooden finials, breathes a sterner, more ancient-seeming spirit.

32 718, 33 806 St. Lawrence Street, 1901–02

How pleasant that these two curvy verandas face each other across the side lawns of their respective houses, as if in constant readiness for a neighbourly chat. The Eastlake-style verandas, topped with a square second-storey balcony, are identical; the houses themselves, outgoing cross-gabled and wide-eaved Queen Annes, are virtual mirror images of each other when it comes to their basic structure. After that,

34 *905 St Lawrence Street*

38 *517 Elgin Street*

count the differences, beginning with the fact that one is clapboard and the other stone, one has three gables and the other two, etc., etc. The local belief is that they were designed by a contractor named William Newman, who built them with a mason named Wilson; Newman lived in number 718, and Wilson in number 806.

34 905 St. Lawrence Street, 1839–61
Merrickville's main street is nicely bounded by the village's two "big houses" – William Merrick's at the north and his son Aaron's here, as St. Lawrence Street merges into countryside. Its position at the edge of town, the four French doors on the first floor, and the full veranda (removed in the 1920s) link it with the relaxed, nature-loving Regency style; the symmetry, two and a half stories, and sharply pitched roof are stricter, more classical notes. The house was probably built by Samuel Langford, an English-born builder and stonemason who became Merrickville's best-known builder; he showed off his stonecutting skills in the window surrounds, quoins, and string course. Hilltop, as the house was called, was owned from 1922 until his death in 1961 by the eccentric businessman and builder Harry McLean, who had a zoo installed on the grounds. It was McLean who removed the veranda and added the side porches, the dormer windows, and the classically inspired portico.

Return to Colborne Street East, and turn east to Elgin Street.

35 118 Colborne Street East, 36 605 Elgin Street, 37 206 Colborne Street East, 38 517 Elgin Street, 39 511 Elgin Street, 40 505 Elgin Street, 1880s
A cluster of red-and-yellow-brick houses ring the changes on a fashion that reached Merrickville in the 1880s. When the architectural critic John Ruskin approved bichromatic brick decoration as an honest substitute for the coloured marble and stone of Italian churches, England complied and Ontario echoed. The fad spread from churches to houses, and embraced all the current styles. Here they include the Italianate with a two-storey bay (118 Colborne), front-facing gabled houses both simple (605 Elgin) and L-shaped (206 Colborne Street East), and a hip-roofed rectangle with a delightful veranda (517 Elgin). The yellow-brick trim includes false quoins, the very Victorian drapery-like swags over the windows, and, at 206 Colborne Street East, jagged window surrounds and quoins like flame-stitching.

41 506 Elgin Street, ca. 1886–91
Samuel Langford, the English mason who built some of Merrickville's early stone houses, could sculpt in wood as well, as this L-shaped house attests. The flushboard construction makes a flat surface that

58

42 *405 Elgin Street*

46 *106 Brock Street East*

shows off all the embroidery, with the veranda trim (temporarily removed for renovation) getting most of the attention. The gabled dormers that interrupt the rooflines, the bay window with elaborate cornice decoration, the Gothic trefoils and quatrefoils in the bargeboard, and veranda treillage are all favourite Langford touches and very conservative for this date.

42 405 Elgin Street, ca. 1855

Nothing lifts the spirits in quite the way that an unpretentious vernacular house does when everything clicks. The veranda, an artful concatenation of bevelled posts and stylized natural forms on the treillage that suggests a vine-laden trellis, is the eye-catcher here. The little Gothic dormer with its own protective hood, the scallops of the tin roof, and even the cheeky brackets supporting it add to the general good humour.

43 306 Elgin Street, 1863

Said to have been built by Samuel Langford as a wedding present for his daughter Margaret, this very vernacular Gothic Revival is strikingly similar to 506 Elgin Street, which he built more than twenty-five years later. Built like the later house in flushboard construction, it has an unusual T-shaped footprint. One of the ways Gothic Revival houses typically parted company with classical styles was their disregard for symmetry, but here the projecting central block is flanked with iden-

tical verandas, side entrances, and gabled dormers. The details, though, are picturesque (and familiar), notably the deep bargeboard on the central gable: a confident, ecclesiastical-looking arrangement of trefoils and quatrefoils.

44 111 Brock Street East, before 1861

Two apparently simple houses on this block – this one and number 105 – are hiding early construction methods. Underneath this demure one-and-a-half-storey clapboard is something more rough and ready: a log house.

45 105 Brock Street East, ca. 1840

Behind its clapboard skin, this house was built of stacked planks, an unusual construction method called Brunswick.

46 106 Brock Street East, ca. 1850

Like a diminutive but impregnable monument, Stephen Merrick's one-and-a-half-storey house is eerily memorable. The typically overpowering Greek Revival doorway, with its tapering Doric columns and pediment, attracts attention first, but the superbly cut ashlar masonry is even more impressive. Note how the house is framed by the stone pilasters at the corners and the entablature that extends across the whole front. All the details have been considered, from the sills that rest on a line of mortar to the panel in the stone entablature that lines up with the little row of

47 *207 Brock Street East*

48 *212 Brock Street East*

dentils in the portico. Behind the splashy portico, this is a symmetrical five-bay neo-classical house like many in the region, save for the exceptional ashlar. (A more "correct" Greek Revival house would set the door at the side with a front gable or string columns across the front.) The view from the side is very different, with broken-coursed limestone replacing the ashlar, and a kitchen tail with a massive, hard-working chimney. Records indicate that Merrick sold the lot to Merrickville's premier mason, Samuel Langford, in 1850. Presumably Langford built the house, or at least the main part; in 1855 he sold it back to William Merrick's fourth son, Stephen.

47 207, 48 212 Brock Street East,
  ca. 1900

Two frame siblings built by a local carpenter, John Petapiece, one outgoing (number 207), the other slightly more reserved (and believed to be Petapiece's residence). You can see number 207's hospitable, open personality in the wider angles of its front-facing gables and its frank address to the street. Number 212 presents a taller, slimmer, and more withheld face, with one porch pediment that turns away and the small-paned windows of the Queen Anne style. Both have the characteristic Merrickville wide frieze and cornerboards that suggest pilasters – indications that the neoclassical style of the village's most prestigious early buildings left a long shadow.

49 206 Elgin Street, 1850s

A log house hidden behind skins from two different eras. Probably as soon as the demands of pioneer life allowed, the original owner gentrified his log house with a frame covering; a more recent owner topped that with aluminum siding. The dormer and second-floor porch are almost certainly an afterthought. The 1861 map of the town marks this as one of the town's two shoe stores.

50 Ardcaven, 206 Main Street East,
  ca. 1890

Merrickville's most aspiring Queen Anne house has many of the style's virtues and vices. The up side includes an expansiveness and an interest in different materials and techniques, the down side a passion for the part that sometimes allows the whole to get lost. The characteristic Queen Anne red brick with matching mortar is fine, as is the trim of sandstone with amethyst streaks; they just aren't good together. The arcaded chimney is handsome but seems to be in the wrong spot. The gable at the top of the two-storey bay doesn't quite cover the balcony and looks like a mistake (although it was a favourite device of Queen Anne builders). Built for Roger Percival, the owner of Percival Plow and Stove.

51 *Public Library, 111 Main Street East*

52 *118 Main Street East*

51 Public Library, 111 Main Street East, ca. 1890

A textbook example of the happily *retardataire* nature of Ontario building. Architects and contractors could build in the very latest styles, as the exactly contemporary house across the street at 206 Main Street East demonstrates, but if the client favoured a picturesque L-shaped Gothic Revival cottage decked out with bargeboard, treillage, and other accoutrements fashionable four decades earlier, so be it. Some of the details here, notably the collar-tie or horizontal brace in the main gable that is always a late-century clue, are later than others, but in the main this house might have been found in an 1850s pattern book. Note the trefoil motif that ties together the ornamentation, especially on the splendidly designed hooded window over the veranda. Built by a contractor named William J. Newman (probably also the builder of **32** and **33** above) and owned for many years by William Pearson, the co-owner of the nearby Magee and Pearson Foundry, the house was given by Pearson's daughter Mary to the village in 1938.

52 118 Main Street East, 1861

With its veranda flaring around three sides, the Sam Jakes Inn looks rather like a heavy-set belle wearing a low-slung hoop skirt. The original two-and-a-half-storey house is a pleasing mix of countrified (the rubblestone construction with roughly cut quoins) and genteel (the regular five-bay arrangement, the cut-stone lintels and sills, and the very fancy cornice). The modern extension to the hotel makes no attempt to blend in, so it's possible to see the original house without distraction. Jakes, its first owner and occupant, was the enterprising Irish immigrant who owned the Jakes Block next door, at the corner of Main and St. Lawrence Streets.

Canal buffs will want to turn back and follow Main Street East for three blocks.

53 441 Main Street East, oldest portion ca. 1815

Local legend has it that Colonel By supervised the construction of Merrickville's locks from the original part of this house, in the north corner at the back. By's clapboard cabin, if indeed it is, was overtaken in the 1860s by the one-and-a-half-storey house, later covered in brick.

Niagara Historical Society Museum

Niagara-on-the-Lake
"A Degree of Neatness and Taste"

N iagara-on-the-Lake is deceptive. Its manicured charm has the high sheen of implausibility, yet it's quite real. No less an observer than the architectural historian Eric Arthur described its base as "a practically unspoiled Colonial village of decent brick and frame houses," mostly built between 1820 and 1840. At the same time, underneath its apparently unchanged surface, at least half a dozen incarnations are more or less imperfectly submerged. Niagara's first historian, Janet Carnochan, boasted that those who knew the history of the town knew the history of Upper Canada, and that's not as hyperbolic as it first sounds.

It's true that no other Ontario town can match Niagara's evolution from glittery capital to tourist town. But its successive lifetimes as a military, legislative, and commercial centre, its slumps and building booms, and its turn-of-the century rebirth as a summer playground for rich Americans echo the histories of many of Ontario's oldest towns. Throw in a near-total burning in 1813 and a history of black settlement, and Niagara's homogeneously placid streets begin to look even more unreal. Still, behind the British teashops and the clapboard houses painted in nineteenth-century colours, Niagara's various lives are there for those who care to look.

Niagara's first layer is the ghostliest, now visible only in the claims for war losses filed by property owners after the Americans burned the town in 1813. The settlement they destroyed was more than thirty years old, founded even before the American Revolution had officially ended. Loyalists who had fought in the fearsome Butler's Rangers and been based across the Niagara River at Fort Niagara crossed to His Majesty's side of the river in the early 1780s. First called Butlersburg in honour of Colonel John Butler, then West Niagara and Lennox, the village was renamed Newark in 1792 by Colonel John Graves Simcoe when he chose it as the first capital of Upper Canada. When Simcoe decided Fort Niagara was too close for comfort and decamped to York with his government in 1796, the town reverted to the name Niagara. Niagara-on-the-Lake was a turn-of-the-twentieth-century appellation devised by the post office to avoid confusion with Niagara Falls; the town's older, shorter name will be used here.

From the beginning, Niagara's clement winters and fertile soil gave the settlement a certain milk-and-honey aspect. An officer from the 42nd Highlanders who visited the town in the 1790s recalled "assemblies, entertainments and card parties" in his thank-you note. William Jarvis, the Secretary of Upper Canada, might complain in 1792 that Simcoe had dragged him to a desolate, fever-infested spot ("People live here from hand to mouth as if they were to be gone tomorrow"). But desolation was in the eye of the beholder: the same Jarvis was considering having a white oak staircase floated down the river to his new house, and his American wife, who prided herself on being one of the "plainest dressed women in Newark," noted "more profusion of dress in our Assembly than I have ever seen in London." (Apparently, an American cuisine was a recognizable entity even in the 1790s: when a Niagaran woman of longer standing learned that Mrs. Jarvis was an American, she made her a welcoming present of Indian meal, pumpkins, sausages, lard, squashes, and carrots.)

By 1806, Niagara's wide, right-angled streets accommodated some 200 houses. Many of their owners were newly arrived Americans, drawn as much by a lenient, non-taxing government as by climate and soil, and their neat Georgian houses gave the town a deceptively settled air. In the same year, the postmaster general, George Heriot, reported that the mostly frame houses were made "with a degree of neatness and taste, for which we might look in vain among the more ancient settlements of the lower province." Somehow Niagara had managed "to assume the garb of wealth, and of long-established culture."

In 1813, the town's population hovered around 1,500, with 300 buildings, many large stores, two churches (St. Mark's Anglican and St. Andrew's Church of Scotland), a circulating library, and a registry office. From war losses claims, we know of some very grand houses. David William Smith's two-storey balustraded Georgian house, set on a four-acre midtown lot, struck the Duc de la Rochefoucauld as stylish and commodious; William Dickson's pedimented brick house, probably on King Street, contained a library of 4,000 to 5,000 volumes.

The War of 1812, referred to ever since by Niagarans simply as "the War," ended all that. In 1813, the Americans captured Fort George (built in 1802 to replace Fort Niagara) and occupied Niagara from May to December. On a windy December 10, they ordered the townspeople, mostly women, children, and old people, to leave their houses. According to legend, a grocer asked for and was given permission to fill his evening orders first, but the clemency was unique and pointless. The withdrawing Americans and the traitorous Canadian Volunteers set fire to the town, destroying all but two houses and the walls of St. Mark's Church (**72**).

If the war losses claims for the town's great houses are impressive, those for more ordinary houses make even more melancholy reading. They tell us that the average Niagara house was a one-and-a-half-storey frame building, from twenty-two to thirty-six feet across, eighteen to twenty-four feet deep, whose central front door was reached by steps. The inside walls were smoothly plastered, sometimes with a stencilled border, and the woodwork painted dark brown, red, or blue. Their goods, as large as "four post bedsteads" and oil-painted floor cloths and as small as mustard-pot ladles, were meticulously itemized in the war claims, none more graphically than by Robert Campbell. He kept a shop on Prideaux Street, and reported that two "hot Shot" passed through the store and "Cut away two shelves ... on all which stood cut Glass Decanters, Tumblers, Glasses & Crokery which was thrown down Broke and destroyed."

It was a drastic, unforgettable act, and six years later a visitor, John Goldie, observed, "Many of the inhabitants here hate the Yankies, as the Devil, and wish to have another opportunity of shooting a few of them." At the same time, the townspeople, returned from the War, and the garrison troops at Forts George and Mississauga were busily rebuilding houses and stores. The original streets had extended only as far as King Street: Queen Street was named for Queen Charlotte, the wife of George III; Prideaux and Johnson Streets commemorated the two commanders who had led the siege of Fort Niagara in 1759. After 1816, with the town enlarged to the south of King Street, Wellington, Picton, and Platoff Streets were named for military heroes in "that titanic struggle of Britain," as a loyal commentator called the Napoleonic Wars. (Platoff Street salutes the Russian general who defeated Napoleon.)

Resisting government pressures to avoid the vulnerable waterfront altogether, Niagarans did move the commercial area as far back as Queen Street, where it remains today. By 1840, as Eric Arthur noted, Niagara's building boom was over. The population numbered about 4,000, of whom 400 were blacks who had escaped slavery and mostly lived around Mary Street.

Niagara flourished in the 1830s and 1840s, supplying provisions to the tiny hamlets of Hamilton and St. Catharines, serving as the legal centre for

Lincoln, Welland, and Haldimand Counties and employing shipbuilders and associated craftsmen at the town's biggest employer, the Niagara Harbour and Dock Company. The town swarmed with lawyers, civil servants, military types; small wonder that Niagara had twenty-eight taverns in the early 1840s.

But by the end of that decade the town's decline was unmistakable. The opening of the second Welland Canal, in mid-decade, signalled the end of the portage route around Niagara Falls and made Niagara a backwater. The Harbour and Dock Company languished in debt. Trying to stave off insignificance, Niagara built a stately Court House in 1847; by 1861 St. Catharines had become the county seat and the Court House was downgraded to a town hall. As St. Catharines and Hamilton waxed, Niagara waned.

Some relief arrived in the last decades of the century, with another wave of Americans. This time there was no burning and pillaging but breezy, leisurely summers spent in refurbished older houses and expansive new ones, often crammed with three generations, family friends, and servants. Grateful businessmen converted houses, such as the Oban Inn (**18**), into hotels or built huge new waterfront hotels, such as the now demolished Queen's Royal on Front Street. A cultural-religious camp, Chautauqua, sprang up at the western end of town, and visitors in search of artistic, intellectual, or spiritual refreshment came from Chicago, St. Louis, Buffalo, and Toronto to listen to orations, sermons, and band concerts.

Just after the turn of the century, the town published a booklet boosting its charms as a summer resort. Accompanied by pictures of holiday houses enjoyed by "well to do business people" from New Orleans and Detroit, the text praised the town's fresh air, modern sanitation, the complete absence of "rowdies or toughs" as well as "puritanical or nonsensical by-laws" that might crimp a tourist's pleasure. Niagara remained a hot-weather favourite until World War I; the rise of the car and the popularity of touring vacations effectively ended its resort era.

Like most of Ontario's small towns, Niagara retreated in the twentieth century, shrinking back into itself as the population migrated to the cities. Unlike almost all of Ontario's small towns, Niagara has had a stunning revival. It stirred shortly after World War II, when preservationists proposed turning the town into a Canadian Williamsburg. Niagarans such as Kathleen Drope, who saved and restored several houses in the late 1950s and 1960s, the master craftsman Carl Banke, who worked on many of the town's old houses, and others were joined by the restoration architect and writer Peter John Stokes, whose *Old Niagara on the Lake* was published in 1971.

Their appreciation of Niagara's old buildings was made immensely easier by the unexpected success of a major theatrical festival in a town of some 12,000 people. The brainchild of a local lawyer named Brian Doherty, the Shaw Festival began modestly enough in 1962 in the Court House; today, with three theatres running for seven months, the Festival generates $8 million and brings 285,000 theatregoers to Niagara. There are some who grumble at the town's success, calling it Niagara-on-the-Take and claiming that Niagara has been ruined. That is simply not the case. In the summer months Queen Street may seem like an unrelieved string of ice cream and souvenir stores, but one street back, on Prideaux and Johnson Streets, the "decent brick and frame houses" advance and retreat from the sidewalk as they have for the past 150 years. The unspoiled Colonial village Eric Arthur noted is still there for the admiring.

Niagara-on-the-Lake

Lake Ontario

Queen's Royal Park

Golf
Course

FRONT ST

18   17   16
          15
        14
          12 11
PRIDEAUX ST
          13 10
        19
          20
30   28   27 26   21   53
QUEEN ST
      29   25 24 23 22
          41   52
                39
          40   42 43 44 46 47 49 50 51
JOHNSON ST
    38   45 48
    37
    36
31   GAGE ST
MISSISSAUGA ST (HWY55)   SIMCOE ST   GATE ST   VICTORIA ST
    35
    34
CENTRE ST
33
32
WILLIAM ST

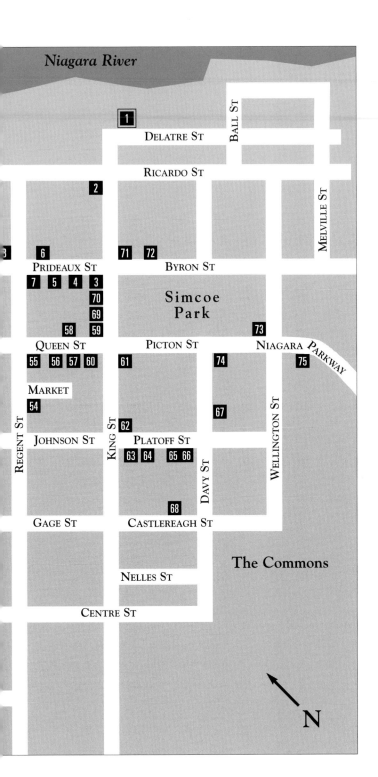

[1] *66 King Street*

[2] *10 Front Street*

▪ **66 King Street,** 1835

Looking startlingly close at this point is Niagara's *raison d'être*: the American Fort Niagara, a mere three miles across the river. For early Niagarans its proximity was truly menacing, yet they continued to live and do business here, sandwiched between Fort George and Fort Mississauga. In spite of a post-1813 policy to relocate away from the water, this was a busy commercial and residential neighbourhood in the 1830s, when 66 King was built as the Whale Inn. Both the Royal Engineers' barracks and the offices of the *Gleaner*, one of Upper Canada's important newspapers from 1817 to 1837, were located on what is now Queen's Royal Park, and the town's largest employer, the Niagara Harbour and Dock Company, was close by to the east.

As for 66 King, except for the taproom door to the left, it looks more like a decorous Loyalist house than a hostelry where a sailor could virtually step from his vessel into a tavern. With its plainish, dignified doorcase and the larger-paned windows typical of the 1830s, the exterior remains very much as originally built. The oval with clasped hands on the frieze above the main door indicated a paid-up subscriber to an insurance company – a crucial time-saver in an era when insurance companies hired private fire brigades, who needed quick assurance of a customer's status.

▪ **10 Front Street,** ca. 1817

Under the stucco bed-and-breakfast with the Victorian veranda beats the heart of a symmetrical clapboard building where early Niagarans did their banking. Thomas McCormick, the agent for the Bank of Upper Canada, was one of the first owners of this house and ran his business from home – parts of a vault are still to be found in the basement.

▪ **Chamber of Commerce Visitor Information Centre, 153 King Street,** ca. 1816

Its hip-roof and cupola balancing on a parade of paired brackets, its façade a self-effacing rhythm of recessed doors and shuttered windows, the Chamber of Commerce Visitor Information Centre has more than good looks going for it. Niagara's Masons built a wooden building here in 1791, and one of their brotherhood, Lieutenant-Governor Simcoe, very probably convened Upper Canada's first parliament in it on September 17, 1792. When it was destroyed in the War of 1812, a new stone building was constructed on this site, reportedly built from pre-War rubble. (It has since been covered with protective stucco.) After use as a residence, school, hotel, and barracks, it was reclaimed by the Masons in 1860.

The first two blocks of Prideaux Street are full of early frame and brick houses.

6 *31 Prideaux Street*

7 *42 Prideaux Street*

4 **18 Prideaux Street,** ca. 1835

The street-facing gable with its deep cornice and returning eaves suggests the newly modish Greek Revival style, but the door's idiosyncratic placement at the side is the mark of a builder beholden to no particular model. Its position close to the street is typical of Niagara's post-War building boom, as are the twelve-over-eight-paned windows on the first floor. The house's first owners were a schoolmaster and his wife, Elizabeth and Alexander McKee (sometimes McKie); Elizabeth's grandfather deeded the property to his three granddaughters in exchange for room, board, laundry, candles, firewood, and medical care.

5 **28 Prideaux Street,** ca. 1817

Built by Dr. James Muirhead to replace a house on this site destroyed in 1813. The stucco finish probably covers the original clapboard; the eared pilasters at the corners add a Greek Revival touch to the prevailing neoclassical order.

6 **31 Prideaux Street,** ca. 1840s

A board-and-batten mongrel with a good deal of charm. The dormers echo the unusual first-floor window and door pediments with their Greek-key corners; the iron fence with its bellicose little posts marks off the deep garden from the street. Although the Second Empire mansard roof and the house's placement on the lot suggest a much later date than its close-to-the-sidewalk Loyalist neighbours, it was probably built in the 1840s. No doubt the mansard appeared when the house was significantly remodelled in the 1870s.

7 **42 Prideaux Street,** ca. 1830

Behind its grandiose façade the original house is only one room deep – a frequent and somewhat puzzling feature of Niagara houses. Arcades, one of the happiest results of the Loyalist love of elliptical shapes and another Niagara hallmark, mark off the five bays. In the central bay, another ellipse – the fanlight – is apparently filled with soap bubbles, a Regency glazing pattern turned sideways in the sidelights. The portico and picket fence are recent and slightly distracting additions. Built for Jemima Stewart, widow.

8 **55 Prideaux Street,** ca. 1820

When she visited Niagara in 1839, the British writer Anna Jamieson complained that a town without a single bookshop had the usual depressing Canadian plethora of taverns. The Promenade House, as 55 Prideaux was then called, was one of them, but even Mrs. Jamieson might have been mollified by this well-behaved little beauty. The graceful Regency pattern in the transom, the raked stone lintels with keystones, and the rosy Flemish bond on the two most prominent façades all contribute to its urbane good looks; the lack of side-

8 *55 Prideaux Street*

10 *78 Prideaux Street*

lights adds to its air of privacy and composure. Described in 1846 as "the most respectable in town" by the British soldier and author Sir Richard Bonnycastle, the hotel provided additional accommodation in a wooden tail that extended down Regent Street.

9 69 Prideaux Street, ca. 1815

"This town is rapidly rising from its ashes," reported Richard Barrett, a Jamaican plantation owner who toured Niagara in 1816. One of the phoenix-like buildings was the house and office of Dr. Robert Kerr, surgeon to the Indian Department, magistrate, and grand master of the Grand Masonic Lodge of Upper Canada. Kerr's original house on this site was said to have been one of the first proper buildings in Niagara, and the replacement, called Demeath, is a confident brick house whose grounds extend to Front Street. Early Niagara builders could be surprisingly willing to breach the Georgian ideal of symmetry, and this house consigns three windows to the right of the door (the centre window originally was the door to Dr. Kerr's office) and one to the left.

10 78 Prideaux Street, ca. 1817

Symmetrical and committed to straight as opposed to curved lines, this house is a convincing Georgian survivor. Unlike the attenuated, sometimes exaggeratedly delicate Loyalist doorcase, this one, which

shelters a lovely six-panelled door with a typically small doorknob, has a compact frieze and a Georgian straightforwardness. But the builder didn't stop there: to light the central hall, he topped the cornice with a six-paned transom, then capped that with a stone lintel to match the windows. (The veranda was added later, probably at the turn of the century.)

11 83 Prideaux Street, ca. 1835

In a town as small as Niagara, tradesmen and lawyers, modest clapboard and imposing brick lived cheek-by-jowl. According to Peter Stokes, this three-bay clapboard house was probably owned by one of Niagara's finest joiners and carpenters, John Davidson. Davidson worked on St. Andrew's (where he built the magnificent pulpit), St. Vincent de Paul, and St. Mark's Churches, and was particularly admired for his splendid curved staircases. His own unassuming house, which seems to have been built a few years before he bought it in 1839, has an appealing combination of dentils and openwork brackets on the frieze.

12 87 Prideaux Street, ca. 1845

Thought to have been built by John Davidson, this front-gabled house is not entirely *comme il faut*: the placement of windows and door is off-kilter, and the slim little vestibule (Stokes likens it to a sedan chair) is undeniably odd. But its simplicity

13 *94 Prideaux Street*

14 *129 Victoria Street*

and small touches such as the acorn-shaped finials at the corners of the bargeboard are attractive. The vestibule, like that at number 83, was probably a practical late-century addition.

13 94 Prideaux Street, ca. 1826

Loyalist builders sometimes got carried away with their detailing, creating door-cases that looked like mantelpieces. The doorcase on this former inn is rather like a piece of fine cabinetwork, but not one that looks out of place on the clapboard exterior. The elliptical fanlight, which spans the sidelights as well as the double doors, and the entablature bordered by recessed pilasters are particularly graceful.

14 129 Victoria Street, 1880s or 1890s

This late-Victorian villa is essentially an L-shaped house with inspiration gathered from hither and yon: the Gothic peak, the bay underneath with its own fringed bell-cast roof, the Italianate round-topped windows, the classical pediment and pillars on the porch, and the Swiss-looking, hooded window surround above the main door.

15 126 Victoria Street, ca. 1884–94

It would be foolish to claim unity of design for this modest clapboard house, but the details have a charm sometimes lacking in less eclectic buildings. The classic Loyalist doorcase and the deep cornice are very old-fashioned for this date, as are the captivat-

ing little window treatments – pediments resting on brackets. The blinkered Swiss windows are very similar to the one on 129 Victoria across the street.

16 80 Front Street, ca. 1820

Regency villas were inspired by Romantic notions about minimizing the barriers between inside and outside: they favoured many and large windows, verandas, exten-sive gardens, and a relatively low-slung, unpretentious profile. The Captain's House, named for Captain Edward Oates, sup-posedly an early occupant, meets all these requirements except for its two-storey height. Its position on a gentle rise over-looking the lake not only satisfied the Regency desire for a picturesque view, it reportedly allowed Mrs. Oates to watch for her husband's boat, the *Richmond Packet*, from the veranda.

17 130 Front Street, 1832

Although only one-quarter United Empire Loyalist, English-born William Kirby (1817–1906) was passionately attached to their cause; among his literary efforts was an epic poem called "The U.E.: A Tale of Upper Canada." So it's only fitting that the house he lived in for half a century has a fine Loyalist doorcase, still visible behind a thick hedge. Kirby's best-known book was *The Golden Dog*, a historical romance about New France; he was also the editor of the *Niagara Mail* and the author of *Annals of Niagara*.

20 *164 Victoria Street*

21 *177 Victoria Street*

18 Oban Inn, 160 Front Street,
    ca. 1822 with later enlargements;
    destroyed by fire 1992 and rebuilt
Even before it burned to the ground on Christmas Day 1992, the little house built by Mary Trumble in the 1820s had been swallowed up in successive enlargements. A hotel and well-loved Niagara landmark since 1895, the new Oban Inn is a faithful re-creation of the original, down to the shingle pattern on the mansard roof.

Walk south on Gate Street, turn left on Prideaux, and continue south on Victoria.

19 153 Victoria Street, ca. 1905–15
A "more-the-merrier" house making unselfconscious use of all kinds of revivalist motifs popular at the start of the century: the Dutch Colonial gambrel roof, the "classical" pedimented porch supported by groups of Ionic pillars large and small, dentils, the oval window, the big dormers. For a purer version of the Dutch Colonial, see the next house.

20 164 Victoria Street, ca. 1915
Dutch Colonial houses are rare in small-town Ontario, because their heyday (after 1910) post-dated the towns' decline. Niagara is fortunate to have a classic example with the signature gambrel roof and a pedimented porch that echoes the central gable. At once stately and homey, as befits a style that symbolized domestic stability,

it rears up on its wide lawn behind a delicate fleur-de-lys fence. As Alan Gowans notes in *The Comfortable House*, the so-called Dutch Colonial house and its gambrel roof are unknown in the Netherlands; modelled on the Dutch farmhouses of the Hudson Valley, this reassuring revival style furnished thousands of suburban American blocks and is still being made today. This one was built for W.R. McClelland, three times Lord Mayor of Niagara and the owner of a local landmark, the grocery at nearby 106 Queen Street (**22**).

21 177 Victoria Street, ca. 1816
The clapboard house built for John Wilson, merchant, has the small-paned twelve-over-twelve windows and the six-panelled door with rectangular transom and no sidelights typical of its decade. Plain to the point of New England, and very satisfying.

As you turn right on Queen Street, look across the street at a row of early shops, beginning with the one at the corner.

22 106 Queen Street, 1835
Niagarans still remember this front-gabled store as McClelland's West End Grocery, which dispensed comestibles for more than 150 years under the old-fashioned sign of the provisioner, the T over the door. The recessed doorway supported by slim cast-iron Corinthian columns was part of an 1880s revamping, but the fanlight in the

25 *126 Queen Street*

27 *165 Queen Street*

gable, the flaring stone lintels, the sills, and the quoins are original.

23 118 Queen Street, ca. 1830 (behind the maple tree, the fourth building from the east end of the block)
The fine cabinetry of the Loyalist doorcase and the first-floor (or display) windows only slightly larger than those above suggest a house, but this dates from a time when domestic and commercial buildings could be indistinguishable. Thought to have been built as a shop by a watchmaker named Jacob Caniff.

24 122 Queen Street, ca. 1840
Roughly a decade later than 118 Queen and distinctly more commercial-looking, thanks to its larger windows.

25 126 Queen Street, ca. 1825
Unique in Niagara and rare in Ontario, the theatrical gable and royal coat of arms must have impressed the citizenry during the building's tenure as a customs house. (When the writer William Kirby was the customs collector, he returned here in the evenings to write his 1877 historical novel, *The Golden Dog.*) Below the shaped gable, Niagara decorum restores itself, with the limestone keystone and imposts emphasizing the primness of its narrow doorway.

26 157 Queen Street, 1817
While the Americans set fire to Niagara on a wintry night in 1813, the sixty-three-year-old Mary Rogers single-handedly rescued her weighty parlour mantelpiece by carrying it out to the street. In 1817, when her son James Rogers announced in the Niagara *Gleaner* that his newly built coffeehouse on Queen Street would entertain "Genteel Company in handsome style and reasonable terms," the mantelpiece was reinstalled in the drawing room. That at least is the family legend. What is certain is that the parlour mantelpiece here is indeed a late-Loyalist fantasia of colonettes and reeded pilasters. (If the house is functioning as a bed-and-breakfast during your visit, as it frequently does, it may be possible for inquirers to see the mantelpiece.) Today the house is a sympathetic partner in one of Niagara's best streetscapes, the original clapboard covered long ago in protective stucco, the regularity of its six shuttered bays pleasingly interrupted by the Loyalist doorcase. Note that the metal strips (called cames) in the slender sidelights are knotted with the embossed oval or rounded ornaments called paterae, in three different styles.

27 165 Queen Street, ca. 1820
A most satisfying strongbox of a house, firmly sectioned off into bays and stories by arcades and a string course. It's best seen in demi-profile, where its impregnable-looking, windowless parapet walls contrast with the rhythm of the arcades and the

28 *187 Queen Street*

31 *307 Mississauga Street*

finely fluted pilasters of the doorcase that entirely fills one arcade. (The virtually blind sides of this house and of 157 Queen suggest that their builders expected the street to be much more closely built up than it was.) Although it was probably built by Adam Crysler, the house's best-known occupant was Colonel David MacDougal, a hero of Lundy's Lane and a charter member of St. Vincent de Paul Roman Catholic Church.

28 187 Queen Street, ca. 1822

Look through the lilac hedge that screens the porch for a glimpse of this house's superb Greek Revival door, copied straight from the New York architect Minard Lafever's 1835 pattern book, *The Beauties of Modern Architecture*. Its bold, stylized effects – a deep plain architrave edged on the inside by bead-and-reel moulding and topped with a flourish of scrolls and palmettes – are characteristic of the style that swept the United States in the 1830s and '40s. The door was an afterthought, probably grafted in the 1840s onto a big Loyalist box built by a well-to-do merchant, Ralph Morden Crysler. Roslyn Cottage, as this house is too modestly titled, is so close to the street that its two-storey pilasters with their beautifully carved Ionic whorls and modillion-edged cornice should be admired from across Queen Street.

29 184 Queen Street, 1909

Best seen in winter, this is a fine example of Tudor Revival, with the requisite half-timbering, self-important chimneys, and strings of tiny-paned windows (some leaded) sheltering behind the shrubbery. The heavy-lidded protruding entrance, where the brick bleeds "naturalistically" into the stone foundation, is particularly delightful. Designed by Charles Wilmot, who was also responsible for the clock tower in front of the Court House, for J.M. Mussen, Lord Mayor of Niagara and a prime mover behind the clock tower.

30 209 Queen Street, 1832

A big, urbane house built by a Niagara member of parliament, Charles Richardson. The four chimneys were set fashionably in from the corners, and the expansive doorcase is surmounted by its own echo in the Palladian window on the second floor. Richardson's Georgian symmetry was a casualty of one of Niagara's periodic "American invasions," when the town became a summer resort at the turn of the century: the side wing and galleries were added by an American owner, businessman Charles K. Birge.

Turn left on Mississauga and walk south two blocks.

31 307 Mississauga Street, 1818

Despite its suburban look, this neighbour-

32 *392 Mississauga Street*

34 *St. Andrew's Manse,*
342 Simcoe Street

hood was part of Niagara's original subdivision, and this one-acre lot was granted to John Servos, a member of a prominent United Empire Loyalist family, in 1816. A town like Niagara, intent on preservation, restoration, and diabolically clever reproduction, can be confusing: this simple and eminently copy-able house in perfect condition could almost be a reproduction. The curious asymmetry of the window placement is a good clue to its age; a modern builder would be very likely to regularize the arrangement.

32 392 Mississauga Street, ca. 1816

John Breakenridge, a barrister from Virginia, commissioned three houses in this neighbourhood in the decade after the War. The builder of this, his second house, had the usual elements – glass and native white pine ("that marvelous material," as Peter Stokes calls it) – and the standard neoclassical repertoire of pilasters, modillions, and friezes to vary and organize as he saw fit. What he created is one of Niagara's handsomest houses, whose disciplined plainness is thrown into relief by the modillion cornice, the elaborately carved doorcase, the two-storey pilasters with their tightly curled Ionic ramshorns. Balancing the horizontal clapboards and the cornice are the strongly vertical lines of the pilasters, the French doors, and the deep end chimneys. The only rest from all these straight lines comes from the curves of the

capitals, the elliptical fanlight, and the patterns in the fanlight and sidelights. The fanlight design, labelled "unfocused" by Ken MacPherson and Douglas Richardson in *Ontario Towns*, is not a success, but the double swags at the top, like strings of beads, are too pretty to miss.

33 240 Centre Street, ca. 1823

John Breakenridge's last house is in sad shape, a ghost with excellent bones. Why Breakenridge left his splendid second house (32 above) is not known, but this one is more restrained, with a simple doorcase and smallish window openings with flared stone lintels. The rosy handmade bricks are set in common bond rather than the more expensive Flemish bond. After Breakenridge died in 1828 at the age of thirty-nine, his cash-strapped widow ran a private school here.

34 St. Andrew's Manse, 342 Simcoe Street, 1836

Built by the Reverend Robert McGill, rector of St. Andrew's, and later bought by the congregation for its manse. Its shape – the compact, hip-roofed Ontario cottage so common elsewhere in the province – is relatively unusual in Niagara. But the four-part Loyalist door is familiar, and the combination of Flemish bond with stone accents complements the church across the street.

36 *289 Simcoe Street*

38 *234 Johnson Street*

■ St. Andrew's Presbyterian Church, 323 Simcoe Street, 1831

One of Ontario's most celebrated churches, St. Andrew's has several faces. From the front, its monumental Doric portico and steeple are daunting. The pinkish brick side, broken by four clear-paned Georgian windows, is more soothing, more domestic, perhaps even a bit short. And the Georgian interior, with its box pews like small living rooms, has the intimacy of a New England church.

A lot of Presbyterian grit and stubbornness underlies St. Andrew's composure. After the original 1794 frame or log Church of Scotland was burned by the Americans, the congregation worshipped for eighteen years in their schoolhouse while they rebuilt homes and businesses and saved for a new church. In 1831, after the Reverend Robert McGill counted 831 parishioners and £400, the cornerstone was laid to the wail of bagpipes.

James Cooper, a member of the congregation, cobbled together a body from Asher Benjamin's 1820 pattern book, *Rudiments of Architecture*, with a Doric portico and an Ionic steeple drawn from Scottish and American sources. As if that were not eclectic enough, Cooper placed the cabinetmaker John Davidson's masterpiece, the black walnut pulpit with its double spiral staircase, with its back to the main door. The sunburst in the tympanum may well date from a post-tornado adjustment

designed by Kivas Tully in 1854.

To see the comely white-painted interior, with slip pews and table pews as well as box pews and long linen-covered tables on Communion Sundays, time your visit for the Sunday service at 11 a.m.

■ 289 Simcoe Street, ca. 1817

The regular march of the early twelve-over-twelve windows is varied only by the equally plain geometry of the transom and sidelights; symmetrical five-bay houses such as this are characteristic of the Niagara region. An early inhabitant was James Lockhart, a merchant, banker, and shipowner.

■ 285 Simcoe Street, ca. 1817

Standing high over a stone basement, with its hip-roof, tall paired chimneys, small-paned windows, and doorcase poised in unobtrusive balance, this is, as its restorer Peter Stokes says, "a microcosm of the early Niagara house." Not easy to see in much detail from the street when the leaves are out, the house is a newcomer to Simcoe Street; it began life on the land owned by the Butler family, of Butler's Rangers fame, and was moved in 1969.

Turn left at Johnson Street.

■ 234 Johnson Street, ca. 1824

The Clench house has everything going for it – setting, history, craftsmanship. Its two-

[41] *233 Gate Street*

[43] *129 Johnson Street*

acre site, which accommodates the sinuous course of One-Mile Creek, provided mid-town privacy and poetry. Ralfe Clench, a lieutenant in Butler's Rangers who went on to be a judge and member of the provincial legislature, may have started building as early as 1816. (Ironically, the original Clench house, one of only two houses to survive the destruction of the town in 1813, burned down in a washday fire short-ly after the Americans left.) Like a sheet of lined paper, the clapboard five-bay front is marked off by six fluted Ionic pilasters and centred with a fine doorcase topped on the second floor by a Venetian window – details familiar from other Niagara houses. Unfortunately the balconied portico (a recent addition) obscures the neoclassical confidence of the original façade. (Extensions to the side and rear also date from this century.)

Walk east on Johnson Street to the corner of Gate Street.

[39] 240, [40] 243, [41] 233 Gate Street,
   various dates
With their stripped-down simplicity, these three clapboard houses may look new but they date from the nineteenth century and were restored by one of Niagara's pioneers of preservation, Kathleen Drope, in the 1960s. Probably the newest and the most interesting of the trio, at least historically, number 243 is known locally as the Slave

Cottage. Its owner, Daniel Servos Waters, was black but was never a slave, having been born to free parents.

Looking very New Englandish with its saltbox shape, number 233 probably dates from as early as the 1820s, although ca. 1840 is the date usually given.

Number 240 Gate Street was built around 1818 (without the vestibule and much smaller in general) as the house of John MacMonigle, yeoman.

Johnson Street between Gate and Victoria is a mixed bouquet of styles, eras, and social levels. Now purely residential, in the nine-teenth century the street was also home to commercial and manufacturing enter-prises that ranged from carriage-making to tailoring.

[42] 135 Johnson Street, ca. 1822
The house of George Greenlees, yeoman, is typical of many early local buildings: close to the street, sparing of detail (a tran-som may have been removed), slightly asymmetrical (to accommodate a larger room on the right). Also typical: its gen-erous three-bay front belies the fact that it is only one room deep, with an attached kitchen. The fine side garden has been part of the property since 1829.

[43] 129 Johnson Street, ca. 1880s
At least half a century younger than its neighbour number 135, this attractive cot-

48 *118 Johnson Street*

50 95 Johnson Street

tage has tempered its picturesque airs, perhaps in the spirit of good neighbourliness. The dentil-like trim on the bargeboard, the stained glass, and the multi-paned windows are late-century variations on a Gothic Revival base.

44 127 Johnson Street, 1912
Something different yet again, this unassuming vernacular house has the look of a farmhouse that somehow found itself on this prim town street. Its first owner was W.H. Curtis, a housepainter.

45 126 Johnson Street, ca. 1828
The fringe of dentils above the doorcase frieze is a charming touch. It was owned for many years by the carriage-making Platt family, whose shops stood next door (where number 134 is now) until the late 1920s or early '30s.

46 123 Johnson Street, 1840s, 1897
An L-shaped bay-and-gable with a complicated history, like number 129 playing down its Gothic Revival inheritance. Originally two small rental units, they were joined together in 1897 when W. Platt, the carriage-maker who lived at number 126, bought them. The porch's pretty treillage was devised from stock trimmings.

47 115–119 Johnson Street, ca. 1840
Niagara's unique surviving example of row housing, built as rental properties for work-

ing-class families and army personnel by tailor George Varey next door to his own house at 105 Johnson. The plain-Jane façade remains very much as built, although two of the original three units have been combined inside. The shiny red ochre paint is typical of the period.

48 118 Johnson Street, ca. 1835
This house, with its paid-up insurance oval over the door, was built close to the sidewalk and moved back later in the century, when fashions in landscaping changed. First owned by a hat-maker with the Dickensian name of Jared Stocking, it served as an inn called the Sign of the Crown, a young ladies' boarding school, and an evening school. In 1837, when its owner advertised the inn for sale or rent, it had eight bedrooms, two dining rooms, stabling for four span of horses, and a half-acre garden "well stocked with the choicest of Fruit trees and Currant Bushes."

49 105 Johnson Street, ca. 1837
A map from 1810 indicates a building on this site, and the fire-scarred foundations of George Varey's rough-cast, gently hip-roofed house may indeed be pre-War. Varey did his tailoring in the room at the northeast corner, painted red ochre; he also played bass viol in the Methodist Church.

50 95 Johnson Street, 1835
Master mason James Blain ran a brick busi-

51 *85 Johnson Street*

52 *Grace United Church, 220 Victoria Street*

ness at the back of his self-made house, which remains an excellent advertisement for the best in materials and workmanship. The soft Flemish-bond brick is accessorized with limestone – the biggish baseline, the sills, and the imposts and keystone that call attention to the reticent little doorcase, minus the usual sidelights. Blain, who probably worked on St. Andrew's Church, inscribed the date of his house in the keystone. Later the house served as the post office (it is known locally as the Post House), and the location of the office door is still visible at the Victoria Street corner. (The large addition to the southeast dates from the late 1980s.)

51 85 Johnson Street, 1813

Not all Niagarans rebuilding after the War were indulging in Flemish-bond brick, arcading, and fanlights. This appealing little Goody Two-Shoes of a house turns its gable to the front to accommodate the narrow lot; the slender clapboards and sober door are clues to its early date. (The garage is an add-on.)

52 Grace United Church, 220 Victoria Street, 1852

As the Gothic Revival progressed, doubts about pointed arches and other popish baggage began to nag at Baptists, Methodists, and Presbyterians. Round Italianate arches sat much better with Niagara's breakaway Free Kirk Presbyterians, and their

steeple-less church has a heft and an independent verve that must have pleased them. Built by William Thomas (who built Niagara's Court House in 1847), when the Free Kirk separated from St. Andrew's, this church has been mistakenly overshadowed by Niagara's Big Three: the Anglican, Catholic, and Presbyterian churches. The bold gable front outlined by the white-brick corbel table, the drip moulds like thick arcs of cake icing, the studded door rimmed with a Romanesque zigzag all do their part in a doughty masculine composition. When the Free Kirk returned to St. Andrew's fold, the local Methodists first rented and then bought this church, in 1875 for $1,500. In 1925, they joined the newborn United Church.

53 Royal George Theatre, 83 Queen Street, ca. 1915

With its flattened wooden pilasters, pediment, and Greek-key frieze, the Shaw Festival's Royal George Theatre looks rather like a cardboard stage set. Built as a moviehouse during World War I and christened the Kitchener, it was Niagara's first cement block structure. It was renovated and Greek-ified in 1978 when owned by a mime company. Now the Shaw Festival's third stage, it seats 351.

Continue east on Queen Street, with a brief detour at the corner of Regent.

57 *Court House, 26 Queen Street*

58 *23–27 Queen Street*

54 The Angel Inn, 224 Regent Street, ca. 1825

In 1826, the *Gleaner* advertised an "excellent TAVERN and STAND known by the Sign of the Angel Inn." One of Ontario's earliest inns still accommodating travellers, the Angel's straightforward charms are obscured by too many signs and all-wrong wide modern clapboard. Its current owners claim the inn is haunted by the ghost of a British soldier massacred on the site in 1813; he manifests a strong aversion to the American flag.

55 46 Queen Street, ca. 1825, reconstructed 1981

The double rows of arcades are familiar from Niagara houses built in this period, but this was one of Queen Street's earliest stores, a dry-goods shop run by John J. Daly. Faithfully reconstructed in 1981, it was the winner of an Ontario Renews Award.

56 32 Queen Street, ca. 1850

This much-modified commercial building has a finely detailed Victorian storefront, the recessed doorways flanked by display windows trimmed with wooden arches. The boomtown façade was designed in the second half of the nineteenth century to conceal the joining of two originally separate buildings.

57 Court House, 26 Queen Street, 1847

The *gravitas* of the Court House is unique in Niagara, but buildings like it – stony, classically inspired hymns to justice and order – were springing up all over Canada West in the middle decades of the century. The architect, William Thomas, had emigrated from England only in 1843, but he was already building St. Michael's Cathedral in Toronto and would go on to design St. Lawrence Hall and the Don Jail in that city. It probably says something about the building's dignity as well as Niagara's aspirations that although this building functioned as the courthouse for only fourteen years, it's still called that. (Planned as the Lincoln County Court House, town hall, market, and jail, the building was demoted to its purely local functions when the upstart St. Catharines became the county seat in 1861.) Although Thomas achieved an undeniable decorum, he mixed his effects in a fairly unorthodox manner typical of the era: the twisted-ribbon design on the string course below the third storey and the bearded-man keystones on the first floor are cases in point. The Court House now houses the Public Library, Parks Canada offices, and the Shaw Festival's Court House Theatre.

58 23–27 Queen Street, ca. 1890

A fine late-century commercial building, unusual in Niagara for its elaborate ornamentation. Lift your eyes to the second

61 *Prince of Wales Hotel, 6 Picton Street*

62 *244 King Street*

storey and admire the four proud chimneys and the deep border of brick-on-brick smocking that stretches across the building. The terracotta Ionic capitals and plaques are *fin-de-siècle* notes typical of the care taken with the entire building. The owner was Samuel Rowley, a Philadelphian who manufactured canning jars.

59 Niagara Apothecary, 5 Queen Street, 1820

The Italianate windows divided into further rounded forms by cable-moulded glazing bars are the attention-grabbers here, but no detail (panelled pilasters, dentils, and tiny pendants) has been spared to make this the very model of a Confederation-era shopfront. When the Niagara Apothecary became a museum in 1970, it was restored inside and out to 1866, when the building began a century's uninterrupted use as a pharmacy.

60 16 Queen Street, ca. 1830

One of Queen Street's most popular buildings is not all it seems. The graceful Gothic Revival glazing is a 1970s reproduction; the floors above are genuine and very workaday. The third floor, probably a storage loft, had a door in the centre with crane beam and hook.

61 Prince of Wales Hotel, 6 Picton Street, 1882

Decorated as relentlessly as a late-Victorian

parlour, from its dormered and turreted roof to the non-stop white-brick trim that outlines every door, window, and building seam, the Prince of Wales probably looked to its early customers like the embodiment of a good time. In spite of its name, no Prince of Wales has yet crossed its threshold; after being called Long's Hotel, Niagara House, and the Arcade Hotel, it was rechristened after a 1901 visit by the Duke and Duchess of York, the future King George V and Queen Mary. (He was created Prince of Wales a few months after his return from Canada.) The original building wrapped around the corner of Picton and King Streets; recent additions extend along both streets.

62 244 King Street, ca. 1828

At times a private school and lodging house, this thirteen-room house was built by Francis Moore, yeoman, in what was then the new part of town. The twelve-over-twelve-paned windows that butt against the cornice and the pilastered doorcase with its deep frieze give the house its disciplined look; the romantic bay window with Gothic tracery was added by the present owner, a restoration architect too knowledgeable to be a purist.

63 10 Platoff Street, ca. 1845

Number 10 looks rather like a poor but proud man's version of a typical Niagara house: note the chaste doorway, the

67 *230 Davy Street*

68 *Niagara Historical Society Museum, 43 Castlereagh Street*

"Niagara asymmetry" of the window placement, and the rudimentary two-way staircase, upscale versions of which can be seen in much grander houses.

64 20 Platoff Street, ca. 1839

Neat as a pin and virtually unadorned except for its board-and-batten skin, this saltbox was owned in its earliest years by two carpenters, Edward Dixon and Thomas Eedson. Eedson briefly ran a temperance house at 244 King Street (62 above).

65 30 Platoff Street, 1908

From the pinnacle on the roof to the wagon-wheels in the Eastlake treillage to the cunning little shed roofs over the windows, this is one of Niagara's relatively rare and most delightful essays in the picturesque.

66 40 Platoff Street, 1859

Looking ghostly but still dignified, Niagara's old public school has been converted into apartments. The fanlight above the main door is no more, but the yellow-brick string course and window treatments that combine stone headers and sills with brick trim contribute an appropriate note of seriousness. The original four classrooms accommodated two classes each; the building functioned as a school until Parliament Oak Public School was built in 1948.

67 230 Davy Street, ca. 1842

Fashions were changing in 1842, when Peter Baikie, shipwright, bought a quarter-acre in "the new survey" and built a two-storey house. His coquettish veranda, with its bell-cast roof and openwork treillage, looked very novel at the time – and still does in this red-brick Loyalist town. The French doors are another fashionable departure from the local norm, but behind the flossy veranda the house itself is the familiar symmetrical three-bay structure.

Go south on Davy Street and turn right at Castlereagh.

68 Niagara Historical Society Museum, 43 Castlereagh Street, 1907, 1875, 1973

A tripartite demonstration of Niagara's attachment to its past. The Dutch-gabled building to the left was built in 1907 by a St. Catharines architect, W.B. Allan, to house the Niagara Historical Society's proliferating collection. (The first building designed as a museum in Ontario, it pre-dates Toronto's Royal Ontario Museum by five years.) On the right, looking like the paradigm of the nineteenth-century schoolhouse, the bracketed and bell-towered high school was very much in tune with contemporary Ministry of Education guidelines: a manual published a year after this school was built in 1875 called for white-brick trim on red-brick schools, a bell that could be heard within a three-mile radius, and windows at least four feet above the

69 *177 King Street*

71 *St. Mark's Rectory,*
17 Byron Street

ground (to avoid distraction). In 1950, when the high school closed, the town donated it to the Historical Society. And finally, in 1973, the two buildings were joined by a board-and-batten wing, lit by eight Italianate windows salvaged from St. Mark's parish hall.

Continue to King Street and return to the corner of Queen.

69 177 King Street, ca. 1886
For the late Victorians, this asymmetrical grab-bag of sawn appliqués, Saracen tower, sweeping porch, and stained glass were standard parts of the fashionable Queen Anne package. But in a town where the finest houses try to outdo each other in tasteful plainness, 177 King looks frankly outlandish. The house was also exceptional in that its mistress was a member of Niagara's sizeable nineteenth-century black community. Most of the blacks lived further south, in the vicinity of John and Mary Streets, but when Fanny Ross married a much older, white American merchant, Samuel Rowley (the owner of 58 above), he built her a mansion close to the centre of town.

70 169 King Street, ca. 1877
The endearing veranda trim, with its twisted spindles and quatrefoils, looks almost too good to be true – and it is. Albeit recent, it suits the little cottage and pro-

vides a welcome variation to Niagara's remarkably homogeneous look. The Gothic-peaked cottage, a staple of most Ontario towns, is rare in Niagara because the style's mid-century popularity coincided with one of the town's periodic slumps.

71 St. Mark's Rectory, 17 Byron Street, 1858
Presenting "An Irregular Villa in the Italian style, bracketed," in his 1840 pattern book, *Cottage Residences,* the American architect A.J. Downing conceded that it was not for every customer. Less sophisticated clients would choose a more symmetrical house, but the cognoscenti preferred irregular designs because they better evoked "emotions of the beautiful or picturesque." Certainly the Niagara Anglicans were persons of taste, and their rectory follows Downing's model fairly closely, with its balconied campanile tucked between two wings. Italianate villas, with their complicated rooflines, towers, brackets, and pairs of round-headed windows, could be playful, sometimes downright hectic. But Niagara's only example of the style preserves a cool Anglican calm, aided by the height of its windows and stories, the classical pediment on the front gable, and the stone-like effect of the so-called white brick. Even the chimneys, panelled and ringed with corbels that echo the brackets on the house, are stately.

72 *St. Mark's Anglican Church*
41 Byron Street

72 *Churchyard*

72 St. Mark's Anglican Church, 41 Byron Street, 1805, 1843

"Do not allow it to be touched," Dean Stanley ordered on an 1890 visit to Canada. "This is a piece of old England." At least part of St. Mark's undeniable Englishness comes from its organic look – as if it had thrust itself up in the midst of its gravestones, like a rock surfacing in the spring. And yet St. Mark's has lived through an impressive amount of New World change. Its beginnings were discouragingly slow: in 1807, the Reverend Robert Addison reported to the Society for the Propagation of the Gospel that the local Anglicans had begun too ambitiously in a mainly Presbyterian settlement, but the floors of the new church were laid and the windows almost ready for glazing.

Originally a stone rectangle with an apse to the east, in 1813 the church was commandeered by the Americans as a barracks, hospital, and storeroom for whiskey, pork, and other non-sacramental sundries. The Reverend Addison found the "horrid scenes" he witnessed during the American occupation impossible to describe. (Look at Charles Morrison's flat, scarred gravestone, east of the church and to the right of the two large Rigg stones, for a legendary piece of American callousness: the army butchers used it as a chopping block.) Burned by the retreating Americans except for its stone walls, the church was not fully usable again until 1820.

The chancel and transepts were added in 1843, very probably to designs by the Toronto architect John Howard, and the interior was Gothicized, as dictated by ecclesiastical fashion and a growing congregation. Today the inside of St. Mark's, with its anecdotal hodgepodge of Greek Revival memorial tablets, "floating" pulpits, Victorian stained glass, and needlepoint flowing with Niagara Peninsula grapes and wheat, is both jolly and poignant.

Cross Simcoe Park to reach Wellington and Picton Streets.

73 St. Vincent de Paul Roman Catholic Church, 93 Picton Street, 1834

Disappointingly featureless from the outside, St. Vincent de Paul deserves a look inside (it is usually open) and a little effort of the imagination. One of the town's three original churches, with St. Mark's Anglican and St. Andrew's Presbyterian, it was built in clapboard with the Gothic windows that made a natural appeal to a Catholic congregation. Now covered in industrial-looking stucco, with a 1965 addition like a rounded modernist distension, the church on the inside has a split personality; once past the strip of bluish marble on the floor that separates the new from the old, you can literally put the misjudged reno behind you. The old windows, the wooden vaulting, the florid late-century Stations of the Cross, and particularly the

[73] *St. Vincent de Paul Roman Catholic Church, 93 Picton Street*

[75] *Festival Theatre, 110 Picton Street*

painted sky with moon and stars above the altar are touching. In the same slightly amateurish vein, the pilasters are a disarming piece of architectural indecision: they apparently end with a Gothic arch and then, as if the carpenter could not entirely forgo his classical training, top that off with an Ionic capital.

[74] Moffat's Inn, 60 Picton Street, ca. 1835

Niagara in the 1830s was flourishing, supplying provisions to the tiny hamlets of Hamilton and St. Catharines, serving as the legal centre for three counties, and busily employing shipbuilders and associated craftsmen at the Harbour and Dock Company. Richard Moffat's was one of the town's twenty-eight taverns, a five-bay Georgian building popular with Harbour and Dock Company commercial travellers and described in W.H. Smith's *Gazette* of 1848 as one of the two best inns in town. Its Loyalist door has given way to a recessed modern one, but the straight-ahead proportions and most of the original twelve-over-twelve windows remain. Its original clapboard now covered in stucco, it still operates as an inn, with an extension towards Davy Street added in 1976.

[75] Festival Theatre, 110 Picton Street (The Commons), 1973

Few Ontario towns have significant examples of modern architecture, but then very few Ontario towns have devised for themselves a new lease on life. After ten years of operations in the Court House, the Shaw Festival commissioned the late Ron Thom to build an 847-seat theatre on the town commons. An interesting choice for a nineteenth-century eastern town, the British Columbian architect was an admirer of Frank Lloyd Wright ("I sometimes call myself Frank Lloyd Thom") and, via Wright, of things Japanese. Admired for his ability to blend new buildings into traditional settings (for example, Toronto's Massey College), Thom designed a dignified build-up of warm brick rectangles that is as classical in its way as the pillared, fan-lit houses of early Niagara. Part of the Wright heritage is Thom's sensitivity to landscape and context (see Peterborough's Trent University); modestly screened by trees, the Festival Theatre manages to be in Niagara but not of it, to suggest that the play, not the building, is the thing. The low-slung shingle roofs that soften the brick modules, the horizontal Japanese/Prairie School feeling of the glass wall and veranda that overlook the rear patio, the interior warmed by tile, wood, and brick are typical Thom notes.

Asa Wolverton House

Paris

Yankees, Cobblestones, and
"the Town of Tall Chimneys"

D riving through Paris, the traveller sees a pleasant, hilly town sprawling along the confluence of the Grand and Nith Rivers. Carved into three unequal parts by the meandering rivers, the place proffers the usual small-town diversions: several smoky cafés, a Chinese restaurant, a few antiques shops, a full denominational set of churches, and some impressive houses on Grand River Street North. Like many Ontario towns, it looks at once bustling and stopped in time.

But a few hours spent walking Paris's streets will bring you face to face with a highly individual history of "pushing, independent, success-at-any-price" Yankees who turned a picturesque spot into the "Manchester of Ontario." (Both descriptions are from *The History of the County of Brant, Ontario*, published in 1883.) Not coincidentally, the town's American forefathers were also responsible for its architectural distinction, a collection of cobblestone buildings unique in Canada.

Paris's first European settler was not an American but a gently reared English Quaker named William Holme. In 1821, he and a small party arrived at the Forks of the Grand, as the place was then called, and began clearing land and selling the plaster or gypsum deposits found on the south bank of the Nith for fertilizer. Holme persisted for eight years, looking upon his land as an Old Country estate rather than as a town to be developed, trying in a rather desultory way to live the life of a country gentleman.

In February 1829, an ex-Vermonter and ironware salesman bought him out: for $10,000, Hiram Capron acquired a thousand acres, the few buildings Holme had erected, and his rights to the plaster beds. Significantly, Holme's neighbours had called him "Squire," while the townspeople of Paris nicknamed the ceaselessly active and inventive Capron "King."

Within six months of Capron's arrival, a blacksmith, a wheelwright, a cabinetmaker, and a joiner were building houses, and – what Capron considered even more heartening – three babies had been born in the village. A shop, a carding machine, and the vital distillery were in preparation. By the end of 1831, the Forks of the Grand had changed its name to Paris, after the plaster of Paris beds that supplied the new settlement's most important industry (and covered the walls of many early houses). Capron had wanted to call his pretty village Paris from the start but, according to Donald E. Smith's *At the Forks of the Grand*, the settlers at first resisted a name they associated with "mobs, guillotines, and ambitious ladies."

From its earliest days, Paris seems to have struck visitors, passers-by, and settlers as unusually beautiful. When he toured "the delightful Village" in 1834, the editor of Hamilton's *Western Mercury* was so charmed by its neatness, the industriousness of its inhabitants, and the picturesqueness of its setting that he hazarded, "European strangers might find here the fairy land of their youthful dreams." In 1846, an English visitor, William Kingston, nominated Paris as "decidedly the prettiest town we have yet seen in Canada," a claim naturally made much of in Paris's accounts of itself. Even the usually tart Anna Jamieson, in *Winter Studies and Summer Rambles in Canada* (1838), responded to the charm of Paris's wooded riverside setting.

But the undulating waterways were divisive as well as romantic. They chopped the town in two rivalrous main parts, Upper Town and Lower Town (the third part, the Flats, was less important). The first settlement began in Upper Town, around Grand River Street South, Church, Burwell, Dundas, and Dumfries Streets. As symbolized by the steeple of St. James Anglican Church, this part of town was staunchly Protestant and populated by English, Scottish, and Northern Irish settlers. The inhabitants of Lower Town, with Grand River Street North as its spine, tended to be Irishmen and Americans. Hiram Capron settled in Lower Town and, a quarter-century after the town's founding, liked to recall the days when bellicose partisans challenged each other:

Upper or Lower
Under which King, Parisian, speak or die!

The "Upper King" was William IV, the "Lower" was Hiram Capron.

Nor was Capron the only eminent American in Paris. Cheap Canadian land and a presumed dearth of local enterprise appealed to many Americans in the decades after the War of 1812, and "success-at-any-price" Yankees were the founding citizens of Paris. They included Norman Hamilton, a businessman from the Rochester area who made a fortune from pigs and whiskey; Charles Mitchell, a New Yorker who owned a carriage-making factory; and Asa Wolverton, another New Yorker, who owned two sawmills.

All three men built handsome Greek Revival houses that still stand, but

Paris's distinctive architectural stamp is the work of a much less prosperous American, a mason from Albany, New York, named Levi Boughton. Because Boughton settled in Paris in the late 1830s, an American folk art found its only foothold in Canada West. Using cobblestones from the west bank of the Grand River, Boughton erected or inspired buildings in a variety of styles, most memorably the grandly allusive Greek Revival. The results of this serendipitous conjunction of geology, history, and architecture are eleven cobblestone houses and two cobblestone churches in Paris and in the neighbouring township of South Dumfries.

The raw materials were in Paris for the asking, and had been since the last ice age, when glaciers ground the loose stones on top of the bedrock into cobblestones. (A pebble is a stone that can be held in two fingers, while a cobblestone can be held in one hand, and a boulder demands two hands. Geologists classify a stone that measures from $2^{1}/_{2}$ to 10 inches in diameter as a cobblestone.) The rubble rounded and polished by the glaciers was mostly local sedimentary sandstone and limestone, but it included smaller amounts of harder metamorphic stones, such as gneiss and quartzite, transported by the glaciers from as far north as Labrador. When the ice melted, the cobbles remained. Some, called field cobbles, are roughly rounded; others, including the ones along Lake Ontario's shoreline and in the Paris area, were subjected to further rounding and polishing by glacial rivers and lakes.

In upstate New York, in the late 1820s, the masons who had recently finished building the Erie Canal noted the plentiful water-rounded stones and the local limestone, which could be crushed and burned to produce lime for mortar. They began to sheathe houses with cobbles set in horizontal courses in mortar, with a raised ridge of mortar between the courses. Some of the masons were English and may have been inspired by eighteenth- and nineteenth-century houses in Norfolk and the southeast of England constructed of beach flints, but the exact source remains unknown. Progressing rapidly from primitive ideas of construction and style to sturdy, highly sophisticated houses, the masons produced hundreds of cobblestone buildings in western and central New York State during the 1830s and '40s.

The vogue crossed the border to Paris in 1839, when Boughton emigrated to Upper Canada. Born in 1804, Boughton had learned his trade in the Rochester area, where the cobblestone fad was particularly intense. He may well have resettled in Paris because the burgeoning town afforded plenty of work for a skilled mason. (Like so many Canadian towns of the era, Paris had more north-south than east-west communication; both Capron and Norman Hamilton furnished their houses with luxury goods from Rochester and Buffalo, transported to Paris in farm wagons.)

It's possible that the great heaps of cobblestones along the Grand River caught Boughton's eye, but no man of business would base a move on such a material. Cobblestone masonry was a labour-intensive architectural flourish to be indulged in sparingly, and Boughton no doubt spent most of his working hours in Paris crafting houses in brick and, less frequently, in quarried stone. But he also found the time to cover the town's most diverting houses with cobbles, and to perfect his own skill in that demanding medium.

Nineteenth-century Parisians would be surprised to read that Levi Boughton's legacy is the single most interesting thing about their town today. To them, Paris was a thriving industrial centre, a fortunate site where enterprising citizens, abundant water power, and rail connections had created a little Manchester at the forks of the Grand. In 1834, the newborn town supported a remarkable thirty-one industries. The town's *raison d'être*, the gypsum deposits along the banks of the Grand and the Nith and in the Upper Town hill, was described by an early historian as "almost inexhaustible." By 1856, when Capron praised the "wonderful patience and toil" of the Cornish miners who extracted the gypsum from subterranean galleries, plaster mills produced both fertilizer and plaster of Paris.

By 1883, Paris's industries included the Paris Tobacco and Cigar Manufactory, a woollen factory, the Canada Land Plaster Company, and factories that produced wool and other textiles, agricultural machinery, buttons, crockery, industrial nuts, and needles, as well as the usual tannery, flour mill, and gristmill. No dark satanic mills here, if the lyrical pen of the historian of Brant County is to be believed: industry had only prettified "the town of tall chimneys" as the long line of "huge square many-windowed stone buildings of graceful architecture" provided interest to the otherwise featureless flats. The effect at night was positively fairy-like: "Standing on the bridge from the Upper Town across the Grand River, it is pleasant to watch, as the evening star appears in the first dusk, a fourfold tier of gas-lit windows burst forth from each of these palaces of industry, starring with dancing lights the impetuous stream below."

Chief among the builders of the palaces of industry was the Scottish-American John Penman, Paris's most prominent citizen after Hiram Capron died in 1872. It seems only appropriate that Penman bought Capron's mansion on Grand River Street North, virtually effaced it, and renamed it. Penman's, his textile mill, was not only Paris's largest employer by far but the biggest knit-goods manufacturer in Canada. At the turn of the century, when Paris's population was 3,500, Penman's employed 1,000 people to produce mainly men's underwear, plus socks, neckties, and gloves. In many ways Penman's constituted a parallel universe: the company recruited mill workers from the English east Midlands, created workers' housing close to the mills, and fostered a distinctive, largely English "women's culture" well documented in Joy Parr's book *The Gender of Breadwinners*.

Today Paris is a town of some 9,000 people and the mills are closed, victims of the move to larger centres. Penman's was the last to go, in the early 1980s, to a new plant in Cambridge. But a whiff of Paris's image as a textile town lingers on. Grand River Street's best known and very old-fashioned business establishment is John M. Hall's House of Quality Linens (many, *mutatis mutandis*, from Hong Kong and Ireland) at 43 Grand River Street North; tourists come from far and wide to shop at Mary Maxim (75 Scott Avenue), purveyors of fabrics, yarns, and craft supplies. And on the banks of the Nith, under the huge beams of Penman's Number 1 Mill, where knitter machine operatives had toiled over men's long underwear (white for outdoor workers, black for miners), shoppers today browse for drapery and upholstery fabrics.

39 *1 Banfield Street*

23 *7 Elgin Street*

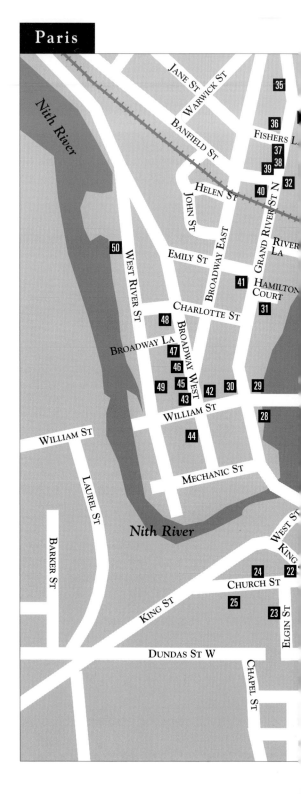

Paris

JANE ST

WARWICK ST

BANFIELD ST

FISHERS L.

35

36

37
38

39

32

40

Nith River

HELEN ST

JOHN ST

BROADWAY EAST

GRAND RIVER ST N

RIVER LA

EMILY ST

50

WEST RIVER ST

41 HAMILTON COURT

31

CHARLOTTE ST

48

BROADWAY LA

BROADWAY WEST

47

46

49 **45**

43

42 **30**

29

28

WILLIAM ST

WILLIAM ST

44

MECHANIC ST

LAUREL ST

BARKER ST

Nith River

WEST ST

KING

24 **22**

CHURCH ST

KING ST

25

23

ELGIN ST

DUNDAS ST W

CHAPEL ST

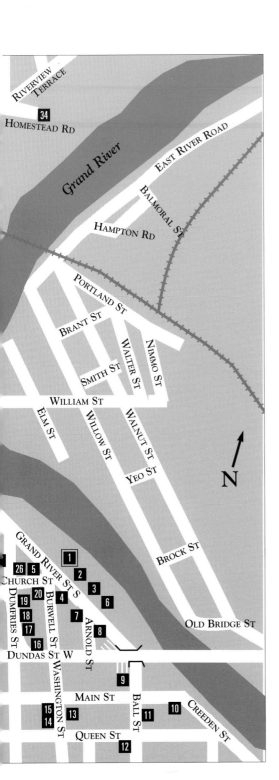

RIVERVIEW TERRACE

34
HOMESTEAD RD

Grand River

EAST RIVER ROAD

BALMORAL ST

HAMPTON RD

PORTLAND ST

BRANT ST

NIMMO ST

WALTER ST

SMITH ST

WILLIAM ST

ELM ST

WILLOW ST

WALNUT ST

YEO ST

N

BROCK ST

GRAND RIVER ST S

1

26 5
CHURCH ST

2

19 20
DUMFRIES ST

BURWELL ST

3

4

6

18

17

7

16

8

DUNDAS ST W

ARNOLD ST

OLD BRIDGE ST

WASHINGTON ST

9

MAIN ST

BALL ST

15
14

13

11

10

CREEDEN ST

QUEEN ST

12

20 Old Town Hall,
13 Burwell Street

32 Penmarvian,
185 Grand River
Street North

[1] *Asa Wolverton House,*
52 Grand River Street South

[4] *St. James Anglican Church,*
Grand River and Burwell Streets

[1] Asa Wolverton House, 52 Grand River Street South, ca. 1851

A compact Southern plantation overlooking the Grand River? Not really, but the two-storey pedimented portico fronted by four Tuscan pillars is an unexpected sight in Paris's earliest neighbourhood. As with many Greek Revival houses, behind the splashy portico is the familiar five-bay neoclassical structure, down to the French doors and diamond-patterned sidelights. Which is not to take away from its effect: with its bold balustrade and balcony and a sideways string (rare in Ontario, usual in New England) of granary, storeroom, carriage house, and stables, Asa Wolverton built himself a dashing house.

As his first name suggests, Wolverton was an American, from Cayuga County, New York, who settled in Paris about 1832 and became the prosperous owner of two sawmills. Naturally enough, he built his house of hand-split laths, covered first in stucco, then with a thinner coat of plaster. The influence of Paris's master of cobblestones, Levi Boughton, can be seen in the smokehouse to the north and in a cobblestone wall that connects the Wolverton house to 60 Grand River Street South.

[2] 60 Grand River Street South, 1850s

This well-proportioned house with a river-facing veranda was also built by Asa Wolverton, who probably lived here while building 52 Grand River Street South.

[3] 64 Grand River Street South, ca. 1856

The last of three very different houses built by Asa Wolverton on the east side of the street, this has a long, low, and utterly un-Ontarian look. What makes it unusual is a modest version of the arrangement at 52 Grand River Street South, the attached, recessed outbuildings that extend the house's street-facing breadth rather than tucking themselves behind in the typical Ontario tail. The home of St. James's second rector, the Reverend Dr. Adam Townley.

[4] St. James Anglican Church, Grand River and Burwell Streets, ca. 1839

In the late 1830s, Bishop John Strachan received £500 from the Duchess of Leeds as well as parishes in Ireland and Scotland, earmarked for an Anglican church in Paris. The terms of the gift stipulated that the church was to be built of stone and named after St. James.

Unfortunately, the original St. James is difficult to see behind the five-sided carbuncle erected in 1989 as a vestibule. Mentally subtract it (which is easier from the side) and the church is revealed as a hybrid typical of its period, a basically neoclassical building with picturesque leanings. Its outline is conservative: the rectangular nave, the vestigial pediment at the front topped with what an early historian dismissed as "one of those nondescript

5 *7 Burwell Street*

5 *Doorcase*

belfries, terminated by a tin-covered spirelet so often seen in country churches." But its dominant accessories, the lancet windows on the nave and belfry, are proudly and fashionably Gothic.

When it came to the stone, the town's Anglicans were equally open to innovation: they gave newcomer Levi Boughton his first cobblestone commission in Paris. A successful cobblestone building gives the effect of fine needlepoint, with similar-sized stones, like stitches, all turned to the same diagonal and the mortar relatively unobtrusive. St. James is not one of those successes. Perhaps Boughton was not given time to collect compatible cobbles; perhaps he had not yet mastered his craft. Unlike his later, more refined work, St. James's cobbles are of differing sizes and textures; they march heedlessly in different directions and compete unhappily with fieldstone, wood, and the complicated tower. The fieldstone chancel was added in 1863, in a more "correct" style of Gothic, known as Early English. The parishioners' most recent addition, the unconvincing cobblestone entrance, has made matters considerably worse.

5 7 Burwell Street, ca. 1845–51

By the time he built 7 Burwell, Boughton's skill had increased to the point where he could build a house of startling simplicity. The tightly knit rows of small, even cobblestones are a silent rebuke to St. James across the street: neither the house's brack-

eted cornice nor its heavy lintels and sills are allowed to distract the eye from the cobbles' fascinating regularity. The house's most bravura feature is a curving corner, so that the two cobblestone walls that face the street unfold in a single seamless sheet. (It was built as a dispensary and living quarters for a druggist, Samuel Sowden, and the door at the rounded corner led to the dispensary.) The back and the side wall to the north are made of fieldstone construction, which was much less time-consuming; the Victorians said of houses like this that they had a "Lady Anne (or a Queen Anne) front and a Mary Ann back." Number 5 Burwell, which has an appealing geometric treillage on its veranda, is a later addition to the north.

Return to Grand River Street South, passing St. James again.

6 66 Grand River Street South, ca. 1870s

A modest Ontario cottage covered with the local plaster, making natty work of commonplace materials – shingles, wooden latticework, a round window – in its gable. The attached wing, which may have come later, has a typically Parisian spooled treillage on the veranda.

7 3 Arnold Street, ca. 1855

Cobblestones could dress the façades of all the mid-century styles, and the Paris area

8 *2 Arnold Street*

10 *5 Main Street*

has a full selection from Greek Revival to Gothic. With its round-headed windows and two-storey bay, Ouse Lodge, as the former rectory for St. James Church was called, is the town's only Italianate cobblestone house. Its limestone quoins are handsome, but even in the best of repair it must have been a rather mechanical exercise; now, with its porch and original doorframe gone and a modern balcony added, it looks downright woebegone.

8 **2 Arnold Street,** ca. 1845
With its monochromatic colour scheme and clunky central chimney, this stucco house is easy to underestimate. But the Tudor labels over the windows, the modest portico, and the returning eaves that cut sharply back into the side walls add up to a vernacular house that makes a fine blend of classical and picturesque elements. Most attractive of all is the lower storey on the Grand River Street South side, with its eight-over-twelve-paned windows and twenty-five precise rows of cobblestones. Built by Thomas Arnold, for whom the street is named.

Continue south along Grand River Street South, passing under the bridge.

9 **3 Ball Street,** ca. 1850
The pleasure provided by this plaster house comes from the rhythm of its four closely set bays (four windows with original

shutters on the second storey, three and an off-centre door on the first floor) and its deep returning eaves. (The porch may be an afterthought.) In spite of the off-centre door, the spirit, if not the letter, of Georgian symmetry is present here. The house also bears the mark of Levi Boughton: three rows of cobblestone foundation are visible from the side.

10 **5 Main Street,** ca. 1880s
The Victorians took their verandas seriously, both as practical summer rooms and as symbolic expressions of domesticity. In his influential pattern book *The Architecture of Country Houses* (1850), A.J. Downing urged builders to concentrate on the veranda rather than the gable, which was less directly connected "to the *life* of the owner of the cottage." Paris has several outstanding porches, which owe as much to the late-nineteenth-century invention of finishing tools as to conceptions of architectural truth. Although this house has been obscured by siding, only a heart of stone would tamper with the wooden crochetwork of its bobbined and medallioned veranda.

11 **22 Ball Street,** ca. 1880s
Another irresistible veranda, on a front-gabled cottage.

12 **19 Queen Street,** ca. 1852
By 1851, Levi Boughton had built the town's most impressive dwellings, but he

12 *19 Queen Street*

13 *22 Washington Street*

and his wife and seven children were still living in a lath-and-plaster house. The census-taker for that year recorded that the Boughtons were building a "handsome" house, in "what is called coble work." Handsome it is, with the painstaking rows of earth-coloured cobbles and finely scabbled grey limestone quoins contributing two more horizontal elements to the typical hip-roofed, low-slung look of an Ontario cottage. (It's a familiar shape in this neighbourhood of old, modest houses, many now hiding behind siding: 17 Queen Street, which began life as a plaster house with a cobblestone foundation, is very similar.) Like many nineteenth-century houses, this one, built to house nine people, is more accommodating than it looks. Levi Boughton Jr., age eighteen, is listed in the same census as mason and plasterer, and he may well have done some apprentice work on the family house: unusually, all the façades except the rear are covered in cobbles.

13 22 Washington Street, ca. 1836
Described in an early history as a "bluff, plain-spoken, kind-hearted specimen of the old time Scottish doctor," Robert McCosh was Paris's first doctor and the founding editor (in 1850) of its Reform Party newspaper, the *Paris Star*. His arresting pedimented and porticoed house, an unusual version of the Greek Revival style in Paris (, Asa Wolverton's house at

52 Grand River Street South is a much grander example), indicates an owner with a streak of individuality. Many of its details, including an elliptical window in the pediment, have been buried under siding, but the pilastered door and the window surrounds are original.

14 19 Washington Street, ca. 1870
Another amiably excessive High Vic veranda on a house now covered by aluminum siding. The cumulative effect of brackets, scrolls, rickrack-like trim, and posts laden with detail is frankly over the top, but the folk-art enthusiasm has to be admired.

15 Sacred Heart Roman Catholic Church, Washington and Main Streets, 1857
For $20,000, the Catholics of Paris acquired a fieldstone Gothic church; the tower was completed in 1880. Calling it "the architectural glory of this part of the town" and the finest by far of Paris's churches, the writer of *The History of the County of Brant, Ontario* (1883) was equally enthusiastic about the interior: "The spirit of true Gothic art is carried out in the minutest detail; everything is real; there are no trashy ornaments, no painted woodwork pretending to be stone." Even more striking than the absence of trashy ornaments are the eleven life-size statues of male saints that line the central aisle. Note the large recessed cross above the side door to the

17 *40 Dumfries Street*

19 *30 Dumfries Street*

south in the priests' house next door (17 Washington Street, built in 1875).

16 40 Dundas Street West, mid-1830s
One of Paris's first hotels. Nineteenth-century inns in small-town Ontario tended to be shoebox-shaped buildings with two-storey verandas; the upper veranda, here with Tuscan columns and French doors, afforded fresh air and sociability for the ladies away from the barroom roistering below.

17 40 Dumfries Street, before 1841
The most prominent non-Yankee of Paris's founding citizens, Hugh Finlayson came from Scotland and settled in Paris in 1836. The owner of a successful tannery, he was the town's first mayor (an office he held six times) and served in the Dominion parliament as well as in the provincial legislature. Finlayson's symmetrical red-brick house with its finely detailed doorcase represents a typically Ontarian merger of robust Georgian and more delicate neoclassical elements. The Paris Mutual Institute, a gentlemen's society that evolved into the public library, met here occasionally for purposes of "mutual improvement" after its foundation in 1841.

18 36 Dumfries Street, ca. 1845
Only the front of this vernacular Georgian is white brick, as the Victorians called it; the sides are cheaper (because local) red brick.

19 30 Dumfries Street, ca. 1860
Avert your eyes from the fried-chicken outlet next door, and admire this Italianate belle who wears her little ironwork cresting like a tiara. The door, with its elliptical brick surround and cast-stone keystone, is its finest feature, and the delicate bead-and-reel moulding around the transom and side-lights is particularly pretty. The owners could not resist a flossy veranda but wisely kept it to the back of their well-behaved brick cube.

20 Old Town Hall, 13 Burwell Street,
1854 (best viewed from Church Street)
The British, French, and Americans used the Gothic Revival style for everything from railway stations to factories. Canadians, as Marion MacRae and Anthony Adamson point out in *Cornerstones of Order*, hewed to a conservative line and reserved it mainly for churches, legislatures, and (in a diluted form) houses. When the Parisians decided on a Gothic town hall, perhaps they were being characteristically progressive. Perhaps they read invocations to civic duty in its cruciform plan, tower, turrets, and fine window tracery. For whatever reason, the Town Hall, designed by a road and bridge builder and surveyor named John Maxwell, is an unusual Ontarian example of a Gothic civic building. A true multi-purpose building, it also served at various times as a school, "opera house," and movie theatre, while continuing to accommodate

22 *22 Church Street*

23 *7 Elgin Street*

the jail, market, and town council. Shorn of official function, in recent years it has been used as a factory and auction house.

21 17–23 Church Street, ca. 1870
Part of a row-housing scheme unusual in small towns, this brick quartet climbs the Church Street hill in nicely calculated steps. The colour of the brick varies slightly from house to house, while the modest quatrefoil detail on the verandas ties the ensemble together.

22 22 Church Street, ca. 1842–45
Another house with a finely worked cobblestone front and a rubblestone back, thought to be Levi Boughton's work. Regency cottages were ideally designed for romantic sites, and this compact one-and-a-half-storey version perches on a hill with a view of St. James's steeples and the Town Hall backed by the surrounding countryside. The big-boned Eastlake porch (a later addition) holds its own with the house's more traditional, horizontal elements – returning eaves, emphatic lintels, hip-roof. The young Alexander Graham Bell lived here for a time in 1870, when it was the home of a family friend, the Reverend Thomas Henderson.

23 7 Elgin Street, probably 1850s
A deft little Gothic exercise, with two different kinds of openwork bargeboard on the gables. The house's owner was Charles

Arnold, whose plant nursery was further up the Church Street hill; he was most famous for his American Wonder Pea. Across the street, 6, 8, and 10 Elgin are worker's cottages that have lost their features, but not their characteristic shapes, to siding.

24 38 Church Street, ca. 1860
With its bay window, loopy bargeboard, and different-sized gables, the Gothic Revival house at 7 Elgin Street has a soft, picturesque air. Number 38 Church Street is obviously a close cousin in "the English style," as nineteenth-century Parisians would have called it, but altogether sterner stuff. The ogee-topped portico, which has been removed, would have mollified the effect, but the two identical gables and determined Tudor labels over the windows give it a very masculine, self-assured personality. Built for a druggist named C.W. Roberts.

25 Cemetery, Church Street
Hemmed in by a low iron fence, a remnant of Paris's original cemetery stands at the top of the Church Street hill. Along with the Victorian iconography of death – clasped hands, weeping willows, doves bearing leaves, scrolls – there is political history here (post-1841 graves marked C.W. for Canada West) as well as the mortality tales of the nineteenth century (a stone commemorating "3 babes of David

and Anne Buchan," a bas-relief of thistles for a "Beloved Brother" from Scotland).

Go back down Church Street and turn left on Dumfries.

26 22–24 Dumfries Street, ca. 1850

Very plain, and one of the most beautiful buildings in Paris. The cut-stone front (the sides and back are variously composed of rubblestone and brick) is unadorned except for lintels and projecting sills made of dressed stone; virtually all the decoration is reserved for the deeply recessed doors, each one subtly different, all equally restrained. On the main door at number 22, what look like pilasters are turned sideways to frame the sidelights. Originally part of a hotel, this building would look convincing on a street in Yorkshire.

27 17 Dumfries Street, ca, 1870

Only a quarter-century apart in time, 17 Dumfries and 22–24 Dumfries are good illustrations of those great architectural polarities, the classic and the picturesque. Across the street from the austere Georgian beauty, 17 Dumfries is a thing of gables, bays, and porches, now projecting, now withdrawing, always energetically decorated with the woodworker's full bag of tricks. (Like a medieval carver sculpting a high corner of the cathedral visible only to God, some perfectionist craftsman spent considerable skill embellishing the sides of the

brackets supporting the floating bargeboard on the third storey.) The solidly carved – as opposed to openwork – bargeboard and the decoration above the collar or horizontal board are typical of the late period of the Ontario gable.

Follow Dumfries north until it merges into Grand River Street, and cross the Nith River.

"The main street, Grand River Street, is gay with stores, glittering and bright coloured, to attract that sex to whom shopping is the best substitute for Paradise." The glamorous 1880s shopping street described in *The History of the County of Brant, Ontario* has a much more workaday look today. On a windy September night in 1900, a disastrous fire that began in a flour mill destroyed half of Paris's downtown. Most of the florid mid-Victorian commercial buildings were replaced by comparatively uninspired straight-topped red-brick structures.

28 91 Grand River Street North has

historical significance as the receiving end of the world's first long-distance telephone call. On this site, on August 10, 1876, in Robert White's Boot and Shoe Store, Alexander Graham Bell heard songs, laughter, and a soliloquy from *Macbeth* from his father and friends in Brantford, eight miles away.

29 *105–111 Grand River Street North*

30 *106 Grand River Street North*

Downtown Paris's few grace notes are above William Street. The bridge to the east, where William crosses the Grand, affords one of Paris's most romantic prospects, of the balconied backs of riverside houses and stores.

29 **105–111 Grand River Street North,** ca. 1870s

Number 111 has the street's only original storefront, the familiar mid-Victorian arrangement of large and small brackets. The block as a whole, with its comely play of planes created by brick corbelling, dog-toothing, piers, and graceful cast-stone surrounds, is no doubt typical of the stores below William Street that were destroyed by fire.

30 **106 Grand River Street North,** 1850s

In 1883, the *Brant Review* reported that an Irish button maker "perfectly wild with drink was creating a disturbance in the centre of the town... With his coat and vest off and his shirt torn to strips, he was a source of terror to females passing and of disgust to respectable citizens. When he was refused liquor at the Bradford House, he shoved his friend clear through the window." Strong drink was one of the things that made pioneer life bearable, and the Bradford House was one of seventeen businesses seeking a liquor licence in Paris in 1859. (The population was around 2,400.)

The inn's founder, Pennsylvania-born O.D. Bradford, sent a trademark yellow omnibus to meet every train and did a brisk business with "the keen and companionable commercial traveller." The second owner, John Ealand, expanded the original plaster hotel, adding the Romanesque arcades on Grand River and William Streets and sheathing the whole in yellow brick. Rechristened the Arlington, it functioned as a local landmark and hotel until the 1980s.

Grand River Street North, rather confusingly labelled Lower Town, became Paris's best neighbourhood by the mid-nineteenth century. In *New Babylon*, a satirical portrait of Paris written in 1931, Marcus Adeney describes "Quality Heights": "Yellow and red brick houses, discreetly set back from the road among tall firs and maples, raise not too discreet eyebrows and seem to be suffering ever so slightly from the burden of their own pretentiousness." Sardonically or not, depending on their vantage point, Parisians actually did know this street as Quality Hill.

31 **Hamilton Place, 165 Grand River Street North,** 1844 (best viewed from Hamilton Court)

Paris's *pièce de résistance* and one of Ontario's outstanding Greek Revival houses. Levi Boughton's own cottage and most of the other cobblestone houses he built in

31 *Hamilton Place,*
165 Grand River Street North

31 *Belvedere*

Paris were unpretentious essays in vernacular styles. When something more grand was called for, the American entrepreneurs in Paris turned naturally to the Greek Revival style. (More American cobblestone houses were built in this style than in any other.) Ironically, when the Asa Wolvertons and Norman Hamiltons decided to settle in stoutly monarchical Upper Canada, they imported the architectural style that most symbolized the democratic values of the republic to the south.

Norman Hamilton, the owner of Hamilton Place, came from the Rochester area and made a fortune in Paris from a clever combination of a distillery and a pork-packing plant: the happy pigs fed on the discarded mash. Hamilton was willing to wait for his dream house: Levi Boughton probably supervised the collection of cobbles of the right size and sheen for several years before beginning construction. The cobblestone façade was tied to the rubblestone wall behind it by every fourth or fifth cobble, which was longer and projected into the rubblestone core. The elliptical cobbles themselves, which are placed at right angles to the wall, are about 9 inches long, and the entire wall about 28 inches deep.

But it's not the cobbles that demand your attention first: it's the striking shape of the building, rather like a deep-crowned hat perched on massive square pillars. Its architect, a Philadelphian named Andrew

Minny, designed a three-storey house whose second-floor windows are set in light-wells concealed by the heavy, unadorned architrave. Behind the severe colonnade (each pillar of which encases an enormous log, to support the roof), the neat rows of humble stones frame a procession of French doors.

32 Penmarvian, 185 Grand River Street North, 1848, renovated 1887

By 1845, Hiram "King" Capron, the founder of Paris, had outgrown his house at what is now 8 Homestead Road (see 34 below), and he began to build the Stone House (also called Riverview Hall), a sober Classical Revival building that required twelve stonemasons and three years' work. In 1887, the industrialist John Penman bought the house (already somewhat fancified by a later owner) and proceeded to bury it under a full complement of late-Victorian architectural icons. He also changed its name to the suitably fanciful Penmarvian, an anagram of his name and that of his wife, Martha McVicar.

Some of Penmarvian's details, such as the slender marble columns on the tower or the triple-arched Romanesque entrance, are pleasing, but as a whole it's a superb example of Gilded Age eclecticism run amok. Arches, gables, Tudor timbering, cresting, carved stone, and terracotta are piled on top of one another without much reason beyond the belief that more is more.

32 *Penmarvian, 185 Grand River Street North*

32 *Carriage house*

Penmarvian is now a retirement home, and it's possible to walk around to the back, where vestiges of Capron's chaste stone house – pilasters, a string course, and a cornice – are still movingly visible. The rubblestone carriage house, which has been converted to a separate house with a minimum of exterior alteration, is delightful.

33 201 Grand River Street North, ca. 1895

This well-preserved villa is most rewarding when the leaves are down or not fully out, and it's easier to admire the subtly patterned slate roof and the two collar-tied gables (the larger edged out by the smaller, both trimmed in turn-of-the-century solid bargeboard). Other *fin-de-siècle* signs are the "classical" porch, the stained glass, and the terracotta panels. Try to find the cherub's head near the bottom corner of the large gable.

34 8 Homestead Road, ca. 1831

The romantic in Hiram Capron described his "spellbound" first view of Paris, when he dismounted from his horse to admire the valley. He claimed that he determined to own "this lovely vale" at that moment, and when it was indeed his, he built his first house with a view of the looping Grand River.

But Capron was also a downright man of business: a hillside spring provided water as well as charm, and the plain-faced one-and-a-half-storey house he built was taxed significantly less than a two-storey house. It was also easier to heat. Exterior details, except for plain sidelights and a front door knocker (probably made in the forge Capron co-owned in Normandale), are virtually non-existent. Even windows, few and far between, seem an unnecessary luxury (the dormers were added later). The town's oldest surviving house is appropriately faced with plaster of Paris. A northern wing, now demolished, held a small store where Capron bartered merchandise for produce and services as well as running a post office.

35 208 Grand River Street North, ca. 1857

Originally built by Hiram Capron for his daughter Elizabeth, this busy coquette probably had a make-over in the 1870s, when slate mansard roofs were fashionable.

36 200 Grand River Street North, ca. 1888

Number 200 and its neighbour 202 began life as near-twins, composed of three advancing, separately gabled blocks, with bays to the side: they are houses that seem to open up gradually. But when number 202 lost its veranda it lost a great deal. Walk up Fishers Lane for a better view of number 200's finely chamfered posts and masculine treillage. The lane was named for the house's first occupant, a member of

105

36 *200 Grand River Street North*

39 *1 Banfield Street*

the provincial legislature and senator named John H. Fisher.

37 198 Grand River Street North, ca. 1880

Not at all glamorous in spite of its size and gently sloping grounds, this is a serviceable essay in the bayed and bracketed style whose two very small gables manage to look both tentative and eccentric.

38 194 Grand River Street North, 1850s

Distant intimations of verandas, French doors, and a central gable are about all the walker can see of the main house when the leaves are out. Built for James Moore, an executive of the Buffalo and Goderich Railway, it was also the home of Andrew Baird, the mayor of Paris on several occasions. Much more fun as well as more visible, its carriage house is around the corner at 18 Baird Street (next to **38**).

39 1 Banfield Street, ca. 1868

On its Grand River Street North side (next to 194 Grand River Street North), a High Vic iron fence hints with every rusty medallion, finial, and scroll that beauty is fleeting and glory must die. Round the corner to Banfield Street, something much less elegiac is on view: a robust and eclectic villa with curvy bargeboard and smashing compound chimney-stacks that was two years in the making. Built by Charles

Whitlaw, the owner of Paris's largest flour mill.

40 Kipp's Funeral Home, 184 Grand River Street North, 1886

When Captain Cox built his expansive villa, it was proudly à la mode. The dominant style was Italianate, signalled by the square tower, brackets, and rounded windows. But the opulent eighties demanded at least a soupçon of other fashions – hence the flirtatious, crested French roof on the tower and two kinds of gables. As at Penmarvian across the street, the alterations are unfortunate and the carriage house, bracketed and trimly banded with red brick, is far prettier than the main house.

41 Presbyterian Church, 164 Grand River Street North, 1894

Romanesque Revival buildings are relatively rare in Ontario's small towns, because it was an expensive style fashionable at a time – the early 1890s – when most large-scale building was finished. But the Paris Presbyterians, newly formed from two older congregations, needed a church that would seat 1,000 people (in a town of about 3,000), and Presbyterians favoured the Romanesque style. To make matters even simpler, a Chatham architect, Thomas J. Rutley, had built a nearly identical Presbyterian church in Chatham in 1889, so the Paris congregation could see what they were ordering. The result is a squared-off

41 *Presbyterian Church,*
164 Grand River Street North

43 *Paris Public Library, 12 William Street*

red-brick mountain bristling with crags and peaks formed by towers, turrets, pitched roofs, and dormers. The multiple rounded arches save it from being just too alpine, and the terracotta shell and Sabbath School plaques on the Emily Street side are endearing 1890s touches.

Two blocks further, turn right at William Street.

42 Paris Baptist Church, 25 Broadway West, 1885
The Gothic Revival refinements include a polychromatic slate roof whose triangles echo the church's many pointed elements: windows, blind arches, louvred triangles, steeples. John Turner, a well-known Brantford architect, lavished most of his care on the larger of the two steeples: its top in particular is a delicately shaped concoction of slate, wood, and brick "carving."

43 Paris Public Library, 12 William Street, 1903
Financed by Andrew Carnegie and designed by a Toronto architect named Frank Wickson, Paris's Edwardian Classical library was built in one of the Classical Revival styles favoured by the American philanthropist. The library was the culmination of an originally all-male Mutual Institute and Paris Circulating Library that had been important parts of Parisian life since 1841. By the end of the nineteenth

century, the financially troubled library (which organized debates, lectures, and discussion groups for mill workers as well as their managers) had asked the town council for its own building. The folly of such a request reminded the *Brant Review* of the "visionary cranks" who also thought electric lights, trolleys, zoos, and museums should be provided forthwith. Luckily, Mr. Carnegie saved the day with $10,000 and his usual stipulation: that no fees should ever be charged, and that the town provide $1,000 a year for upkeep.

44 16 Broadway West, 1840s
Another transplanted American, Charles Mitchell, settled in Paris in 1836 and established a carriage-making factory. The temple-plan house Levi Boughton built for him in the 1840s indicates what a splendid marriage could be made between cobblestones and the sophistications of the Greek Revival style. The nubbled effect of the cobbles domesticates the Doric columns and pilasters, the deep cornices, and the severe porch; they in turn dignify the commonplace stones.

The house's details – the ironwork grilles that half-heartedly lit the bedrooms at floor level, the classical wreaths, palmettes, and Grecian lady on the architrave above the door, the curvaceous limestone ornaments at the porch steps – would have been available to the unknown designer from contemporary pattern books. But the amalgam he created,

44 *16 Broadway West*

49 *45–47 West River Street*

at once rock-solid and refined, is one of the most accomplished Greek Revival houses in the province.

The cobblestone masonry is among Boughton's finest achievements, and the side addition, built as a doctor's office in 1885, is an extremely good match. (Although Paris's masons continued to build with cobbles well into the 1860s, long after the vogue had ended in New York State, the 1885 addition is definitely a postscript.) The ironwork cresting on the belvedere probably dates from this period, and the dormers are also a later addition, built when people were willing to compromise the classical cube shape for a little light and ventilation.

45 30, **46** 32 Broadway West, ca. 1870

The nineteenth-century American architectural writer A.J. Downing warned that Italianate houses could err either by "entire baldness" or "frippery ornament." This urbane pair steers neatly between those two extremes, with yellow brick used lavishly for cornice, string course, quoins, and unusual window trim. The two-storey bay suggests a scaled-down version of the Tuscan tower seen in more elaborate Italianate villas; the portico on number 32 is original.

47 36 Broadway West, ca. 1875

A beautifully proportioned and detailed example of an Italianate villa. Unfortunately for the passer-by, it's shielded by

a screen of evergreens, but the driveway permits a view of the harmony achieved by a two-storey bay, rounded windows, lacy ironwork cresting, and a porch that makes joyous work of brackets, dowels, openwork, and rickrack.

48 St. Paul's United Church,
48 Broadway West, 1875

A bold, rather challenging idea favoured by Methodist and Baptist congregations: a big gabled front with no eaves and no spire, outlined in undulating corbelling and sectioned off by five turrets. The double-doored entry, which detracts from the gaunt impressiveness of the original, was added in 1926.

49 45–47 West River Street, ca. 1850

Not all Greek Revival houses came with porticoes, pillars, or particularly grand aspirations. This early double house covered in stucco announces its classical leanings with two gravely outsize Doric-pilastered doors; both their off-centre location and their massiveness were hallmarks of the Greek Revival style.

This modest riverside street, once close to the factories along the Nith, is still lined with early workers' cottages, many now renovated or covered with siding. Closer to Penman's, there are several company-built houses, available to employees at low rents or for purchase. Number 97 West River

50 *Penman's Number 1 Mill,*
140 West River Street

50 *Main entrance*

Street was built about 1880 for relatively high-status employees; 99–101 West River (ca. 1880) and 105–107 (ca. 1917) are company houses built to serve as rooming-houses or multiple family dwellings.

50 Penman's Number 1 Mill, 140 West River Street, 1874

Anxious to scotch rumours about the immorality of factory girls and convinced that architecture could have a morally elevating effect, Penman's paid careful attention to its looks. Whatever the effect on morals, the original Penman's Number 1 Mill is as pretty as a factory could be. The gently belled mansard roof (with a slate pattern in mauve and green), the round-headed, many-paned windows surmounted with two layers of brick swags plus keystones on the front, the bays delineated by strengthening piers all contribute to a building justly described by an early viewer as "spacious and stately, quite unlike the popular ideal of a factory." As Joy Parr notes in *The Gender of Breadwinners*, nine-teenth-century reporters responded to the detailed delicacy of the mill's architecture, describing it in feminine terms and discussing the "wonderful discretion" with which machinery was placed in the "commodious departments" as if treating home decorating.

There are six additional cobblestone houses outside the walking tour area. In Paris:

• Luck Farm house, at the end of Barker Street
• 33 Oak Avenue

And in South Dumfries Township:
• Paris Plains Church, 709 Paris Plains Road, east side of Highway 24A
• 207 Golf Links Road, about one kilometre from the Golf and Country Club
• 899 Keg Lane Road, west of the Paris Fairgrounds and before Ayr Road
• 963 Keg Lane Road, the second house on the north side of the road past Ayr Road

125 Gore Street

Perth

"An Ontario Shangri-La"

Festina lente sed certo. Make haste slowly. Never has a town's motto suited it better, suggesting a place both leisured and focussed, conservative and progressive. At least that's how Perth likes to think of itself.

And with some justification, certainly as far as its famously good looks are concerned. The Tay and Little Tay Rivers that meander through the smart military grid of the streets, the Scottish severity of the commercial buildings and the lavishness of some of its earliest houses add up to a backwater with a disarming combination of self-important bustle and languid charm.

Perth's beginnings were all purposefulness. Its creation was arbitrary and instant, the result of a government decision to settle Upper Canada through a series of interior corridors. The War of 1812 had impressed the colonial authorities with the vulnerability of the St. Lawrence River Corridor, both because of its location and because it was populated by ex-Americans whose loyalty was dubious. At the same time, the United States was becoming an increasingly attractive competitor for desirable British emigrants. The solution, announced in 1815, was a two-pronged policy of military resettlement and assisted emigration in the area around the Rideau River and Rideau Lakes.

A spot on the Tay River was called Perth, after the town in Scotland, and designated the central depot for the new settlements. The site, chosen in haste and largely because more strategically located land had already been granted to absentee Loyalist owners, determined much of Perth's history: it has always been just a little off the beaten path, several miles from what became the Rideau Canal, on a small artery with unimpressive millpower.

By the spring and summer of 1816, pioneers were making the twenty-six-mile journey from Brockville by wagon, scow, ox-sled, and scow again. By the fall of that year, there were twenty houses under construction in the new village of Perth. If the location was not ideal, the pioneer population looked promising, at least on paper. The original 700-some assisted emigrants, half Lowland, half Highland Scots, were given free passage, 100 acres, six months' food, agricultural equipment at cost, and the promise of a minister and a schoolteacher. As it happened, most of the Highlanders settled in Glengarry County, leaving Perth peopled mainly by Lowlanders from the Glasgow area. A deposit of £16 required of every male over sixteen and £2 from every married woman (refundable two years after settlement) was designed to attract self-reliant settlers and to discourage migration to the States; it also kept the numbers down.

The arrangements for soldiers were similar, but the pot was significantly sweetened for officers. They were offered 200 acres, town lots, and half-pay pensions. Although the Scottish settlers and the soldiers became Perth's farmers as well as its butchers, bakers, and candlestick purveyors, the retired officers were responsible for the town's glamorous social tone. Winnifred Inderwick, one of Perth's twentieth-century preservationists, called the infant village "very, very snooty." As early as 1817, the censorious Reverend William Bell, Perth's long-time Presbyterian minister and chronicler, noted: "Most of the officers built houses in the village, and tended not a little, by the politeness of their manners, to render a residence here desirable... The whole number amounts to between thirty and forty, and most of them are justices of the peace. This gives them a greater influence in the settlement, than is perhaps agreeable to the civilians."

Bell was ambivalent about their influence, sometimes praising their good manners, at other times scorning "the haughtiness, pride, vanity and dissipation of the half-pay officers and their ladies. They minded nothing but dress, visiting and amusement." The amusements for the gentlemen included swearing, fighting, Rabelaisian drinking bouts (which eventually drove Bell to the temperance movement), and horse racing down Drummond Street. (Bell found a woman of almost ninety making her laborious way to the first Drummond Street race, in June 1823. Scandalized, he recommended that she spend her time preparing for the next life. She was dead by the end of the year, a fact he noted with some satisfaction in his journal.)

It's hard to know how much of the mystique of the half-pay officers is just that, and how much a few dozen military men and some splendid houses really affected the life of a muddy village. Whatever the truth, Perth was a place that excited fantasy, seen in particularly high relief in an 1894 article in *Toronto Saturday Night* magazine by Charles Lewis Shaw: "Isolated from the rest of the world, living almost entirely under semi-military laws, like the Bourbons forgetting nothing and learning nothing, the settlement for the first twenty-five years of its existence presented a curious anomaly, an Old Country village of the previous century in the backwoods of Canada. It was known as the half-pay officers paradise."

Overwrought as that picture is, the masculine, honour-obsessed ethos that Shaw describes undeniably prevailed in a segment of Perth society. It played itself out most tragically in what is considered Canada's last duel, fought in 1833. All the male principals were lawyers, at the very top of the town's rambunctious, rivalrous elites. When John Wilson, the twenty-year-old law clerk of James Boulton, killed Robert Lyon, the nineteen-year-old law clerk of Thomas Radenhurst, because of a supposed insult to Boulton's governess, the younger men were only aping the histrionic enmity of their elders. Boulton and Radenhurst were two of Perth's three most prominent lawyers; the third, Daniel McMartin, was not directly involved in the last duel, although he was very much part of their hyper-competitive circle, which numbered public insults, duelling threats, and horse-whipping as normal pastimes.

In his fine history, *Perth: Tradition & Style in Eastern Ontario*, Larry Turner discusses (with John J. Stewart) the three senior lawyers' social differences in terms of the architecture of their houses. All three are still among Perth's most prominent houses, and their styles mirror their owners' values almost uncannily; the owners, in their turn, are a microcosm of Upper Canada's elites. Boulton, a scion of the Family Compact Boultons, built a simplified version of their Toronto house, the Grange, which is itself a simplified version of an English Georgian house – ordered, refined, aristocratic. McMartin, a pugnacious country boy, harked back to his Loyalist New York State origins with a Federalist mansion, the most complex and preening house of the three. Thomas Radenhurst, although an Anglican and (like the other two men) educated by the future Bishop Strachan, was a Reformer: his front-gabled stone house is the least pretentious and the most rooted in the Rideau Corridor idiom.

The duel marked an end to the worst excesses of Perth's would-be aristocrats, although a certain afterglow persists to this day. Boulton, widely vilified by the Radenhurst forces, left town for Niagara soon afterwards. Wilson followed Boulton after his acquittal. McMartin and Radenhurst stayed in Perth, practising law and watching the town grow at its own odd, herky-jerky pace.

At first it hurtled forward, with its designation in 1823 as district town for the new Bathurst District and the accompanying influx of lawyers, bureaucrats, innkeepers, and merchants. The construction of the Rideau Canal, from 1826 to 1832, was a further stimulus to Perth's shopkeepers and labourers as well as to the crucial business of road-building in the area. (Perth's first stone buildings pre-date the canal; the Scottish settlers and the easily workable sandstone deposit on which the town stands saw to that. But the British engineers and masons imported to build the canal, many of whom settled in the region, built the majority of Perth's trademark stone buildings.)

The Rideau Canal made Perth's out-of-the-way location distressingly obvious, and plans for a local link to the Rideau took shape. The resulting Tay Canal was, in Larry Turner's words, a "debt-ridden, shallow, inadequate trough where the hopes of Perth were gradually drowned." Misconceived by a group of half-pay officers, businessmen, and magistrates, it was badly built and finished two years late (in 1834), and had failed by the late 1840s. It was also the first sign that, for whatever reasons – geographical, psychological, economic – Perth's leading men of business would not succeed in bringing their town into the mainstream.

When the Town Hall was built in 1863, Perth's population was around 2,500 and silvery sandstone buildings were lining up on Gore and Foster Streets. Ironically, the inauguration of the handsome Town Hall signalled a narrowing of Perth's influence and a drawing in upon itself. The completion of the St. Lawrence Canals in 1847 had reduced the Rideau Canal to a purely regional system and Perth to an unlikely immigration site. When the Bathurst District was succeeded in 1850 by Carleton, Renfrew, and Lanark Counties, Perth eventually became merely Lanark's county town. Bytown, later Ottawa, which had been non-existent when Perth was a busy market town, rapidly became the area's most important centre.

On the other hand, as Perth shed some of its dreams of glory, businesses closer to home were thriving. Haggart's flour mill, a small but optimistic mining industry, McLaren's celebrated distillery of pure malt whiskey behind the Town Hall, the cheese factories that proliferated in eastern Ontario in the 1870s all gave the town a new, more realistic lease on life.

If the duel of 1833 was a tragic exaggeration of Perth's silver-spoon beginnings, the production of the Mammoth Cheese of 1893 was a comic exaggeration of Perth's ongoing agricultural life. A few shards of the monstrous cheddar that earned Perth international fame are still to be seen in the local museum. Its eleven-ton bulk broke the floor at the Chicago World's Fair, where it was displayed before going on to an English tour that included a London parade in its honour and a special exhibition hall. First acquired and then rejected by Sir Thomas Lipton, the British tea importer, who claimed it was spoiled, it was finally bought by a London caterer who set up ladders to allow closer inspection; garden spades were used to provide samples.

Tepidly praising Perth's "generally satisfactory condition" in 1880, the

Illustrated Atlas of Lanark County conceded that to those "more acquainted with the activity and push of western life, the place at first sight looks 'slow'... The buildings are for the most part rather ancient looking, being composed chiefly of hewn stone, but many of them are exceptionally good ones." (Note that the "rather ancient looking" buildings of hewn stone, today considered Perth's chief charm, were decidedly not a drawing card in 1880.)

Although the *Atlas's* commendations were lukewarm at best, Perth was on the eve of its most prosperous decade, thanks to two railroad projects and a second Tay Canal. As usual with Perth, progress was temporary or partial. The town swelled with more than 1,000 construction workers and the Canadian Pacific Railway became the town's biggest employer for three decades, with factories for the assembly of every kind of passenger and baggage car. When the car works burned in 1904, the CPR decamped to Montreal, and Perth lost hundreds of jobs. The second Tay Canal, a public enterprise that was as financially disastrous as the first, nevertheless became an important touristic asset, prettifying the downtown Tay Basin and securing Perth's importance in the area's network of rivers, lakes, and canals.

And, as with other small Ontario towns, tourism remains a crucial part of Perth's modern "success," more dependable than its periodic attempts at local enterprise. Although Perth's population has actually increased from 3,500 to 6,000 in this century, the history of the region as a whole is the usual twentieth-century story of migration to the cities and the centralization of industry. In spite of that, partly because of the local commitment to making haste slowly, partly perhaps through pure good luck, Perth's downtown core has remained both intact and vibrant.

In 1965, the planned destruction of the Matheson House (now the local museum) galvanized preservationists; after some initial skirmishes, Perth became the pilot project for Heritage Canada's main-street revival program in 1980. It was a fitting choice because, unlike most Ontario towns whose charm is in their residential streets, it is Gore's and Foster's commercial blocks that are Perth's most delightful parts. Their stony Scottish character, warmed by the unusual creamy undertone in the sandstone and softened by the looping river, is unique in Ontario.

When a New Yorker named Peter Davidson moved to Perth in the 1940s, he wrote an affectionate essay about it called "An Ontario Shangri-La." If not quite born old, Perth has always been slightly out of time; Davidson's title sounds less fanciful with every passing year.

9 *Bathurst District Court House,*
43 Drummond Street East

23 *77 Gore Street East*

49 *29 Drummond Street West*

N

QUEEN ST

VICTORIA ST

BOULTON ST

49

47

DRUMMOND ST W

ISABELLA ST

48

46

45

D'ARCY ST

50

GORE ST W

BOULTON ST

WILSON ST W

KIPPEN ST

LESLIE ST

JOY AVE

ALVIN ST

CLYDE ST

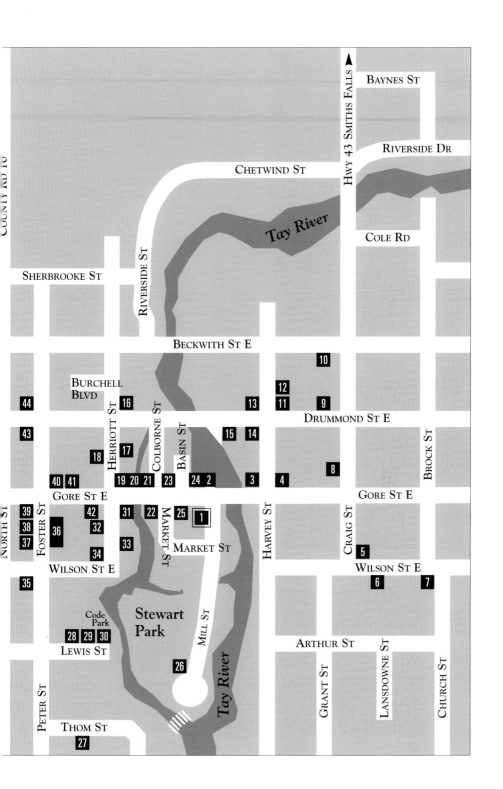

2 *93–99 Gore Street East*

4 *125 Gore Street East*

1 9 Mill Street, ca. 1820

Mill Street was one of Perth's first streets; many of its simple early houses are now obscured by siding. Believed to be Perth's oldest stone house, number 9 is so basic it's almost featureless. Unlike later buildings, where the stonework on the front was more carefully arranged than on the sides and back, this is all one rough-and-ready piece, without quoins, without the central peak typical of later houses. (The dormers are not original.) Built by Captain John McKay, who arrived in Perth in 1816 with the military settlers.

2 93–99 Gore Street East, ca. 1830

What a difference a decade makes in a pioneer settlement. About ten years after Perth's first stone house was built, the bluff Scottish good looks of number 93–99 were possible. Nine bays across, the first floor designed for shops with apartments in the upper floors, the building is sophisticated enough for a good-sized Scottish town. The cut-stone quoins, sills, and lintels were marks of distinction; the use of rougher stonework on the sides and back is typical.

3 105–109 Gore Street East, ca. 1840

Scottish builders were fond of reversing the usual Palladian arrangement, recessing the centrepiece and projecting the side wings. Other self-confident Scottish touches in merchant James Allan's dwelling-cum-store include the prominent string

course and extra-large cut-stone quoins and window surrounds.

4 125 Gore Street East (facing on Harvey Street), 1830

The arrogant, carefully controlled display of Daniel McMartin's house is still disconcerting in a little Ontario town; in 1830, when livestock roamed the unpaved streets and the population stood at about 350, it must have been flabbergasting. One of Perth's first lawyers, McMartin harked back to his New York State Loyalist origins when designing his house. The legends about it proliferate: in all versions, the Federalist style and bricks were Yankee imports; in some the workmen were imported, in others even the trees. (Proud Mac or Haughty Mac, as he was called, is said to have rejected Canadian maples in favour of cottonwood trees.)

Whatever the truth, McMartin's house is a very tony, academic exercise in the Federalist style, with the arcades, the mixture of brick and local marble accents, the cupola flanked by lanterns, and the daunting double chimney-stacks that spelled ostentation of the very best kind. There are houses like this aplenty in American towns and cities on the eastern seaboard, but not many in Canada.

McMartin's original white picket fence was topped with urns copied from Asher Benjamin's 1830 American pattern book, *The Architect; or, Practical House Carpenter;*

 66 *Craig Street*

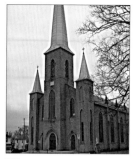

7 *St. John the Baptist*
Roman Catholic Church

the current fence is an approximation. The McMartin house is now owned by the Ontario Heritage Foundation.

5 66 Craig Street, 1824

Inge-Va, as this much-photographed house is called, looks as though nothing untoward ever happened here, but it is forever connected with Perth's famous 1833 duel. The victim, Robert Lyon, was a relative by marriage of the house's owner, Thomas Radenhurst, as well as his student at law, and his lifeless body was brought back here. (A violently drunk Radenhurst, according to the Reverend William Bell, was found the next day "running about the streets" with a pistol, bent on avenging Lyon.)

Even without this romantic connection, Inge-Va would be celebrated by connoisseurs of the Ontario cottage. It was planned with care for Perth's first Anglican rector, Michael Harris, who lived here about eight years. The lime for the mortar was seasoned underground for a year so that the bricks did not need repointing until the 1960s; the interior has five Adam-style mantelpieces. All the trademarks of the eastern variant of the Ontario cottage are in evidence: Scottish-mason-quality stonework on the front with less painstaking work on the sides, twelve-over-twelve-paned windows, an unexpectedly elaborate Loyalist door. The original cottage had a plain roof with side gables, like many eastern Ontario cottages of the time; sometime after 1833,

the front gable appeared, a characteristic of post-1830 houses in the Rideau corridor. The house was named Inge-Va, which is Tamil for "come here," by its third owners, Cyril and Winnifred Inderwick. The Inderwicks donated Inge-Va to the Ontario Heritage Foundation, but the house is not yet open to the public.

6 St. John Parish Centre, 36 Wilson Street East, 1905

Commissioned to design a convent for the Sisters of Providence of St. Vincent de Paul, the Smiths Falls architect George Martin repaired to the nearby Hughes Quarry for the rich, amethyst-tinged sandstone he favoured. The deep zinc roof, the niche for the statue of St. John the Baptist, and the two big gables flanking the pretty central bellcote give it the look of a Québécois religious institution.

7 St. John the Baptist Roman Catholic Church, 38 Wilson Street East, 1848

An undeniably arresting sight, best seen from halfway up the first block of Brock Street, St. John's is easier to admire than to love. Its alarmingly vertical outline and stern organization of elements into symbolic groups of three – towers, doors, lancet windows – no doubt impressed the Irish immigrants fleeing the famines of the 1840s for Lanark County; whether it consoled them is another question. The side, with the interlaced tracery of the windows

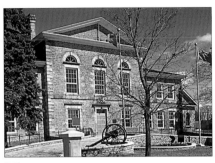

8 *53–55 Craig Street*

9 *Bathurst District Court House, 43 Drummond Street East*

and the buttresses topped with pinnacles like witches' hats, is less daunting than the front. The lancet windows in the towers have unfortunately been filled in with cast stone, and the doors are modern, but the pink-and-white Gothic confectionery of the interior is mostly original. (Just before or after 11 a.m. Sunday mass is a likely time to see the interior.)

Retrace your steps along Wilson and Craig past Gore Street.

8 53–55 Craig Street, 1816

Believed to be Perth's first building, this oak log house was built as a tavern by an army officer named John Adamson, but its uses only began there. The Reverend William Bell preached the town's first sermon at Adamson's Inn on the second Sunday in September in 1817. It accommodated Perth's first school and the premises of the *Examiner*, a precursor of the Perth *Courier*. Rough as it was, this was the local officers' social club: when dancing was called for, the central hinged wall on the second floor was hooked to the ceiling.

While staying here in 1819, the governor general, the Duke of Richmond, who had been bitten by a rabid fox some weeks earlier, first showed signs of hydrophobia; he died a few days later. Bell, who regretted attending the costly dinner for the duke that was held at the inn, noted in his diary that His Grace drank seven glasses of

brandy and water on arrival; also that innkeeper Adamson "behaved very ill" during the duke's stay, beating his wife and servants. It was the duke who suggested that the log house be sided with red clapboard, hence its mystifying local name the Red House. It has been white since 1822; both the logs and the original basement hearth are intact.

9 Bathurst District Court House, 43 Drummond Street East, 1842–43, Registry Office, 1872

Perth was planned as an orderly gridiron by Reuben Sherwood according to Lord Dorchester's 1789 design for inland settlements in Upper Canada. But the town's repetitive square blocks made an important allowance for hierarchy: public buildings were to be clustered at the highest point. Originally the Drummond Street hill held the courthouse and jail as well as the Anglican, Presbyterian, and Roman Catholic churches.

When the original 1820 courthouse needed replacing, Malcolm McPherson designed a Palladian-inspired building. A civil engineer, McPherson was sufficiently unsure of his plans that he took them to the Toronto architect John Howard, who emended them and charged McPherson £5.10s. Their collaboration, a "temple with wings," as Marion MacRae and Anthony Adamson call it in *Cornerstones of Order*, is full of familiar Perth touches: the

9 *Registry Office*

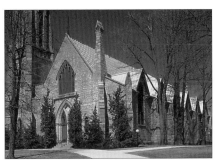

11 *St. James the Apostle Anglican Church,*
Drummond Street East and Harvey Street

hammered quoins, the prominent relief joints of the mortar, the emphatic string courses. Note the variations in the apparently simple window treatments, especially the floating half-round windows on the second floor.

The last public execution held in Perth took place in front of the Court House in 1851. The *Courier* commented sarcastically on the presence of local women ("how amiable, how consistent with the tender feelings of the other sex") who gathered to watch the execution of Francis Beare for murder.

The 1872 Registry Office to the right follows the usual Ontario plan for such buildings, probably designed by Kivas Tully. The typical one-storey, three-bay strongbox is executed here in local broken-coursed sandstone, with rusticated quoins and a smoother body – the reverse of the Court House arrangement.

Follow the path between the Court House and the Registry Office, cross the courtyard parking lot, and take the stairs down to the right. A sidewalk along the side of the building leads to Beckwith Street.

10 Perth Jail, 62 Beckwith Street East, 1862–63

If architecture could serve as a deterrent, the Perth Jail might well have lowered the crime rate. This unyielding piece of rock-faced masonry is basically Palladian in out-

line, but its rough skin, its long thin proportions, and its dearth of openings make something forbidding of this usually genial style. The thick swaths of cut-stone trimmings don't offer much in the way of reassurance either; as Ken MacPherson and Douglas Richardson finely observe in *Ontario Towns*, the keystones "seem to grip the sash with the bite of a vise." The designer was Henry Horsey, a Kingston architect. Unfortunately, the modern door and the new parts of the ramped entrance detract from what was a most intimidating ensemble. The jail was closed in 1994.

Retrace your steps back to Drummond Street.

11 St. James the Apostle Anglican Church, Drummond Street East and Harvey Street, 1861, tower and spire, 1888

Perth's first Anglican church, a frame building, was built on this site in 1822. Its Gothic replacement, built of local sandstone for $17,000, was first designed by William Thomas of Toronto in 1856 and built to his plans up to the window arches; at that point, about 1860, his design was scrapped and the building was completed by Thomas Fuller and Chilion Jones, the architects of Parliament's original Centre Block. In keeping with its image as a "garrison church," the side walls were prominently buttressed, and a tunnel connected

13 *The Summit, 33 Drummond Street East*

14 *15 Harvey Street*

it with the Court House. A "remarkably handsome building," as the *Ottawa Citizen* called it in 1875, its chief beauty came later: the tower and spire that constitute a full arsenal of pointed forms in wood, copper, and stone. In 1836, William IV proclaimed St. James a Royal Charter Church, a rare honour in Canada, which allows servers and choir to wear red cassocks. The interior is well worth seeing, especially for the dark pine ceiling, like a Gothic barn.

12 St. James's Rectory, 12 Harvey Street, 1875

St. James's "tasteful rectory" (as the *Ottawa Citizen* described it) was designed by King Arnoldi, a well-known Ottawa architect, and cost its parishioners $5,000. The bold bargeboards are well in evidence, especially on the Harvey Street side, but other tasteful details – the dog-toothing on the string course and the handsome window surrounds – are obscured by the modern porch and shrubbery.

13 The Summit, 33 Drummond Street East, 1823

Soon after he arrived in Perth to practise law, the twenty-two-year-old James Boulton built the town's first brick house on its highest hill. Overweening as that sounds for a young man, Boulton's house was only a more modest version of Toronto's Grange, built six years before by his brother D'Arcy

Boulton Jr. The Perth house, called the Summit by a later owner, has the same symmetrical five-bay, two-storey structure, with tall first-floor windows and shorter ones above. The fanlight hidden by the portico and the rounded light in the gable are other familiar neoclassical touches but, unlike the Grange's projecting frontispiece, the Summit's face is flat. Brick houses were rare in the Rideau Corridor, especially at this early date, but Boulton may well have insisted on the dominant Toronto building material. (The side addition came later.)

In spite of Boulton's legal eminence, his ambitious house, and the fact that two of Perth's streets commemorate his family (Boulton Street and D'Arcy Street, named after his son), he stayed in Perth only about a decade. Public feeling against Boulton was so strong after the 1833 duel, when his law clerk killed Thomas Radenhurst's law clerk, that he left for Niagara, but not before he was burned in effigy on the Summit's lawn.

14 15 Harvey Street, 1834 or earlier

A district town spawned many hotels, one of which was this neoclassical sandstone house convenient to the courthouse. William Cross, a Perth innkeeper, advertised in the *Bathurst Courier* in 1834 that he had moved to a "Commodious Stone House" and would supply his guests with "choice Liquors of all kinds" and a larder

15 Drummond Street East

18 *37 Herriott Street*

stocked "'in the good old English style.'" Originally called St. George Hotel, its sobriety and deep hip-roof give it a Georgian look that was old-fashioned by this date.

15 30 Drummond Street East, ca. 1836
Looking much more ancient and primitive than the Summit across the street, this house was built more than a decade later. Like the first stone house on Mill Street, it has no quoins, no central peak, and no differentiation between front and sides. From its position close to the turning basin of the Tay Canal, its lack of shutters, unusual for a private house, and indications of a bar in what is now the dining room, it seems likely that it was originally an inn. Built by James or Daniel Campbell, both early Perth merchants.

16 15 Drummond Street East, 1834
Another homespun-looking stone cottage, this one with rudimentary quoins and very simple window treatments. It is said to have been built in one day in a bee involving the work of some 100 men, for a carpenter named James McPherson.

Among Perth's original streets, the ones parallel to Gore were named for military types, the ones parallel to Foster for administrators. Herriott Street is a misspelled memorial to George Heriot, postmaster general for British North America and watercolourist.

17 Fire Station, 30 Herriott Street, 1855, 1883
The Second Empire tower that was added in 1883 to the red-brick firehall of 1855 had more than good looks going for it: the fire hose was hung in it to dry, helped along by a blazing stove at the foot of the tower.

18 37 Herriott Street, 1860
As befits the house of one of Perth's cultural elite, John Hart's Italianate box is soigné from the urn that tops the bell-shaped dormer to the diamond appliqués at the bottom of the portico posts. Part of the house's harmony can be traced to the repeated variations on a few basic shapes: as well as the rounded Italianate windows, the dormer's curve is echoed and widened in the surround of the double window below it; even the diamonds on the portico posts are related to the pediment-topped first-floor windows. Scottish-born John Semple Hart (1833–1917) ran a bookstore and *de facto* cultural centre in the block he owned at 15–31 Gore Street East; in 1887, the Toronto *Mail* called it the finest bookstore in the country outside Toronto and Montreal. As well as books, Hart purveyed international newspapers, stationery, wallpapers, musical instruments, and sheet music; he also founded *Hart's Canadian Almanac*, which was published for sixty-five years.

Continue south to Gore and head towards the Town Hall and Mill Street. Cross and

20 *51–53 Gore Street East*

22 *56–62 Gore Street East*

stand with your back to the Royal Bank for the best view of the next three buildings.

19 45–49 Gore Street East, 1846
Brooke and Grays Emporium, with living quarters above, nodded to the Palladian style with its pediment and to the neoclassical with its elliptical doorcase and fanlight. Its builder, Thomas Brooke, was a Halifax-born merchant and long-time town clerk.

20 51–53 Gore Street East, 1846
Also built by Thomas Brooke, this building was gutted in a 1979 fire and painstakingly rebuilt. The riverside view, with its parapet wall, quadrant windows, cut-stone quoins, and balconies, is one of Perth's most charming.

21 57–61 Gore Street East, 1841
Like its neighbour number 51–53, this sturdy piece of oatmeal-coloured sandstone looks its best at the riverside. Built by a harness-maker named Francis Halliday, it was known for many years as the Sheriff's House because the second owner, James Thompson, was the sheriff of Lanark and Renfrew from 1852 to 1893. In 1918, the centre-plan house was converted into a store with apartments above.

22 56–62 Gore Street East, ca. 1830
Built by masons who had worked on the Rideau Canal, this may originally have served as housing for the canal workers; by

1837 it was a hotel called Allan House. Thomas Radenhurst and his ill-fated clerk Robert Lyon practised law at number 62, where Radenhurst's name is still visible in blue paint to the left of the elliptical doorway.

23 77 Gore Street East, formerly Carnegie Library, 1907
With $10,000 from Andrew Carnegie earmarked for a library, Perth approached the fashionable Toronto architects Darling & Pearson. The corner site must have put Frank Darling in mind of the Bank of Montreal building he had designed at the corner of Toronto's Front and Yonge Streets some twenty years earlier when he was in partnership with S.G. Curry. The Perth version has the same Beaux Arts structure – a corner door flanked by two pediments, topped by a high closed balustrade – but its grandiosity was scaled down for a small town. While the stone bank in Toronto was elaborately encrusted with carving, the library is a homelier combination of orange-red, yellow, and white bricks, purple-streaked sandstone, and yellow-painted wood. Not a colour scheme for the squeamish, but this unabashed building has some fine details, such as the terracotta Ionic capitals and the oak leaves carved on the brackets. A 1980 fire destroyed the book collection and gutted the building, which is now used for offices.

25 *Town Hall, 80 Gore Street East*

26 *41 Mill Street*

24 81–83 Gore Street East, 1931

The Art Deco style (1925–40) could incorporate any number of earlier styles, typically by abstracting and flattening them. Here Perth's former post office, now converted to offices, is topped with a stylized pediment; the pilasters that section off the building and the consoles or long brackets over the door are more straightforwardly classical, and well matched to Gore Street's older buildings.

25 Town Hall, 80 Gore Street East, 1863 (best viewed from 81–83 Gore Street East)

While less purely beautiful than some of its more severe, Scottish-inspired buildings, Perth's Town Hall, designed by John Power of Kingston, has become an emblem of civic pride – especially the cupola, which was added in 1874. Grafting Italianate accessories on a Palladian body was a popular 1860s strategy for public buildings, at a time when $12,000 bought the best of local materials (creamy Potsdam sandstone) and craftsmen (Scottish masons). The elongated rounded windows, the use of vermiculated stone on windows and the banded front door, the meticulous outlines formed by string course, quoins, and dentils make for a civic building with just the right amount of dignity for Perth's size. And just behind the Town Hall, the Dodds & Erwin grain elevator, originally positioned on the river for power and in its fourth generation as a family business, injects a salutary note of reality.

Follow Mill Street through Stewart Park.

26 41 Mill Street, 1837

More easily seen from the carriage entrance than from the front, this is a Scottish mason's version of Regency. The mason was John Haggart Sr., born in Breadalbane, Scotland, who built Chaffey's Lock on the Rideau Canal. His two-storey house, with long first-floor windows that stop short of the usual full-length French ones, is more upright and less casual than the pure, low-slung Regency. Regency builders did favour stucco, which is here applied to stone and scored to look like ashlar. The two broad chimneys set close to the centre of the hip-roof are an important part of the house's proportions. Haggart lived close to his four-mill complex on the Tay, which included an oatmeal mill, a sawmill, and a flour mill. The house was later lived in by his son, John G. Haggart, mayor of Perth, MP, cabinet minister, and the main mover behind the second Tay Canal, popularly known as "Haggart's Ditch" because he had it extended to accommodate the family mills.

Continue west, crossing the falls via the hump-backed bridge called the Rainbow Bridge to Thom Street. Named for Alexander Thom, a military surgeon who

29 *9 Lewis Street*

30 *1–3 Lewis Street*

was Perth's first doctor, this was part of his 500-acre grant.

27 **9 Thom Street,** ca. 1850
Looking like an image of mutability, set in a ruined garden, this frame neoclassical house originally had grounds that included an apple orchard. The neoclassical calling cards are still here: corner pilasters, the finely moulded cornice, the plainish doorcase, and the returning eaves that hint at a classical pediment. The first owner was a tanner, fuller, and carder named Richard Code, one of various Codes who were involved in milling operations in the Perth area.

From Thom Street, turn right and follow Peter Street to Lewis Street.

28 **11 Lewis Street,** pre-1833
Rock Cliff cottage, as this was called, was very likely the unpretentiously genteel residence of one of the half-pay officers, bureaucrats, and lawyers who first settled Perth. The Ontario peak probably dates from mid-century, and the late-Victorian four-paned windows definitely result from an 1890s make-over.

29 **9 Lewis Street,** 1880s
Even a board-and-batten worker's cottage could claim acquaintance with Greek Revival stylishness: in this case, the front gable, door placed to the side, and eared trim on the second-floor windows are

Greek Revival hallmarks. As well as being classy, the front-gabled, side-hall house plan was practical for a town that expected to grow: it could occupy a narrower lot than the more expansive side-gabled houses popular before 1850 in the Rideau Corridor.

30 **1–3 Lewis Street,** 1883
Bolts, beer, and boxes were made at various times in this small-scale factory, now converted to condominiums. The Tay River that supplied power for the busy little nineteenth-century industrial district now obliges the owners with balcony views of absolute tranquillity.

Walk between 11 Lewis and 9 Lewis, around the back. Cross Code Park, admiring the Queen Anne house and Code's Felt Mill to the left, and walk up Herriott Street to the corner of Herriott and Gore. The next four buildings were built for the textile manufacturer T.A. Code by the Smiths Falls architect George Martin.

31 **44 Gore Street East,** 1830, 1911
Enamoured of the dark sandstone yielded by the turn-of-the-century Hughes Quarry, Martin used it as a linking element in the complex of buildings he designed for Code. In 1911 Martin enlarged this early building to three stories and faced it with rocky Hughes stone. The over-delicate classical swags in the frieze were a favourite touch in the first decade or so of this century.

126

[33] *50 Herriott Street*   [34] *Code's Felt Mill, 53 Herriott Street*

Retrace your steps down Herriott Street for the rest of the Code complex.

[32] 45–47 Herriott Street, ca. 1906
From Georgian classicism to the square Italianate style was an easy step, as indicated by this sandstone duplex. The same restraint and symmetry prevail in both styles, in this case outlined by George Martin with brackets at the top and darker stone quoins at the sides in strong contrast to the coursed rubblestone body. Built for the manager of Code's Mills.

[33] 50 Herriott Street, 1906
Another of Martin's designs, Kininvie, as this house was called, was a present from T.A. Code to his wife, Jennie Leslie, who died soon after the house was built, in 1907. With typical Queen Anne high spirits, dormers laden with half-timbered effects and giant dentils burst out all over the roof; porches sprout Corinthian and Ionic columns of varying heights along with rounded and pointed pediments. Tempering all this excess (and connecting it to the Code factory) are the purplish Hughes Quarry voussoirs, quoins, lintels, and string courses. Kininvie was heated by steam tunnelled from the Code factory across the street.

[34] Code's Felt Mill, 53 Herriott Street, 1902
For Code's office wing, Martin punctuated the workaday coursed rubblestone with amethyst-toned string courses and voussoirs. (The older part of the complex, on Wilson Street, dates from as early as 1842 and represents a more traditional, straightforward mill design.) Begun in 1876 with a commission from the North-West Mounted Police for socks, Code's is still producing and selling felt from this mill and factory outlet. What is now Code Park served in the nineteenth century as a drying field for the felt.

[35] Perkins Motors, 2 Wilson Street West, 1937
With its links to industrial design, the Art Moderne style was well suited to a car dealership. Perkins Motors, which served Perth from 1937 to 1990, has all the earmarks of this swanky, streamlined 1930s style: the rounded corners, the flat roof, the long line of windows (incorporating novelty glass), and the use of metal accents. Now transformed into a small shopping centre, it has a restored five-pin bowling alley upstairs.

Foster Street, now Perth's "second" shopping street, was originally the main street. Begin on the corner closest to Perkins, looking across the street.

[36] 56–78 Foster Street, various dates
Number 56–58, the oldest in this commercial group and the only one with a slanted roof, was built in 1855 as a bakery. The

37 *61–63 Foster Street*

38 *57 Foster Street*

brick building next door, number 60–64, with a frieze of brick fancywork, was built three decades later, in 1885. Originally a hotel, its carriageway remains. Number 66–68, a stone building with rounded second-floor windows, was built in 1874 as a harness and saddlery shop. The yellow-brick ensemble was built in two stages, first number 70–72 in 1865. A more thorough-going example of the Italianate style than its stone neighbour, this has a fine brick frieze and rounded window surrounds. When a Mrs. McComiskey built a drug-store at number 76–78 in 1878, she continued in the style of her neighbour.

Now cross to the opposite side of Foster.

37 **61–63 Foster Street,** ca. 1900–08
In 1908, this "up-to-date building," as the *Courier* called it, housed a business school and other offices; around 1916, the Bank of Nova Scotia took possession. Significantly younger than its neighbours, it's compatible while remaining true to its own more flamboyant decade. Using rich purply stone from the Hughes Quarry to pick out the pilasters, string courses, and radiant voussoirs, the designer capped his work with a tin cornice decorated with semicircles, brackets, and dentils. Note the bead-and-reel capitals, also made of tin, on the second-storey pilasters.

38 **57 Foster Street,** 1871
A drugstore has stood on this site since 1846, two and a half decades before John Coombs built this little classic. Except for the large-paned late-nineteenth-century shop window arrangement, it could pass for a building erected in Britain almost a century earlier.

39 **41–47 Foster Street,** 1848, with 1883 additions
The "most extensive mercantile house in the County of Lanark" was located here for more than sixty years, part of an empire that occupied more than an acre of downtown land and dispensed grain, millinery, cheese, crockery, and virtually everything else needed to sustain life. The owner, Arthur Meighen (a cousin of the prime minister who shared his name), arrived in Perth in the 1840s with his widowed mother and four brothers from Northern Ireland. In 1867, he moved his enterprise into this stone building, so business-like that the raked cut-stone window surrounds and projecting sills are its only ornamentation.

Stand at the northwest corner of Foster and Gore, and look across the street.

40 **Shaw's of Perth, 1 Gore Street East,** 1840
Roderick Matheson arrived in Perth in 1816 as a half-pay lieutenant in the Glengarry Light Infantry Fencibles, opened a

 Perth Museum, 11 Gore Street East

42 30 Gore Street East

store in 1820, and set about becoming the richest man in town. (At his death in 1872, he was a senator in John A. Macdonald's government.) When he built his plain-faced sandstone saddle and harness shop at the corner of Gore and Foster in 1840, it fronted on Foster, then the main street. It became Shaw's in 1859 when Matheson's daughter Flora married Henry D. Shaw. The Heritage Silversmiths building behind it on Foster Street served as stables and coach house.

41 Perth Museum, 11 Gore Street East, 1840

Twenty years after he opened his first store, Roderick Matheson built himself a walled compound of house, store, and warehouse at Perth's main intersection. The warehouse is no more, but Shaw's of Perth continues in business and Matheson's house, saved from demolition in 1966, is now the town museum.

Definitely one of Perth's four finest houses, with its Scottish Palladian composure and the plain beauty of its stonework, it is arguably the finest of all. The very slight projection of its wide frontispiece contributes to the general air of restraint, as does a tiny but significant detail such as the lack of a doorknob: this was a house designed never to be without a servant. Note the careful patterns formed by the broken-coursed, prominently mortared stonework, with quoins and window surrounds made of large dressed stones. The formality does not extend to the tweedy, uncoursed rubble of the side and back walls. Mathesons lived in the house until the 1930s, after which it served as a tea room and home to the Canadian Legion.

42 30 Gore Street East, 1884

Modern taste probably favours Gore Street's spare classical buildings, but in its day the Bank of Montreal was considered the *crème de la crème* of downtown Perth. The 1887 Toronto *Mail* (which commended Perthites for having "the money-saving faculty to a remarkable degree") went further, calling the bank "the most elegant piece of architecture in the county." Picking and choosing elements from hither and yon – the Second Empire mansard roof, the Bank of Montreal sunburst insignia in the gable, the Tudor small-paned windows, the Romanesque arches – the bank manages to be both picturesque (and hence "modern" in the 1880s) and dignified enough for its context. Designed by Sir Andrew T. Taylor, a Montreal architect, and built by Duncan Kippen and J. Scott using the local grey-white Bathurst sandstone, the bank was drastically renovated in the 1960s. In the 1980s, as part of Perth's main-street revival, it was expensively (to the tune of almost $250,000) returned to a state closer to the original.

Return to Foster Street and turn right.

43 *31 Foster Street*

44 *25 Foster Street*

43 **31 Foster Street,** ca. 1865

After plans for a symmetrical Italianate house with a projecting frontispiece appeared in the *Canada Farmer* in 1865, variations were built throughout rural and small-town Ontario, usually in brick. For $9,000, William McNairn Shaw, a lawyer and member of the Ontario legislature, procured himself an exceptionally handsome sandstone version of the plan. The extras include double chimney-stacks with flaring chimney pots, cut-stone window surrounds with leafy centrepieces, quarry-faced quoins with dressed margins, and a handsome cast-iron fence. Originally the veranda swept around three sides; the square portico is early-twentieth-century, and the dormers were added after the 1940s.

44 **25 Foster Street,** ca. 1862

Relatively overlooked but one of Perth's loveliest buildings, this pale sandstone cube was first the Commercial Bank of Canada, then the Merchants Bank of Canada. As was the nineteenth-century custom, the bank housed its agent as well as its offices. The double string course makes the middle look rather indecisive, but the plainish double and triple chimney-stacks, the subtle flourishes in the rounded window and door surrounds, and the very slight contrast between the sandstone blocks and the cut-stone mouldings and quoins add up to a building with understated finesse. The prettiest view is on Foster Street.

Drummond Street West between North and D'Arcy Streets is a potpourri of styles, including an Eastlake porch at number 5, a classic Rideau Corridor stone cottage at number 12, an exercise in the Bracketed style at number 13, an Italianate house at number 14, and a Gothic Revival house at number 16.

45 **11–15 D'Arcy Street,** 1851

J. Kennedy makes teeth of bone,
For Those whom Fate has left without;
Or else makes something for his own,
By pulling other people's out.

So ran a poetical tribute published in the Perth *Courier* in 1866 to Dr. J.F. Kennedy, who lived in the north unit. A relative of Alexander Graham Bell, Dr. Kennedy had one of the world's first telephones installed here in 1876 to communicate with his dentistry office on Foster Street. The citified house itself is said to have been built by a cobbler named James Robertson, using only Edinburgh masons. Whether or not that's true, its cut-stone front, rubblestone sides, and parapet walls look convincingly Scottish. Originally called the Temperance Hall, it provided meeting space for temperance societies as well as touring musicians. Robertson claimed to be using his second-floor "music hall" for sacred music, but the *Courier* reported complaints about the inclusion of comedy and non-religious acts; a chastened Robertson promised they would stop.

46 *22 Drummond Street West*

48 *26 Drummond Street West*

Once lined with sugar maples, Drummond Street West between D'Arcy and Isabella was Perth's premier residential street during the prosperous 1880s.

46 22 Drummond Street West, ca. 1885
Two of the houses on this block, numbers 22 and 23, are variations on a favoured Ontario model with a central gable, bracketed cornice, and bays. Number 22 relies on textural brick framing and string courses to tie together windows and provide a horizontal element; its front porch is early-twentieth-century and replaces a wraparound veranda. Built for Francis Hall, a lawyer and one-time mayor (1881–82).

47 23 Drummond Street West, 1878
More elaborate than its neighbour across the street, number 23 has Tudorized the prevailing Italianate look by adding leaded bay windows on the second storey, plus a *porte-cochère*. Built for $12,000 by J.T. Henderson, it was home for more than sixty years to his daughter and son-in-law John Stewart. Stewart was a well-known lawyer and distiller who served two terms as Perth's mayor; Stewart Park is named for him.

48 26 Drummond Street West, 1880s
Eclecticism triumphant. Why limit yourself to one style when it was possible to have rounded Italianate windows, two French mansard-roofed bays (one slim, one

chunky), and a graceful Eastlake porch? Surprisingly, it makes an appealing mélange. So-called white brick, the preferred building material on this street, was promoted in centres like Toronto for its stone-like effect. Its presence in Perth may reflect that fashion or a late-century scarcity of old-style stonemasons. Known locally but inaccurately as "the house that Prohibition built," it was the residence of Fred Girdwood, who was one of the few people allowed to sell alcohol during Prohibition, at his pharmacy at 57 Foster Street (**38**). Since the house pre-dates Prohibition, more likely this is the house that Prohibition bought.

49 29 Drummond Street West, ca. 1870
Built like its dressier neighbours of white brick, this house is distinguished by its dignified Gothic door and boxy, relatively uncomplicated shape. It was built but never lived in by another mayor, H.D. Shaw, of Shaw's of Perth.

50 19 Isabella Street, 1870s
Another version of Ontario's favoured Italianate plan, this one has the style's signature double door and windows and a winsome sculptured cornice on the bays and roof. A so-called vista house that closes off the end of Gore Street, it also concludes the walk.

2 Hill Street

Picton

"One of the Pleasantest Places Imaginable"

A notched and nooked island floating in Lake Ontario, Prince Edward County is not quite like any other place. For Loyalist descendants from across Canada who come on pilgrimage, combing its abundant cemeteries for family names, admiring the neoclassical houses their American-born forebears built, it is holy ground. For more casual visitors, it is a stubbornly conservative outpost, an island slightly lost in time that seems much more remote than it actually is. For residents, uninterested in Ontario's other twenty-five counties, it is simply "the County."

Picton, the island's geographical and administrative centre and its largest town by far, is less obviously "County" than the backroads and smaller settlements. But behind Picton's preoccupied market-town face, the island's past shows itself in layers that reach back two centuries to its Loyalist beginnings.

Human settlement before the Loyalists was almost non-existent. In the late summer of 1615, Samuel de Champlain paddled through the Bay of Quinte accompanied by 500 Indians and fifteen French explorers. (The Bay of Quinte separates the County from the rest of Ontario; what had been a peninsula became an island in the 1880s when the Murray Canal severed the County's slim link with the mainland.) Probably the County's first European observer, Champlain found "a rich and cheery country" with excellent fishing and a profusion of vines and walnut trees that made the banks look almost landscaped.

In spite of its Edenic qualities, the place was not popular with the local Algonquins: the small peninsula (about thirty miles across) afforded poor hunting and was too vulnerable to attack from rival tribes. For a half-dozen years in the seventeenth century, two Sulpician priests established a mission at the region's western edge, but it took the American Revolution to populate the County.

In the summer of 1783, tens of thousands of homeless Americans "whose

133

only offence has been their attachment to the King's service," as Sir Guy Carleton put it, were waiting in makeshift camps along the St. Lawrence for land. By the fall, surveyors were at work around the Bay of Quinte. What became Ontario, which had been virtually uninhabited when the American Revolution began, acquired 5,000 to 6,000 Loyalists, and the Kingston–Bay of Quinte region was one of three main areas of settlement. The County attracted a typically mixed bag of British soldiers, Hessian mercenaries, Quakers, and farmers from New York and "the Jarsies" (New Jersey).

But the completeness of the Loyalist invasion of Prince Edward County was not typical. Unlike the other early settlements, where the proportion of Americans was diluted by later immigration, the Loyalists filled the little peninsula to capacity within a single generation. As Richard and Janet Lunn point out in *The County*, the population of Prince Edward County in 1842 was 14,945; 452 had been born in England, 1,584 in Ireland, 103 in Scotland, 10 in Europe. All the rest were born in America or native to the County.

They were a special subset of Americans, who combined an obstinate independence with a special attachment to the Crown. By 1792, the County had been named for the fourth son of George III, future father of Queen Victoria, and the original townships were christened Ameliasburgh, Sophiasburgh, and Marysburgh, after three daughters of George III. Picton itself began as two settlements at the head of Picton Bay, both named for heroic royalists. The first, on the west side, was called Hallowell after Benjamin Hallowell, a Loyalist and commissioner of customs in Boston; the second was first nicknamed Delhi, for reasons that remain unclear, and later called Picton for Sir Thomas Picton, a hero of Waterloo.

Today, more than a century and a half after the two settlements were amalgamated, the differences remain marked. The former Hallowell includes the business area, the town's "best street" of High Victorian mansions, the high school, the fairgrounds – in other words, a fairly complete town. Delhi, on the other hand, has what one family's fortune and the established church could confer: the original Anglican church, the "big house" (in this case also the rectory), the impressive Courthouse. Still surrounded, as they were in the nineteenth century, by mostly modest houses and shops, these three landmarks give Delhi the air of a fief or a village with a very prominent squire.

The squire was William Macaulay (1794–1874), for fifty-one years its Anglican rector, chief landowner, and determined town planner. Most land grants awarded to Loyalists by the British government were around 150 or 200 acres, but Macaulay inherited 500 acres around Picton Bay from his father, Robert, a Loyalist merchant supplying troops in the Kingston area. Educated in Cornwall by the Family Compact's doyen, John Strachan (later Bishop Strachan), and at Oxford, William Macaulay was ordained and settled on his land in Picton in the 1820s. He built a handsome brick church and a rectory at the foot of a hill still known locally as Macaulay Mountain, donated land for the nearby Catholic church and the courthouse, and fancied himself a developer. In reality he greatly overestimated his business talents and owed what success he had to his brother and business agent.

By the second or third decade of the century, it was clear that Picton-Hallowell – in the centre of the island, on the important Danforth Road, with the county's best harbour – was destined to be the leading town. Hallowell was a going concern, with three doctors, three lawyers, several churches, inns, shops, and small factories in 1831. Cargo ships, yawls, and twice-weekly steamboats to and from Kingston thronged the harbour. Mr. Cole's singing school met twice a week, there was a public reading room from 1833, and a boarding school for young ladies.

The Delhi or Picton side had the Anglican church, plans for the limestone courthouse – and the Reverend Mr. Macaulay. When people began to talk about amalgamating Hallowell and Picton, Macaulay was opposed, but finding "that the folks in the village were pertinacious," as he wrote his wife, he acquiesced. In 1837 the Legislative Assembly officially melded the two villages. Macaulay lost his battle to keep his own little fief separate, but he won the smaller skirmish – the new town was called Picton, and not Port William as the Hallowellites wished.

Macaulay's portrait shows a man with pouchy, narrow eyes and a generous mouth firmly closed, a patriarch in the nineteenth-century mode who saw no reason to look attractive or affable. With his real estate and his ties to England, the Family Compact, and the Anglican church, he should have been the natural leader of Picton. And so he was for its elite, but only for its elite. In the usual Anglican way, his church extracted rent for the pews, a sure way of discouraging cash-strapped settlers, and neither Macaulay nor either of his two wives was much inclined to democracy. The twenty-two male parishioners who presented their minister with "a perfect bijoux" (as the Picton *Gazette* called it) of silver plate for a New Year's gift in 1861 represented the town's aristocracy; his first wife's obituary commended her for occasionally extending hospitality to "the more respectable members" of her husband's congregation. Just as Macaulay's side of town was overtaken by the go-getting Hallowell side, his stiffly hierarchical Anglicanism was overtaken by Methodism. The doers in Picton were not landowners but merchants, not Anglicans but Methodists, the profoundly democratic purveyors of "the Hot Gospel."

The County was the cradle of Methodism in Canada, a dynamic religion originally spread by circuit-riding American preachers. A Methodist Organization was founded in what became Picton in 1793; Canada's first Methodist place of worship, Hay Bay Church in nearby Adolphustown, had been built in the previous year. Belden's 1878 *Historical Atlas of Hastings and Prince Edward Counties* noted, "Being what might be termed an 'aggressive' church, the Methodists have let go no hold, but pushed their conquests further and further" until they were the County's most numerous congregation. Direct, emotional, demonstrably willing to travel to the settlers and share their fortunes, the Methodist preachers made converts undreamed of by the unbending Macaulay. By mid-century many of Picton's leading citizens belonged to the First Methodist Church on Chapel Street.

The nineteenth-century history of Picton, the County's shipping, marketing, and manufacturing centre, follows the agricultural fortunes of the region. The coming of the railroads and a direct cross-country line to the north reduced the region to an inconvenient backwater serviced by a branch line. (Accustomed to transportation by boat, Prince Edward County resisted even the branch line until 1879.) Its golden age, the Barley Days, lasted from 1860 to 1890, a frantic time when County farmers and shippers got rich trying to meet the New York State brewers' insatiable demand for barley and hops. The unique example of prosperity in Prince Edward County's rather hardscrabble story, the Barley Days built the showplaces on Picton's Main Street as well as the fine farmhouses on the country roads. But when midwestern brewers, who procured their barley and hops closer to home, began to challenge the New York State brewers, the County's pre-eminence wobbled. It ended definitively in 1890 when the McKinley Tariff imposed heavy duties on imported grain.

With the demise of the Barley Days, most County farmers, shippers, and businesses simply adjusted their expectations downward in a characteristic show of stoicism. (Sir John A. Macdonald, who practised law for four years in Picton, reputedly said, "I love the people of Prince Edward County. They vote for me time after time and they never ask me for anything. And they never get anything.") Some smugglers defied the tariff, setting up business in the nooks and crannies of the island's shoreline; the same spots served rum-runners during Prohibition. County farmers returned their attention to local stand-bys, especially cheddar cheese; in 1874, the island had twenty-eight cheese factories. The canning industry, which began in Wellington Boulter's Mary Street factory in Picton in 1881, was bigger business, expanding in Boulter's case to a repertoire of apples, pears, jams, beans, chicken, turkey, and pork and beans. In 1900, there were eight fruit and vegetable canning factories in the County, half of the national total. By 1930, there were about thirty-five factories, and a quarter of the County's cultivated land, about 25,000 acres, was devoted to crops for canning.

Today the canning factories have centralized and moved to larger centres, and the island's small farms concentrate on dairy products, apples, and other fruit. Picton's population has hovered around the 4,000 mark for a century, sometimes dipping below, sometimes rising tremulously above. In many ways the town and the region it serves have kept their nineteenth-century ways – an independent conservatism, a self-sufficiency that can look like incuriosity and makes do with relatively little.

In the rhetoric of 1878, Belden's *Historical Atlas* noted Picton's "beautifully shaded streets, well-built business blocks, fine public buildings, and splendid private residences" and pronounced it "one of the pleasantest places imaginable." Is it? The streets, the business blocks, the public buildings, and private residences are commendable and still here, but Picton is delightful only in parts. The commercial part of Main Street has been defaced and neglected, and the Reverend Macaulay's side of town requires a dose of historical imagination to appreciate it. But Picton is rewarding in a way that may be better than delightful, in its naturalness and the discrete miniaturism of its quarters (the "best street," the Anglican buildings, even a minute factory complex). Here is a town where fifteen minutes' walk will take you from the timeless country burial ground of Old St. Mary Magdalene to the artfully naturalized High Victorian romanticism of Glenwood's garden cemetery, from the frigid elegance of the neoclassical courthouse to the Hollywood potpourri of the Regent vaudeville house. Like all nineteenth-century towns whose history has not been obliterated, Picton is a palimpsest, but its size and unpretentiousness make its layers particularly vivid.

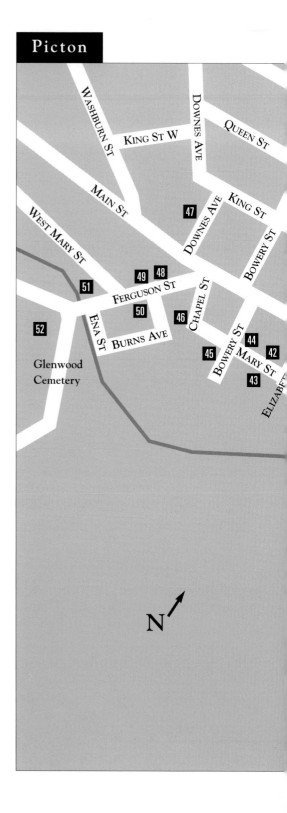

Picton

WASHBURN ST
KING ST W
DOWNES AVE
QUEEN ST
MAIN ST
DOWNES AVE
KING ST
WEST MARY ST
BOWERY ST
47
49 48
51
FERGUSON ST
CHAPEL ST
50
52
ENA ST
46
BURNS AVE
45
BOWERY ST
44
MARY ST
42
43
ELIZABETH

Glenwood
Cemetery

N

37 237 Main Street

39 Regent Theatre,
222–226 Main Street

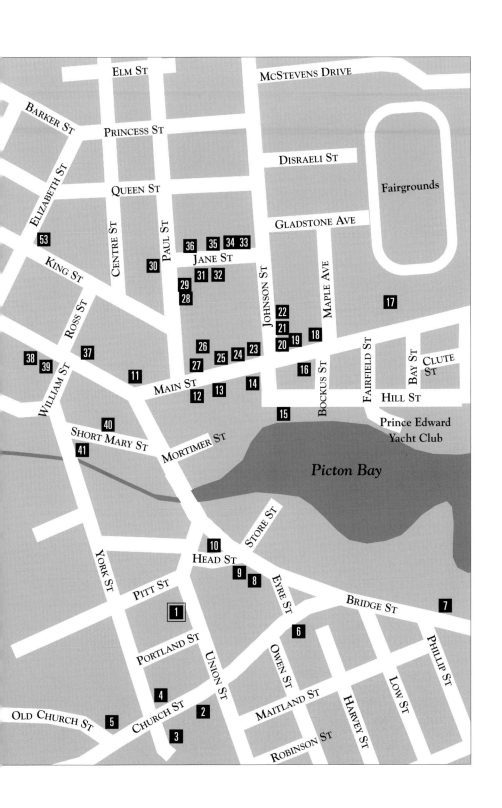

1 *Prince Edward County Courthouse,*
44 Union Street

1 *Jail and courthouse*

The walking tour of Picton falls naturally into three parts. The first is the oldest part of town, the fiefdom of William Macaulay, now looking somewhat neglected but full of early buildings including an important cluster of church, rectory, and courthouse. The second is Main Street east of Town Hill and its environs, an idyll of Victorian prosperity that came into its own beginning in the 1860s. The third and most heterogeneous part ranges from commercial buildings and residential streets to a tiny industrial district and a Victorian garden cemetery.

I. THE REVEREND
MR. MACAULAY'S PICTON

1 Prince Edward County Courthouse,
44 Union Street, 1832, **Jail,** ca. 1864

Tastes change. To modern eyes the Courthouse, one of the oldest in Ontario, is monumental and, given its context, almost startlingly imposing. But to Smith's *Canadian Gazeteer* in 1846, the building was "light and elegant." "Elegant," yes, with the severe beauty of its cut limestone unornamented except for string course, bevelled quoins, and the neoclassical doorcase and central window. (Quarried in Kingston, the stone arrived by boat.) "Light" is harder to grasp, because of the same severity, the portentous Tuscan portico, and the magnificent setting overlooking the harbour.

The setting was the work of William Macaulay, determined to play Lord Bountiful as well as increase the value of his real estate. Until 1831, Prince Edward County's trials and judicial matters had been decided in Kingston; once the County became the master of its own courts, Macaulay offered two acres in his subdivision and £200 for the new jail and courthouse. Although rivals from the Hallowell side complained in the *Hallowell Free Press* of its distance from the "business part of the village" and the "noxious effluvia" from the nearby marsh and millponds, Macaulay's lure won the day.

Marion MacRae and Anthony Adamson (*Cornerstones of Order*) credit Thomas Rogers, an English-born architect who was responsible for an early courthouse in Belleville, with the design. Whoever the architect was, he crafted a building that could easily have been a Georgian gentleman's country house. The portico that was added in the 1840s and the cupcake cupola that appeared in the 1860s to improve ventilation gave it a more public cast.

Originally the jail cells were at the rear and below ground. When the inspector of asylums declared them substandard in 1857, a new two-storey jail was designed by Henry Horsey. Twelve of the eighteen cells measured eight by three feet, with twelve-foot ceilings; the remaining six, reserved for debtors, were slightly larger. The rough-faced stone, set in broken courses to display

2 Old St. Mary Magdalene Anglican
Church, Church Street at Union Street

2 Macaulay gravestones

its various colours, and the cut-stone surrounds on windows and doors make a suggestive contrast between rough-hewn nature and the refining hand of civilization. Last used for prisoners in 1981, the jail now houses the county archives.

2 Old St. Mary Magdalene Anglican Church, Church Street at Union Street, 1825

When St. Mary Magdalene was formally consecrated in 1831, Bishop Charles Stewart wrote, "It appears that a pious and zealous missionary can gather a large congregation from a sparse population." It also appears that a wealthy missionary who knew what was *au courant* in England could achieve handsome results with his village church.

Perhaps the first brick building in the settlement, Macaulay's church began fashionably enough, with broad, clear-paned windows with interlacing Gothic tracery. (Each of the windows, still intact, has fifty-seven panes of glass.) As the Gothic Revival became more scholarly and Macaulay's fortunes waxed, stone extensions to the nave were made in the 1860s; a stone tower with buttresses and a broach spire, designed by John W. Hopkins of Montreal, replaced the first tower in 1860. (The parishioners' money-raising efforts for the spire included a floral bazaar and oyster festival.) No attempt was made to mask the alterations, and the difference between

the original windows and the later, more "correctly" angular ones is clearly seen on the side wall.

The gravestones in this country churchyard mark the short and simple annals of pioneer parishioners with the usual clasped hands, open Bibles, and crosses, as well as a stone that made it into Ripley's *Believe It or Not* for commemorating William Pierce, "Died Feb. 31, 1860." The Macaulays – rector, first and second wives, and an infant daughter – are laid to rest behind a wrought-iron fence. After Macaulay's death in 1874, the rationale for a fashionable congregation's worshipping in the unfashionable part of town disappeared and the parishioners took steps to move to Hallowell, finally completing the new St. Mary Magdalene on Main Street in 1913. The old church has been used as the county museum since 1970.

3 Macaulay House, 35 Church Street, ca. 1830

Fresh from a trip to Rome and awaiting ordination in England, Macaulay reassured his brother John, "Nothing that I have seen in England or elsewhere has made me repine an instant that I was born in the wilds of Upper Canada." Certainly not, when the wilds afforded him a symmetrical brick house in the best Loyalist taste that money could buy.

In this case money bought sidelights and transom in a very à la mode pattern

3 *Macaulay House, 35 Church Street*

6 *St Gregory the Great
Roman Catholic Church*

of diamonds and lozenges, a dainty portico, and a cornice supplied with dentils, triglyphs, metopes, and an up-to-the-minute cornice gutter. (On no account miss the rainwater heads, a winsome folk composition of lions, fans, feathers, and stars copied by twentieth-century restorers from another County house.)

The portico is a restoration of the original from the 1830s; the scars of two later verandas can be seen on the front. Very much a gentleman's residence, Macaulay House is also a practical County dwelling: the formality of the Venetian windows on the first floor gives way to the countrified twenty-four-paned windows on the second. Similarly, the house is faced with uniformly rosy-coloured (and costly) Flemish bond on the front and a tweedier mix of brick colours in common bond on the sides.

The tail here goes on and on, a story in itself of the domestic economy of the day – beginning with kitchen and servants' quarters, then summer kitchen plus hired hands' quarters, woodshed, drive-house. At the very end is a separate fieldstone stable. Macaulay House is now a museum, with the interior finely restored to the early 1850s, when Macaulay married for the second time.

For history buffs, two other early houses associated with Macaulay are nearby.

4 57 York Street, ca. 1835
The Curate's House, as the cottage Macaulay built for his assistant is known, was handy to church and rectory and appropriately humble. Underneath its stucco, applied in the 1970s, the original house is brick.

5 36 Church Street, ca. 1825
"Our little cottage is a very comfortable one," Macaulay wrote to his mother in 1829 while waiting to move into his new rectory with his bride. Tradition has it that the honeymoon cottage was this house, whose massive chimneys (recently removed) and flanking wings are clues to its early date. The so-called White Cottage was certainly one of Macaulay's many properties; now hemmed in by suburban development, it may well be Picton's oldest house.

Retrace your steps on Church Street, heading east three blocks.

**6 St. Gregory the Great Roman
Catholic Church, 7 Church Street,
1892**
For the full effect of St. Gregory's sturdy asymmetry, position yourself on Eyre Street. Macaulay sold an acre of land to the local Roman Catholics for five shillings and they built themselves a stone church and cemetery in 1839.

Although the County remained predominantly Protestant, the Irish famines

 97 *Bridge Street*

[8] 64 *Bridge Street*

increased mid-century immigration to the point that a larger Catholic church was needed. The second church on this dramatic site was designed by Joseph Connolly, an Irish-born disciple of Augustus Welby Pugin, the architectural patron saint of the Catholic Gothic Revival. Connolly, whose masterworks are the Church of Our Lady of the Immaculate Conception in Guelph (designed 1875) and St. Paul's on Power Street in Toronto (1887–89), built thirty Catholic churches in Ontario. For Picton, he concocted something that from the front, with the lean-to on one side and the rotund tower on the other, looks more earthbound and less attenuated than the classic soaring Gothic profile. Inside, the slender nave, lined with splendidly sentimental late-nineteenth-century stained-glass saints, produces a more aspiring impression.

Walkers more interested in Picton's oldest neighbourhood may skip the next house, a Colonial Revival extravaganza, and proceed to 64 Bridge Street.

▐7▌ 97 Bridge Street, ca. 1906

Like the wine in the *New Yorker* cartoon recommended for its amusing pretensions, there is something likeably risible about the full-blown Colonial Revival style. As the name suggests, this turn-of-the-century style began with memories of eighteenth-century American houses but quickly

parted company with their carefully proportioned restraint. With its colossal portico, frenetic fenestration, and balconies and verandas at every turn, Claramount is a classic of this genially distorted genre. Designed by William Newlands, a Kingston architect, for a lawyer and canning magnate, Edward Young, and named for Young's wife Clara, it originally dominated ten elaborately landscaped acres.

Three very early houses in a row are sited, in the fashion of the day, right on the Danforth Road. A major thoroughfare built from 1799 to 1801 by the American surveyor Asa Danforth, the road extended from Kingston to York (now Highways 2 and 33).

▐8▌ 64 Bridge Street, ca. 1835

Thomas Eyre's original inn, which began operating on this site in 1807, was more than a watering-hole. Tradition has it that the titanic struggles over the town's name were waged on Eyre's premises; certainly the annual town meeting was held here in the first decade of the century. Eyre's first inn was replaced by this stucco-over-stone building, centred on a fine-boned Loyalist doorcase with its deep entablature and slim pilasters. The five French windows with their unusual thick-and-thin glazing pattern extend across the front and around the corner of the gallery.

9 *58 Bridge Street*

12 *Registry Office, 334 Main Street*

9 58 Bridge Street, ca. 1847

There's something almost primeval-looking about this rubblestone cottage with its modestly pitched roof, near-complete lack of ornamentation, and the way it widens on Head Street to become a trapezoid. In 1847, William Macaulay's business agent reported that William Owens, a "steady, industrious" young carpenter, had bought the lot and was preparing to build on it. Owens was indeed industrious: he became in turn a lumber merchant, shipbuilder, potash manufacturer, farmer, and Picton's mayor for seven years. His family owned the house until 1920.

10 54–56 Bridge Street, 1840

The third in this group of houses set close to the street was built for a local merchant named John Foster. Four-bay houses were unusual because County builders preferred symmetry; in this case, two of the first-floor windows are larger than the third, which may indicate that Foster intended combining home and store. (A modern conversion to a duplex has robbed the house of its original door.) Belden's 1878 atlas shows the Foster house with a lavish side garden that included three fountains, more than a dozen trees, and a fetching bargeboarded barn.

II. RESIDENTIAL MAIN STREET AND ITS ENVIRONS

11 North American Hotel, 303–309 Main Street, ca. 1835

As if its position at the top of Town Hill were not prominence enough, the North American Hotel was an unusually lofty three stories high. Compared with Eyre's Inn down the hill, built at the same time and with many of the same elements, this hotel seems almost big-city: note the parapet walls, the full two-storey veranda, the elliptical fanlight over the recessed main door. (The smaller door with the rounded transom led to the taproom.) Although it has not operated as a hotel since 1917, the building has recently been restored to a state that closely approximates George Ackerman's 1869 watercolour of the Main Street landmark.

12 Registry Office, 334 Main Street, ca. 1871

The bars on the windows look almost *de trop*, because this little strongbox breathes such confidence in its ability to safeguard land titles and whatever else might be necessary. Form and function are closely allied here: aside from the iron door and windows, its compact shape, triple-arcaded front, and stout pilasters also proclaim its protective function. The three acroteria (the ornaments on the pediment) add a touch of non-functioning class not seen in

 346 Main Street

 *2 Hill Street*

other registry offices, but in general this follows the standard plan used across Ontario in the decades after Confederation. (Kivas Tully, the architect for the provincial government at that time, may have been responsible for the design.)

The location was chosen for its proximity to Shire Hall, the county's administrative offices (332 Main Street, built 1874); unfortunately, compared with its diminutive neighbour, Shire Hall looks too big and banal. Since 1975, the Department of Land Registry has been housed in the courthouse, and the Registry Office is now used for committee rooms.

13 338 Main Street, ca. 1870

Prim and more self-contained than the brick show-offs that line this prosperous street, this clapboard house was built by Kate Dunlop, from a family of clothiers. The simple bracketed windows and door, the corner pilasters, and the frame construction might suggest a date before 1870, but the house's unusual proportions – the peak that accounts for virtually half the house's height, the exaggeratedly long, slender first-floor windows – suggest a stylized version of an older style. (The removal of its veranda has accentuated its height.) The bargeboard, so tactful that it apparently appears only intermittently except at the apex, is also a "late" variety.

14 346 Main Street, ca. 1859

When Elisha Sills, merchant, built his Italianate stone house, there were only a few farmhouses east of Town Hill; by the time he died, in 1879, the street was well on its way to becoming Picton's best address. Set far back on its broad lawn, Sills's house draws the eye up, block by rectangular block – first the projecting entrance, then the second-floor sunroom, finally the house's signature, the belvedere. When the sun lights the red and blue glass in the belvedere, it looks like a glass miniature of the main house, edged with the same S-shaped brackets like long swooping commas. (The best view of the belvedere is from Johnson Street.)

15 2 Hill Street, ca. 1879

Before turning down Johnson Street towards Hill, look back across Main Street to the Merrill House (343 Main Street, **24** below) for a close cousin to this spiky nine-gabled creation. Edwards Merrill, a Picton lawyer and judge, built 343 Main first and almost immediately decamped to this site overlooking Picton Bay. Here the angularity that is so striking a feature of the earlier house is present but softened – by the lovely rounded Italianate door, the wider gables, two stories rather than three. A typically Ontarian mixture of Gothic and Italianate elements, the house is thought to be the work of J.W. Fegan, the master builder who also built Merrill House.

16 *352 Main Street*

17 *Crystal Palace, Main Street*

16 352 Main Street, ca. 1897

The pastel colour scheme makes it look more like a San Francisco Painted Lady than an Ontario Queen Anne. But the shape, a conglomeration of porches, gables, a balcony, and the signature polygonal tower, is real enough. Big-city Ontario architects favoured red brick for their Queen Anne villas; builders (rarely architects) in the smaller centres were often content with wood, which was thought more appropriate to a country setting. Here the clapboard is varied by three different kinds of shingles, another favourite Queen Anne material. Dentils, seen on the tower and under the main gable, were a County perennial, but they were also a classical component in the typical Queen Anne mix of classical and picturesque elements.

17 Crystal Palace, Main Street, 1887, **Prince Edward Old Boys Memorial Entrance,** 1920

The County's annual September fair isn't what it used to be: the Best Baby Show ("open only to Prince Edward born babies") and competitive needlework sections in such arcana as lambrequin bracket, Mount Mellick embroidery, and Kismet tracing are no more. But the County celebrates its agricultural life as it has for more than a century, in what may be North America's only remaining Crystal Palace.

The original Crystal Palace, Joseph Paxton's glass building for the 1851 Great

Exhibition in London, was copied all over North America for agricultural and industrial fairs, but especially in Canada, where a visitor remarked in 1861 that there were as many Crystal Palaces as government buildings. (Appropriately, John Ruskin had called Paxton's Crystal Palace "a giant cucumber frame," and Paxton had indeed based it on a greenhouse where he had worked as a gardener.)

Picton's version was built by a local contractor named Frank Wright. A cruciform building of board-and-batten, shingles, and great stretches of glass, it was centred on a cupola with a prettily flared roof. The delightful Prince Edward Old Boys Memorial Entrance, a faux-Tudor gatehouse complete with tiny-paned windows and half-timbering, was built as a memorial to the 150 County soldiers who died in World War I.

18 355 Main Street, ca. 1921

Elegant it isn't, but that's the point: this is an easygoing California Bungalow, crossed with a bit of Tudor half-timbering. The big, mildly pitched gables, overhanging roofs supported by rafters, the massive porch supports, the combination of simple building materials and the general lack of ornamentation were hallmarks of a style that originated in the plain, horizontal houses in India. (The bungalow gets its name from the province of Bengal.) By the beginning of this century, the North Americanized

19 *353 Main Street*

21 *2 Johnson Street*

style came to symbolize modernity, informality, and sensible middle-class living. When John Hubbs bought this lot for $2,500, it carried a proviso that the buyer must construct a residential building costing at least $9,000.

19 353 Main Street, 1868

The composure of Gideon Striker's symmetrical house suggests that it has been untouched since 1868, the date proudly displayed over the balcony window. Not so: subsequent owners discovered the flexibility afforded by a neoclassical house and added the polygonal bay to the side late in the nineteenth century, and the imposing doorcase and French doors probably during the 1920s, when revival styles were fashionable. A grandson of James Striker, a well-known Loyalist from Dutchess County, New York, Gideon Striker was an early partner in what is now Teasels, said to be the oldest pharmacy in Canada and a local landmark. He was also a successful Reform politician.

20 349 Main Street, ca. 1890

This house and the two adjoining on Johnson Street span a sixty-five-year range and represent three very distinct styles. The delightful 349 Main is a checklist of domesticated Gothic Revival features: the L-shaped plan, the demure bargeboard (in a popular County pattern) topped with finial and drop, the veranda with sculptural

treillage. The style was old-fashioned for this date, but nothing that would make a house-proud Victorian feel at ease is missing, and not a railing out of place. The circular forms in the middle of the veranda posts are a typical Picton touch and an example of what carpenters could do with stock turnings. The first owner was Walter McKenzie, who ran a dry-goods business.

21 2 Johnson Street, ca. 1900

Like a great piece of midnight brown velvet unfurling, this house has one *raison d'être*: its wooden shingles. Appropriately called Shingle style, the late-nineteenth-century American fashion has links with the Colonial Revival (the rediscovery of a favourite colonial building material) as well as the Queen Anne style (less busy, more horizontal, but with the same delight in porches, towers, and rounded forms in general). The earthy shingles flare out under the front balcony, at the bottom of the porch and at the side of the house; they take the place of railing on a porch that suggests iced tea, Judy Garland movies, and other summertime half-memories. The little second-floor balconies are absurdly topped with urns, a reminder of the classical motifs popular at the time, but the real message here is sensuousness. It was built by a Picton lawyer, James R. Brown, on land severed in 1893 from the Johnson farm (see next house).

 4 Johnson Street

24 *343 Main Street*

22 **4 Johnson Street,** ca. 1835
Paradoxically, this farmhouse looks much more citified than its voluptuous next-door neighbour. Farmhouses in the 1830s could have a certain cool elegance, when they were in the Loyalist style as this one was, but the Johnson house is exceptional. Flemish bond, which covers the front and the west side, was expensive and unusual; the fine doorcase has sidelights in a bold diamond-and-circle design and a rectangular transom that cleverly mimics the Loyalist elliptical fanlight. Even the flaring stone lintels and sills repay close attention: they are very decisively tooled, then bordered with tooling in the opposite direction. Built by Joseph Jewell Johnson on what was already a family farm, the house originally had an unobstructed view of Main Street; except for a replacement veranda and the expansion of the kitchen tail to two stories, the house has not been significantly altered.

23 **Royal Canadian Legion, 347 Main Street,** ca. 1863
In its glowing account of Walter Ross's general store, Belden's 1878 atlas reported that "everything about the establishment wears an air of 'business.'" The same might be said about Ross's stolid, hip-roofed house, but that isn't entirely fair: in his day, verandas on the side wings and two triple-stacked chimneys crowning the central roof added some badly needed lightness and variety.

What's left now, aside from the sternness of the Tudor labels and the plain brackets supporting the broad eaves, is sheer size. Ironically, Ross's business failed the very year Belden's praise was published, and the house was later bought by the American railway magnate George McMullen. Nationally famous for blowing the whistle on the Pacific Scandal that brought down Sir John A. Macdonald's government in 1873, McMullen and his heirs lived in the house until the 1930s; it is now the local Royal Canadian Legion headquarters.

24 **343 Main Street,** ca. 1878
This house has taken the verticality of the Gothic style so seriously that it's almost comic-sinister: if the wicked witch had lived in Picton, she might have tried to entice Hansel and Gretel in under that particularly skinny central gable. Even the round-topped Italianate double windows on the second and third floors look malnourished. The original shutters and more generously undulating bargeboard, as illustrated in Belden's 1878 atlas, helped some, but clearly the master builder J.W. Fegan and the owner Edwards Merrill loved gables: this house has twelve, including three on the unusual central tower.

25 **341 Main Street,** ca. 1883
It's only necessary to glance back next door at 343 Main to see that architectural fashions in the late 1870s and early '80s were

26 *339 Main Street*

29 *18 Paul Street*

fanciful, idiosyncratic, and wholeheartedly asymmetrical. Dr. W.W. Colton, the builder of this classically regular house, must have had a conservative streak. Wexford, as it was called by later owners, has more in common with houses built twenty years earlier such as 347 and 353 Main Street (**23**, **19**). The porch with its paired columns on brick platforms is a typical early-twentieth-century renovation.

26 339 Main Street, ca. 1835

This Loyalist farmhouse and the Johnson farmhouse (**22**, 4 Johnson Street) were the original houses in this part of town; like the Johnson house, it's surprisingly urbane. Walk up the driveway past St. Mary Magdalene's parish hall to see the stylish Greek-key trim and modillions under the eaves. Why a house without near neighbours would have the high parapet walls designed to keep fires from spreading in a crowded town is unclear, but they contribute to its urban look. The original owners, the Washburns, were among the leading families in Hallowell, and the builder of this house, Simeon Washburn, was a justice of the peace and judge of Surrogate Court. In 1890 the Anglican church bought the house and land, and built the new St. Mary Magdalene and its parish hall; the Washburn house became the rectory.

27 (New) St. Mary Magdalene Anglican Church, 339 Main Street, 1912

When the Anglicans determined to move to Picton's establishment street, they chose a church made of cement blocks for $22,000. (A comparable stone building was estimated at $26,000.) Custom-made by H.W. Bedell's cement works in Picton, the blocks were economical and innovative, but they give the building a rather grimy industrial look. Designed by Joseph Power of Kingston, the church is a stylized early-twentieth-century version of Gothic with the *de rigueur* large stained-glass window and a chunky Norman tower.

At about the same time that Main Street was acquiring its upper-class prestige, **Paul Street** (named for Paul Washburn, son of Simeon and the man who set up this subdivision) was becoming a pleasant neighbourhood for shopkeepers and their families. It's lined with boxy red-brick houses, most Italianate but some Gothic, trimmed with white wood.

28 16 Paul Street, ca. 1875,
29 18 Paul Street, ca. 1880,
30 19 Paul Street, ca. 1880

Three comely examples of square two-storey brick houses, their wide eaves bracketed and their round-headed windows equipped with working shutters. Number 18 is probably the prettiest (its more balanced arrangement of three second-storey

33 *15 Jane Street* **34** *9 Jane Street*

windows gives it the nod over its near-twin, number 16); notice how the wide curves of the treillage echo the round-headed windows and door. Their first owners were, respectively, a chief constable, the owner of a canning factory, and a shoemaker.

Jane Street

As far as we know, no one famous lived here and nothing terribly significant happened on the prosaically named Jane Street. (Jane Washburn was the wife of Paul, for whom Paul Street was named.) It's simply an excellent example of the good life, architecturally speaking, as lived by working people at the end of the nineteenth century. A block of mostly frame houses, many front-gabled with the door to one side, set close to the street but with deep gardens to the side and back – a Stephen Leacock street, minus the vinegar.

31 **4 Jane Street,** ca. 1888

A two-storey rectangle with a bell-cast veranda trimmed with eyelet-like treillage and the characteristic Picton roundels in the posts. The first owners were John and Emma McGillivary, a shoemaker and his wife.

32 **6 Jane Street,** ca. 1885

The bells and whistles on this brick-veneered house include three finials with drops on the gables, and a veranda that shades two sides of the L. The treillage is a familiar Picton pattern: acorn-like shapes

in the centre and quatrefoils-with-comma at the bottom.

33 **15 Jane Street,** ca. 1874

Late-century treillage tends to be solid rather than openwork and the posts become more prominent: note the diamond motifs and panels on the bevelled posts and the sculptural complications at their tops. The curve of the veranda roof, the double Italianate door, and the deep cornice add to this house's air of self-reliant contentment. Built for Samuel Love, a lumber merchant.

34 **9 Jane Street,** ca. 1875

Looking like a boxy, L-shaped piece of white-on-white embroidery, this is the fanciest house on the block. Note the spindled porch, the appliquéd cornice, and – especially – the superb brackets that from close to the house look like rows of sea-horses supporting the broad eaves. Built for Stephen N. Seeds, a purveyor of groceries, flour, and feed.

35 **5 Jane Street,** ca. 1870

There's an appealing naiveté about number 5, with its Italianate door extended by louvres and the asymmetrically arranged windows, as in a child's drawing of a house.

36 **1 Jane Street,** ca. 1865

The pleasing features here are the two-sided veranda, the corner posts, and the

37 *237 Main Street*

38 *Picton Public Library, 218 Main Street*

deep cornice. The first owner was Elisha VanBlaricomb, listed in the 1881 census as "gentleman."

III. THE COUNTY TOWN

Retrace your steps to Town Hill.

Main Street's commercial spine is busy but not particularly attractive: too many uncongenial modern storefronts, not enough attention to the traditional buildings behind them. Even its busyness is not entirely positive, but partly a result of the lack of through streets.

37 237 Main Street, ca. 1860

Lift your eyes above the banal first-floor storefronts to appreciate Main Street's finest commercial block. Even when Reuben Chapman and Gideon Striker's building had some competition, it's doubtful that anything in Picton surpassed its rich mixture of cast-iron window surrounds, white-brick corbels, and brick pilasters and quoins. Most delightful of all are the mustachioed men apparently chinning themselves on the brackets in the centre of the second and third floors, and the bearded gentlemen functioning as keystones on the third floor. Originally the building housed the Chapman and Striker Drug Store and a dry-goods store on the first floor, a dentist's office and picture gallery on the upper floors.

38 Picton Public Library, 218 Main Street, 1906

In 1831, the *Hallowell Free Press* announced a meeting to form a public reading room. The reading room, one of the first three in the province, evolved in the usual Ontario way into a lecture and self-improvement society, a Mechanics' Institute, and finally a Free Public Library. The American philanthropist Andrew Carnegie, who endowed 125 libraries in Ontario, favoured towns with populations ranging from 1,000 to 15,000 with no previous library buildings: Picton qualified on both counts. He also favoured the temple-form or other classical revival styles for his libraries. Designed by Peden & McLaren of Montreal, Picton's library is a compact piece of Edwardian Classicism, with the deeply hipped roof, banded brick pilasters, keystones, Venetian windows, and affably pompous portico that often earmarked this eclectic style.

39 Regent Theatre, 222–226 Main Street, ca. 1830, remodelled 1920, 1931

An unlikely casserole of Hispanic and showbiz with a few odd garnishes, the Regent began life as a sober commercial building. In 1920, a theatrical manager named George Cook transformed it into a 1,100-seat theatre with ample backstage facilities for live touring shows; in 1931, he gave the front a face-lift, with non-functioning tile

39 *Regent Theatre, 222–226 Main Street*

43 *57 Mary Street*

rooflets, neon crowns and signage, a fringe of coloured glass under the marquee, coloured tiles above the windows. Once the heyday of touring shows had passed, the Regent served as a scaled-down movie theatre until it closed in the 1980s. It is now under renovation by the Regent Theatre Foundation. The lobby, with its classical frieze of gambolling cherubs, can still be seen through the glass doors, but the oddest touch is outside, on the pilasters under the marquee: an Old World/New World match of classical urns, garlands, and two Indian chiefs!

Short Mary is the picturesque local name for a backstreet lined with nineteenth-century houses built into a steepish hill. Mostly frame, they are not all in the best of repair and many are covered in siding, but it's a streetscape of great charm that winds up to Mary Street proper.

40 **24–26 Short Mary Street,** ca. 1880
A three-storey house, beginning with stone and ascending to brick; its appeal comes partly from the adroit mixture of materials, partly from the closely set shuttered windows and the ornamented porch with its serpentine brackets.

41 **33 Short Mary Street,** ca. 1900
Much bigger than the way it presents itself on Short Mary, this house steps downhill on its stone foundation. The double row of dentils at the cornice and above the

unusual Chinese Chippendale–style treillage ties this boxy rambler together.

42 **50–52 Mary Street,** ca. 1838
Today the front of this early five-bay Loyalist house is plain to the point of dour, but the finely planned and executed cornice and eaves ornamentation – with a border of dentils and paired modillions – suggests an ambitious builder as well as owner. It was built for John Wilson, innkeeper and later wagon-maker. One of John Wilson's relatives and a co-owner of this house was Stewart Wilson, whose foundry and terrace housing for his workers are located at the corner of Mary and Bowery Streets.

43 **57 Mary Street,** ca. 1875
A Victorian classic, with its chunky come-hither portico, bay window, and, under the broad eaves, a County favourite: brackets dripping acorn drops. Owned by William German, who was listed in an 1871 directory as a "Speculator."

44 **62–68 Mary Street,** ca. 1851
A market town the size of Picton can hardly be said to have a factory district, but this corner is a unique and remarkably intact example of a factory and terrace housing designed for workers. Stewart Wilson and Archealus Tupper ran the Phoenix Foundry, which produced engines, extractors, and various kinds of small machines. The

44 44 *62–68 Mary Street*

46 *First Methodist Church,
8 Chapel Street*

foundry specialized in stoves, and it was said that customers came from as far as Port Hope. Wilson built this four-house terrace for the foundry workers; the factory itself is thought to have been on the east side of Bowery Street as well as at 69 Mary Street. The verandas were probably considered essential and were there from the beginning; the two gables with bargeboard and finials were probably added in the 1880s.

**45 69 Mary Street, 13–21 Bowery
Street,** ca. 1844
Evidence suggests that this two-storey building began as a workshop in Wilson's business and was converted to terrace housing, possibly in the late nineteenth century. It's not entirely workaday, as the two quarter fanlights (recently filled in with stained glass) and the rickrack trim on the raking cornice attest.

**46 First Methodist Church (now Picton
United Church), 8 Chapel Street,**
1898; **Methodist Parsonage,** ca. 1901
Some significant church history happened on this strikingly positioned piece of land. The Canadian and American Methodists split during the Canada Conference held here in 1824; the location of the Methodist Seminary at Cobourg (now Victoria College at the University of Toronto) was decided at Picton's Methodist Church in 1831. Less seriously, one of the County's favourite John A. Macdonald stories has it

that, as a young lawyer, he and a few friends positioned a dead horse in the pulpit, with its front hooves on the reading desk. This church, known as the Stone Church and the third erected on this site for the County's most populous denomination, follows turn-of-the-century taste with its rock-faced limestone, emphatic Gothic crenellations, and large stained-glass window. The Kingston-based architect Joseph Power designed the handsome interior in the Methodists' favoured "Akron plan": semicircular seating directed to the pulpit. The parsonage, to the side of the church, was built in the same rock-faced limestone but in a more eclectic style. Alas for the modern porch, which distracts mightily from its handsome Tudor gable and polygonal tower.

47 1 Downes Avenue, ca. 1858
It seems particularly unfair that John Pepper Downes's garden, which once extended to Main Street, should be rudely curtailed and his Gothic cottage exiled behind the Bank of Montreal. Born in Devonshire, Downes settled in 1832 in Picton, where he served as the clerk of County Court for two decades. He is better known as the chronicler of Picton's mid-nineteenth-century streets and buildings, through twelve invaluable pencil drawings, most done in 1847. Downes's own house, called Grove Place, is a stylish composite of pattern-book Gothic elements unusual in the

48 *16 Ferguson Street*　　　　　**51** *75 West Mary Street*

County but fitting for a man with Downes's architectural interests. The American A.J. Downing's widely disseminated 1850 pattern book, *The Architecture of Country Houses*, illustrates "A Cottage-Villa in the Rural Gothic Style" that strongly resembles Downes's front-gabled house with two magnificent twin chimney-stacks standing guard at the edges of the hip-roof. (Unfortunately, one of the stacks now has one modern chimney.) The strong bargeboard, recommended by Downing, who detested "gingerbread" frippery, the oriel window, and the stern finial and pendant are also seen in the pattern book, and Downes's house tosses in a buttressed Tudor vestibule for good measure.

48 **16 Ferguson Street,** ca. 1890
Picton has several dashing little Italianate houses like this, with rickrack trim under the cornice and a two-storey bay like an abbreviated tower. Built for Angus Lighthall, cabinetmaker and undertaker. (Number 20 Ferguson is well-nigh identical.)

49 **18 Ferguson,** ca. 1835
This plain-Jane rubblestone cottage was the First Methodist's rectory after 1880.

50 **23–25 Ferguson Street,** ca. 1857
Often taken to be made of oversized, handmade bricks, this double house is the best known example of an unusual method of

bricklaying in which the bricks are laid on edge. Picton has about ten examples of rowlock-bond construction, as it is called, and this house was built by and for Robert Welsh Jr., a mason with connections to other rowlock houses. Marginally more economical because it added about 1.6 inches to each row, rowlock construction never became more than a curiosity.

51 **75 West Mary Street,** ca. 1880
Strategically set on a V between Ferguson and West Mary Streets, this villa was definitely planned to be noticed. Its builder picked and chose from just about all the available styles: here a lacy bit of bargeboard, there a mansard tower, throw in a conical turret at the end of the superbly woodworked porch, and don't forget brackets and ironwork cresting. Strictly speaking it doesn't quite compute, but the verve is undeniable. Even the carriage house, with its pedimented windows and five-over-three-paned windows on the doors, is a charmer. Built for Richard Hadden, a harness-maker and saddler.

52 **Glenwood Cemetery,** incorporated 1871, **Superintendent's house,** 1875, **Chapel,** 1901
A turn-of-the-century souvenir booklet called *Picturesque Picton* enumerated the town's chief attractions: "fine stores, well kept lawns, and its beautiful cemetery." A beautiful cemetery would not be among a

52 *The Cemetery Chapel*

53 *51 King Street*

town's proudest claims now, but our fore-fathers felt differently. Beginning in the 1840s with the invention of garden or rural cemeteries (the forerunners of our public parks), even the Victorians who could not afford a plot tended in perpetuity enjoyed strolling and picnicking in a rustic burial ground.

Glenwood, a 150-acre site formerly occupied by a morocco leather factory, was carefully designed along principles popularized by the American landscape architect Frederick Law Olmsted. The resulting park, very different from the country churchyard at Old St. Mary Magdalene, is a series of mounds where tilting obelisks, draped urns, and crosses appear to have been naturalized like wildflowers. Most are sober Protestant memorials, several to the Washburns, Strikers, Chapmans, and Laziers who loom large in County history. The occasional flight of fancy – an angel, a sculpted tree split into two trunks that seems to commemorate two sisters – plus real ducks and un-shy hedgehogs is a good antidote to the solemnity.

As well as restfulness, consolation was in order, something the fanciful architecture of the little step-gabled mortuary chapel was designed to supply. The promotional pamphlet of 1910 explained, "The treatment of the interior has been so designed that those depressed by grief may in some measure be cheered by the brightness about them." (If you knock on the superintendent's door, he may well show you around inside; the interior today is more neglected than cheerful, but the stained glass is delightful.) The exterior also aspired to cheer, especially the vestibule, which is literally a pile-up of jovial details: gables, shed roof, finials, ironwork signboard.

Glenwood was very much a business, selling plots beginning at $15 and promising "most courteous aid" in the selection. The courteous aid was available in the superintendent's house, itself a reassuring piece of vernacular building with eared windows and the typical County protruding central bay.

For Octagon Buffs

53 Not on the walking tour but at **51 King Street**, in the downtown area, is one of Picton's two octagons (the other is at 16 Main Street). The Fralick brothers' ca. 1862 version of the American phrenologist Orson Fowler's "invention" (see page 181) is unusually attractive. That's mostly because the brothers diverged from Fowler's chosen (and dismal-looking) material, grout, and chose a cheerful red brick. The small paired windows were another good idea – octagons could look featureless – and they originally also appeared on the first floor. The Fralicks ran a carriage-making factory behind the octagon, on Elizabeth Street.

St. Mark's Anglican Church

Port Hope

"Endless Variety of Hill and Dale"

From the seventeenth century onwards, the place itself, the valley of an impatient little river that flows into Lake Ontario, never lacked for inhabitants – or names. The French fur traders and Sulpician missionaries who settled there in the 1660s and '70s called it Ganaraske. To the Mississaugas who had displaced the Iroquois, who in their turn had displaced the Cayugas, it was Cochingomink, or "commencement of the carrying place" – the trail north to Rice Lake. In the 1770s, a handful of American traders and trappers who built cabins at the river mouth called their settlement after the busy stream – Pemitiscutiank, which meant "fat fire creek." One of those trappers was Peter Smith, and by 1788, the tiny place was known as Smith's Creek.

By then, the American Revolution had kick-started Ontario into serious settlement, and the Loyalists, waiting in Niagara-on-the-Lake, needed homes. Two entrepreneurial exiles from New York State, Jonathan Walton and Elias Smith (no relation to Peter), undertook to settle forty families in the area around Smith's Creek and erect a sawmill and gristmill. In exchange, they received the land that is now Port Hope. Their first boatload of twenty-seven refugees arrived in 1793 and, so the story goes, was greeted suspiciously by the devotedly royalist Mississaugas. After some discussion, the Indians accepted that the newcomers were no "Yankees" but were as loyal to the Great White Father in England as they were.

Walton and Smith had settled their full quota of families by 1797, and many of them must have congratulated themselves on their dwelling-place. Blessed with "an endless variety of hill and dale" (as a 1916 promotional pamphlet described it), the settlement was more than pretty. The rich soil suited the growing of grain and fruit, the surrounding forest was full of game, and the Ganaraska River, which flowed into a natural harbour on Lake Ontario, was so choked with salmon and trout that fish stories were taken seriously. (In one of the earliest, the local fishing champion, James Sculthorpe, and his uncle refused $50 for a single night's catch of 300 salmon.)

In spite of these natural advantages, the village itself did not grow particularly quickly. By 1813, there were a few shops, a school, a public hall, a registrar of deeds. In 1817, a traveller named Charles Fothergill counted about fifteen houses, two of which were inns. He must have liked what he saw, because he settled in the hamlet and became its first postmaster. Perhaps Fothergill found Smith's Creek too banal a name or too common (there were several in the province); in any case, he tried to rename the place Toronto but met with resistance. In 1819, a public meeting unanimously chose Port Hope as the name of the village, in honour of the surrounding Hope Township, which commemorated a former lieutenant-governor of Quebec.

In addition to the happy promise implied by the name, the British emigrants who swelled Upper Canada's population after the Napoleonic Wars found the shoots of civilization in Port Hope. Steadily and with little apparent fuss, much of the "modern" town developed throughout the 1820s and '30s. In 1822, its tiny establishment built itself an Anglican church, St. John's (later St. Mark's), on King Street. One of the prime movers behind St. John's was Elias Smith's son John David Smith. By this time, the Smiths were firmly established as Port Hope's premier family, and Elias's descendants built some of its finest houses.

On the other side of the river from the church, Walton, Queen, Mill, and John Streets were filling up with wooden buildings that housed distilleries (eight in 1826), smithies, hatters, shoemakers, inns, and factories producing malt, wool, and chair parts. Enlarged and improved throughout the 1830s, the harbour was the departure point for the region's main exports, timber and agricultural products. Port Hope itself, ideally placed to serve as an outfitting and market town for the new settlements to the north, was incorporated in 1834, thereby acquiring a police force and a public market.

The influx of Britishers did not mean that the town forgot its links with the United States. Smith's *Canadian Gazeteer* for 1846 reported daily steamship service between Port Hope and Rochester during navigable weather, at a time when the town's population was about 1,200. Canadians who could afford it resorted to upstate New York for the latest in luxury goods – some as cumbersome as Greek Revival mantelpieces – as well as entertainment. The Masons, Oddfellows, and other groups from Rochester and Port Hope frequently organized elaborate excursions to their brothers across the lake. At least three of Port Hope's most important buildings were designed by a Rochester architect, Merwin Austin.

But the red-letter days in Port Hope's history usually had British origins. The life of Queen Victoria was a rich source of solemnity, beginning with her accession to the throne in 1837. When the news reached Upper Canada, the sheriff of the United Counties of Northumberland and Durham rode into Port Hope in state, accompanied by a trumpeter and a troop of cavalry, to proclaim the news to a cheering throng.

Two years later, a town decked with banners celebrated the Queen's marriage to Prince Albert with a twenty-one-gun salute and a triumphal arch over the bridge. The townspeople lined up for wedding cake, and the *Port Hope Gazette* was slyly confident that the "fair and lovely portion of the community" would place their pieces under their pillows in hopes of similar good luck. That night every building in town was illuminated, some displaying the initials of the nuptial pair in flaring lights.

In 1841, another general illumination – a genuinely spectacular event in an era before gas and electricity – marked the birth of the royal couple's first child, the future Edward VII. When the object of the rejoicing visited Port Hope nineteen years later, on September 7, 1860, the town choreographed its greatest royalist splurge.

With seven days' notice that the Prince of Wales would be making a brief stopover on his Canadian tour, most able-bodied townspeople were mobilized to line the Market Square and the main thoroughfares with evergreens and to craft wreaths, swags, and, especially, triumphal arches. A peculiarly Victorian species of special-effects architecture, the evergreen-upholstered arches on this occasion spanned the width of a main street and rose as high as the third storey of a building. The huge Mechanics' Arch straddled the railway track (the Prince arrived by train from Peterborough) and featured flags, bunting, and emblems suitable to that trade. The Merchants' Arch was gay with international flags and the motto "Let Commerce Flourish," while the Agricultural Arch was festooned with fruits and vegetables.

After the speeches and the dignitaries' luncheon, the guest of honour departed on "the Prince's Walk," a specially built and decorated elevated platform that led from the Town Hall to the train for Whitby. As he made his way along its carpeted length, women and children threw flowers in his path.

Behind the scenes all was not so joyful, and the visit exposed one of the darker strains in Ontario culture. The Prince's mentor and the secretary of state for the colonies, the Duke of Newcastle, had forbidden Ontario's powerful Orange Order from greeting the Prince officially, explaining that the future monarch of Christians from every denomination could not countenance an organization that was divisive at best and violent at worst. The governor general, Sir Edmund Head, seconded the interdict. In Kingston and Belleville, where the Prince arrived on a steamer, the defiant order prepared to welcome him in full regalia. As a result, to the disappointment of two crowded and elaborately decorated towns, the Prince did not leave the boat.

An emergency meeting in Port Hope resolved to accept the directive, but the town fathers pledged "at the right time and in the right place to support the Orangemen in resenting these insults." The right time and place turned out to be the Market Square, soon after the Prince's train left town. In a hastily arranged, ironic reversal of the ceremonies for the Prince, thousands of spectators watched a torchlight procession drag the governor general in effigy through the streets. (He was chosen rather than the Duke of Newcastle because it was considered discourteous to burn a guest of Canada in effigy.) As the dummy burned, the crowd groaned in disapproval of the governor general. Once the effigy was no more, loyalty reasserted itself, and the departing crowd gave three cheers for the Queen and the Prince of Wales.

Not all Port Hope's great moments were lived in the shadow of royalty. The description of the cornerstone-laying of the Town Hall in 1851 evokes a town in its heyday, and a complex and highly organized society. Virtually all the men in town marched in the procession under the banners of two bands, the various fire companies, the Sons of Temperance, the St. George's, St. Andrew's, and St. Patrick's Societies, the Orange Lodges, and the Masons. The ceremony could not proceed until the presiding Masonic official had been satisfied, by means of the square, level, and plumbline, that the foundation was Masonically correct. The toasts at the banquet included "Success to the Anglo-Saxon Race," "The Countess of Elgin and the Fair of Canada," and "The Sons of Temperance." The *Watchman* reported, "It went off, as such things universally do in Port Hope, with eclat."

During the 1850s, most things did go off with éclat. Walton Street's harmonious spill of commercial buildings dates from this prosperous decade. The age of the iron horse, so long awaited, began. The first Toronto-Montreal train stopped at Port Hope on October 27, 1856. Even more important for the town's economic future was the railway route to the north, which local entrepreneurs had been scheming over for two decades and finally managed to launch in 1853. At first Port Hope lagged behind its arch-rival Cobourg in the race to Peterborough, but the slower and steadier Port Hope and Lindsay Railway triumphed after the Cobourg line's bridge over Rice Lake gradually collapsed in the winter of 1861–62.

Bolstered by the trade with the north (and ultimately with the west, as far as Midland on Georgian Bay), the good times lasted until the 1880s. Part of

Port Hope's decline can be pegged to its reliance on the timber trade, which suffered in the '80s from high American tariffs and overzealous felling. The late-century move to the cities was also significant: the percentage of Ontarians in rural areas fell by a staggering 20 per cent in the last thirty years of the nineteenth century. In 1881 Port Hope had a population of 5,585; it would not have that number again until 1948.

The town's failure to fulfil its mid-nineteenth-century promise has meant mostly good things for its appeal and liveability. With a population of some 12,000, Port Hope is now probably best known to outsiders as the home of Trinity College School, the boys' private school that has been a local presence since 1868, or as the location of Cameco, formerly Eldorado, the controversial uranium refinery that has dominated the harbour since the 1930s. But to those with a taste for history and architecture, Port Hope is notable for its early and sustained passion for preservation.

How and why some towns fall successfully in love with their past is a mystery. (Perhaps it is significant that until 1883, Port Hope set its clocks about half an hour behind Montreal time, and adamantly rejected attempts to standardize them.) The town has some undeniable factors in favour of preservation: few houses have been built since the 1880s, and most of the old ones have survived. Walton Street is widely acknowledged as one of the finest main streets in Ontario, and the threatened demolition of its St. Lawrence Hotel in the 1960s mobilized the preservation forces. As a result, Port Hope has the second-largest branch of the Architectural Conservancy of Ontario, more than 150 designated buildings, and many townsfolk who talk historic colours and original storefronts at the drop of a hat.

But Port Hope's attachment to its history is neither arid nor precious. Walton Street is primarily for Port Hopers and only secondarily for tourists: a good shoe store or barber's is considered more desirable than another antiques shop. At the same time, it seems perfectly unaffected, even ordinary, in Port Hope that the bookstore (Furby's) is named after an early newspaperman, a recently departed gift shop (Farini) commemorated a local nineteenth-century aerialist, and the town pub (the Beamish House) bears the name of a nineteenth-century merchant. Peter John Stokes, the restoration architect responsible for the good repair of many local buildings, puns about the "treasured combination of faith, Port Hope, and charity" that animates the town. As a witticism, it leaves something to be desired; as a pointer to the town's "particularity," it's not far from the mark.

Port Hope

YEOVIL ST

BRUTON ST

CLAYTON'S LA

VICTORIA ST N

BRUTON LA

BRUTON ST

CHARLES ST

JULIA ST

HAGERMAN ST

PINE ST N

67

68

55 54

56 BALDWIN ST

57 53

62

61

60 59 58

52

RIDOUT ST

BRAMLEY ST

LITTLE HOPE ST

CHURCH ST

THOMAS ST

HILL ST

WALTON ST

51

63 64

65

66

SULLIVAN ST

The Commons

ROSS ST

STRACHAN ST

GIFFORD ST

PINE ST S

THOMAS ST

SHERBOURNE ST

47 46 45 44 43

AUGUSTA ST

48 49 50

DURHAM ST

42

VICTORIA ST S

TRAFALGAR ST

36

41

35 34 33 32

31

30 40

37

DORSET ST W

38

CATHERINE ST

SMITH ST

PERCY ST

PARK ST

39

HAY ST

ELIZABETH ST

HARRIS ST

POINTER LA

N

HAYWARD ST

ALEXANDER ST

HAYWARD ST

CHOATE ST

MARSH ST

ELDORADO PL

28 *First Baptist Church, 59 John Street*

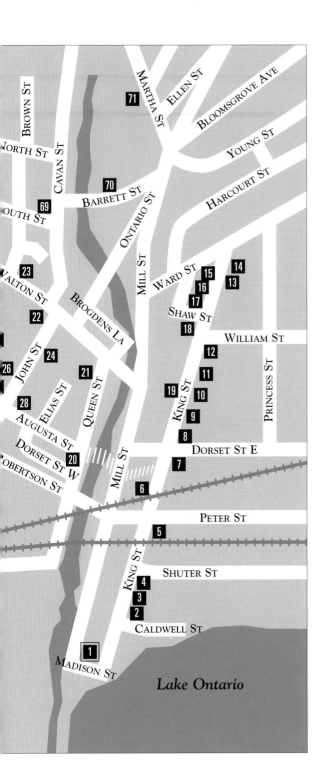

BROWN ST

NORTH ST

CAVAN ST

SOUTH ST

MARTHA ST

ELLEN ST

BLOOMSGROVE AVE

YOUNG ST

HARCOURT ST

71

70

BARRETT ST

69

ONTARIO ST

MILL ST

WARD ST

SHAW ST

WILLIAM ST

23

VALTON ST

BROGDENS LA

22

JOHN ST

24

26

21

QUEEN ST

ELIAS ST

28

AUGUSTA ST

DORSET ST W

20

ROBERTSON ST

MILL ST

KING ST

PRINCESS ST

15

14

16

13

17

18

12

11

19

10

9

8

7

6

5

DORSET ST E

PETER ST

KING ST

SHUTER ST

4

3

2

CALDWELL ST

1

MADISON ST

Lake Ontario

38 *115 Dorset Street West*

20 *Town Hall,*
56 Queen Street

3 | *127 King Street*

5 | *Little Bluestone, 117 King Street*

1 168 King Street, ca. 1822

"They heard the inn before they saw it–music and men's voices, laughter and the odd curse. When it loomed into view, lit against the dark lake, it appeared, even from the rear, to be in a state of great agitation, the structure vibrating with the activity it contained."

Jane Urquhart, *Away*

With Lake Ontario glinting at the foot of King Street, this rather neglected but scenic part of town is a reminder of Port Hope's origins as a lake port. Across from the tiny sandy beach is one of the town's oldest houses, a straightforward vernacular Georgian building whose second-storey veranda once swept around three sides. Aluminum siding now obscures the clapboard, but the fine pilastered doorcase, wide chimneys, and twelve-over-twelve-paned windows are original. It belonged to Captain J. Wallace, a grain and lumber merchant who owned three schooners and is said to be the builder of the town's first wharf. The builder was Wallace's brother-in-law, Norman Brogdin, who built St. Mark's Church further up the hill at about the same time. In the 1850s the house became an inn, first called the Seaman's Inn; an early-twentieth-century incarnation, called Canada House, was a favourite destination for visitors who came on the Rochester ferry.

The house's most recent distinction is its appearance in Jane Urquhart's 1993 novel *Away*. As the Seaman's Inn, the white house that "shone in the Great Lake harbour like a lamp," it is bought by Liam O'Malley and floated twenty-five miles down Lake Ontario to Loughbreeze Beach near Colborne.

2 131, 3 127, 4 123 King Street, ca. 1875

Three sensible houses, said to be built for officers on the Great Lakes schooners. All three follow the same plan: a front-facing gable, off-centre door, veranda, and Gothic lancet windows in the side gable. Number 127, with interesting jagged trim on the entablature of its front windows, is the only one to have retained the bargeboard on its gables. The best preserved, 123 King has a dapper little veranda with bevelled posts and a glassed-in mud room.

5 Little Bluestone, 117 King Street, ca. 1834

In the early 1830s, the Smiths, father and son, married and built two houses on the family estate, which stretched from Dorset Street south to Lake Ontario. The father, John David, was the son of one of Port Hope's founders, Elias Smith; he celebrated his second marriage with the construction of an impressive residence called the Bluestone (see **7** below). John David's son Elias Peter took up residence with his bride, Sophia Soper, in a house

6 *92 King Street*

7 *The Bluestone, 21 Dorset Street East*

closer to the lake, called Little Bluestone.

Both houses are American-inspired variations on a classical theme, built of the same bluish limestone ledgerock and covered with stucco. Their common elements – the graceful doorcase with semi-elliptical transom and sidelights, the deep cornice and returning eaves, the half-round fanlight in the gable – may suggest a single builder. Whoever the builder of Elias Peter Smith's house, he was careful not to upstage the Bluestone: Little Bluestone, with its deeply set off-centre door, gabled front, and a limestone basement so high the house seems to be standing on tiptoe, is a handsome but more modest essay in the Greek Revival mode. The house was restored in 1980 after years of neglect, but its location near a car wash and the railway bridge is more than a little desolate.

6 92 King Street, ca. 1844

Constrained by its parapet walls and four tall chimneys, punctuated by the regular rhythm of its prim windows, this townhouse is all self-assurance. Its style is essentially neoclassical, although the rectangular glazing pattern in the sidelights and transom of its fine doorcase is characteristic of the Regency style.

7 The Bluestone, 21 Dorset Street East, 1834

When John David Smith married Augusta Louisa Woodworth in 1833, he was a wealthy forty-seven-year-old, one of the town's leading citizens, and the widowed father of ten children. She was twenty and came from Oneida County in New York State. The limestone house Smith built for his bride was also American, an upstate New York variant called Genesee Greek Revival, which married the masculine symmetry of the Georgian house with the femininity of the Ionic portico and doorcase. The Bluestone, named for the stoneblue stucco that covered its walls, depends heavily upon the American architect Asher Benjamin's 1830 pattern book, *The Architect; or, Practical House Carpenter* for its "Grecian manner": its frontispiece and all nine of its mantelpieces derive from Benjamin's handbook.

Perhaps the house was planned to make its American mistress feel at home, but John David Smith was himself a native of New York City. In any case, the Bluestone has many of the characteristics found in the houses of American settlers, at least as observed by John McTaggart, a Scottish traveller to Canada in the 1820s. The "mansion of Jonathon, or the United Empire Loyalist," he noted, typically had an ornamented fanlight, prominent chimneys, nine windows and a door on the front, and seven windows on the gabled side with a semicircular one almost under the roof. (The number of windows in Upper Canada often impressed Britons, who lived with a window tax.) All that describes the

9 *57–59 King Street*

10 *55 King Street*

Bluestone, but, as a matter of fact, very few houses were built on so lavish a scale or detailed so meticulously; more than a century and a half after it was built, it remains the town's most splendid house.

8 61 King Street, 1858–59

In September 1858, the *Weekly Guide* reported that Robert Charles Smith was building a "brick dwelling house" across the street from his father's house, the Bluestone, and that it was too early to tell its style. Now it seems too late, as mature plantings and additions to the back obscure what was probably always a pleasantly solid house of no strongly pronounced style. If some of the details, like the fretwork on the veranda or the ogee window in the front gable, seem too dainty for the house, it's unlikely that this bothered the Victorians. In 1884 a foundry owner named John Henry Helm bought the house for $5,000; he probably contributed the ironwork fence and roof cresting.

9 57–59 King Street, ca. 1875

Port Hope has few houses in the Second Empire style, an urban craze of the 1870s that petered out with the decade. And duplexes in this showy mode were relatively uncommon throughout Ontario, although a style that often involved twin two-storey bays and complicated symmetry is eminently bisectable. This house has most of the earmarks of the genre, including

the essential mansard roof, the dormers so elaborately framed they might be miniature houses, the subtle variations in the brick planes. In spite of all this careful detail, there's something slightly heavy about it, at least partly due to the blank modern portico that replaces the much prettier original. The side veranda and cedar roof have been restored according to the original design.

10 55 King Street, 1909

A reassuring twentieth-century interpretation of Tudor, with a solid, asymmetrical form, a "rustic" shingled roof, and the requisite small-paned windows, often in groups of three. Houses in this style that overdid the mock half-timbering came to be known as Stockbroker Tudor; this one confines it to the sides, with just a whisper in the one-storey bay to the south.

11 St. Mark's Church, 51 King Street, 1822

With its white clapboard skin and Christmas-card Gothic trimmings, St. Mark's looks both timeless and tentative. And well it might, since it has changed shape, colour, and name while stubbornly continuing to live as one of Ontario's oldest frame churches.

In 1822, an Anglican missionary visited the "flourishing village" of Port Hope and noted with approval that a church was being built. Dedicated to St. John the

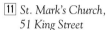 St. Mark's Church, 51 King Street [11] Churchyard

Evangelist, the "neat church" was a grey-painted frame rectangle. The Smith family were major donors, and Jonathan Walton himself presented the bell; the builder was Norman Brogdin. In 1851 the fashionable Irish-born architect Kivas Tully was hired to build what the local paper the *Watchman* called an "elegant and commodious transept" and to Gothicize the windows. (The equally Gothic crenellations on the tower may have been added at this time.)

But even as early as 1851, there were murmurings that Port Hope's population had shifted away from Protestant Hill, as this part of town was called, towards Cornhill, on the west side of the Ganaraska. In 1865, a new brick church was commissioned on Pine Street, and in 1869 the congregation of St. John's held its last regular service in the King Street building. Although most of the original congregation moved to the new church, there were hold-outs, unhappiness, and the persistent legend that a "devoted warden" had buried Jonathan Walton's bell rather than have it grace the upstart church. By 1873, the bishop had been petitioned to reopen the old clapboard church; it was repaired and rechristened St. Mark's, and the bell rehung. Thus Port Hope is one of the few Ontario towns of its size to have two Anglican churches.

As the local Anglican church goes, so goes a significant part of the life of an Ontario town. The annals of St. Mark's are rich in social history: the early rectors who were also classical schoolmasters and educated the town's elite; the surpliced and mortarboarded church choir of the early twentieth century, thought by some to be evidence of dangerous leanings towards Rome; the forty-two gallons of paint that in 1948 transformed the church from grey to white; the never-to-be-forgotten day of July 26, 1959, when Queen Elizabeth II and Prince Philip attended morning worship at St. Mark's with Vincent Massey, the governor general of Canada and a parishioner.

A walk in the cemetery is recommended, the better to admire Tully's windows with their crisscross glazing and balled labels as well as the tombstones of Smiths, Waltons, Masseys, and other early parishioners.

12 33 King Street, ca. 1850

Sir John A. slept here, when he came to town to unveil the statue in front of the Town Hall; the town's first school was also located on this site from 1813 to 1826. The original tall Loyalist townhouse was amplified at the turn of the century with a two-storey wing whose rounded windows and veranda hail from a very different sensibility.

13 13 King Street, ca. 1845–50

A pilastered townhouse with brick corbels under the wide eaves, built close to the street line. Originally the front door faced

15 *8 King Street*

16 *18 King Street*

the street on the north side. Now it's at the side, underneath the gingerbread veranda facing the garden.

14 5 King Street, ca. 1853
John Hatton, a Walton Street shopkeeper, commissioned a very rectangular townhouse with a handsome border of brick corbels and high parapet firewalls, which probably indicated that close neighbours were expected.

15 8 King Street, ca. 1850
Whether or not he intended it as a professional calling card, this spiky creation by Robert Mitchell, one of a family of local carpenters, demonstrated that he was a dab hand at Gothic gables and windows as well as graceful ogee transoms. The shuttered French doors on the main floor are a vestige of the Regency style's more easygoing, hospitable airs, but in general this is copybook Gothic. Not exactly cosy (although the porch, a later addition, undercuts the house's verticality), but very *au courant* at the time, the house is finely kept today.

16 18 King Street, 1840s
Modest but with a few endearing frills, this clapboard and stucco saltbox was built by William Mitchell, another member of the carpentering Mitchells. Originally it was probably an all-stucco Ontario cottage; the clapboard façade with its unusual wooden quoins and the gable with its pointed

window seem to be early alterations. The outsize, simplified Greek Revival door emphasizes the house's ground-hugging solidity.

17 20 King Street, ca. 1870s
A very neat brick box. The richly dimensional frieze and brackets on the bay and portico are composed of stock late-Victorian turnings.

18 22 King Street, 1914
With its symmetrical five-bay arrangement and the sharply pitched hip-roof whose rounded dormers echo the curve of the portico, this handsome Georgian Revival house harks back to the eighteenth-century houses of the American colonies. Soon after the centenary of the American Revolution in 1876, American architects rediscovered various Colonial and Federal styles, and inevitably the fashion crossed the border.

19 48 King Street, ca. 1860–65
Port Hope has lots of houses like this – a High Victorian two-storey red-brick structure in stretcher bond with wide eaves, a full-length veranda, three windows on the second floor, two windows and an off-centre door on the first. (Imagine away the addition to the side.) So many, in fact, that the type came to be called Port Hope vernacular; this one, with its round-headed windows and the wider curves of the

[19] *48 King Street*

[20] *Town Hall, 56 Queen Street*

eyelet-like veranda trim, is particularly appealing.

Opposite the Bluestone, descend the stairs cut into Church Hill. Continue straight ahead to the footbridge, where there is a good view of the Town Hall.

[20] Town Hall, 56 Queen Street, 1851
While Port Hope increasingly flexed its civic muscles during the 1840s, the board of police met in a coffeehouse and the town council rented a room on Walton Street. Such makeshift arrangements ended when a Rochester architect named Merwin Austin was commissioned to design a town hall worthy of Port Hope's importance. By the time it was occupied in 1853, the building had cost almost $30,000, nearly triple its estimate, and had reportedly ruined its contractor, Philip Fox. The broad-shouldered neoclassical result – balancing the rounded first-floor windows and the jolly cupola with the straight lines of the second-floor windows, the pilasters, and the cornice – is careful to the point of mechanical. But if the red-brick building is short on soul, it was definitely serviceable: in addition to the civic offices, it originally housed shops, a lock-up, and a large hall on the second floor where Port Hopers attended dances, concerts, and plays. The hall was rebuilt according to the original design after it was gutted in an 1893 fire.

The statue of Arthur Williams, a local

hero of the Battle of Batoche, was unveiled by Sir John A. Macdonald in 1889.

Retrace your steps back across the footbridge and continue up Mill Street to Walton Street. Before beginning your promenade of Port Hope's nineteenth-century core, make a brief detour to a twentieth-century landmark on Queen Street south of Walton.

[21] Capitol Theatre, 14 Queen Street, 1930
Thought to be the first movie theatre in Canada built expressly for talking pictures, the Capitol was designed by a Toronto architect, Murray Brown, for Famous Players. A so-called atmospheric theatre, it has clouds that move (by means of projectors) across the blue-painted ceiling, and a décor based on a walled English garden. The theatre closed in 1987, but the Capitol Theatre Heritage Foundation is now engaged in its restoration.

Walton Street
"Instead of low, ungainly two storey buildings which at one time lined Walton Street and other of our business streets, is to be seen a fine chain of three storey brick buildings of the very best description, reminding the traveller at once of a manufacturing town in England."
Weekly Guide, 1853

Walton Street

22 *St. Lawrence Hotel, 87–97 Walton Street*

And a "fine chain" it is, often described as the handsomest main street in Ontario. Part of Walton Street's success is a matter of timing: its commercial buildings, stretching from Mill Street to Pine Street, were built within a thirty-year span – the 1840s to '70s – when architects and contractors took the classical virtues of harmony, proportion, and sobriety seriously. The earliest buildings are essentially neoclassical, followed by the compatible rounded regularities of the commercial Italianate style. Because of the homogeneity that allows for abundant variation and the skilful adjustment of rooflines, doors, and windows as the street descends to the river, Walton Street as a whole is more delightful than the sum of its parts. Which is not to say that the parts lack delight: such as, among many, the beautifully made stone pilasters and window trim on 1–3 Walton, the pediment of the North American Hotel (number 28–32), which looms up at the end of Queen Street, the rounded corner on number 29–33, the slenderness of number 94–96, the bombé mansard roof and richly sculpted window surrounds of the street's only Second Empire building (number 114), the carriageway between numbers 150 and 152. Note the subtle dimensional effects achieved on many buildings with brick piers. Walk up to Pine Street and down again to John, admiring the total effect and chancing on your own favourites. Two buildings along the way deserve special attention.

22 **St. Lawrence Hotel, 87–97 Walton Street,** 1853

Walton Street's *tour de force*, and the building whose threatened destruction alerted Port Hope to its inheritance. Designed by Merwin Austin, the Rochester architect who had designed the Town Hall two years earlier, the St. Lawrence is usually considered a very early manifestation of Italianate grace and lightness. But the slenderness of its windows is also conservative, a reminder of the still fashionable verticality of the Gothic Revival. Designed as a seventeen-bayed hotel with first-floor shops carefully adjusted to the sloping street, the St. Lawrence might easily have been overwhelming. It isn't, thanks to sure proportions and windows gloriously embellished with cast-iron surrounds – crowned on the first floor, a lacier acanthus effect on the second, and more simply rounded on the third. (The St. Lawrence, the Town Hall, and Smith's Block at 48–60 Walton Street were definitely designed by Austin. In addition, the architectural historian Stephen Otto believes that most of the Walton Street buildings erected in the 1850s can be attributed to Austin.)

23 **134–136 Walton Street,** 1852–53

An urbane Greek Revival terrace that takes apparently effortless possession of its

23 *134–136 Walton Street*

25 *47 Pine Street South*

hilly site. Probably designed by Merwin Austin for a local chemist, Tristram Walker Metcalfe, it was advertised in 1855 as "Three Handsome Brick and Stone Dwelling Houses...well adapted for Stores and Public Offices." (One of the original apartments faced on Brown Street.) Its horizontal elements – the deep cornice inset with grilles, the finely raked limestone lintels weighing down the many-paned windows, the eared trim on the main door, the cast-iron fence – are offset by the two-storey painted brick pilasters and the tall, slim chimneys.

Retrace your steps and turn onto John, which is lined with commercial buildings in the same mix of neoclassical and Italianate styles. The Midland House, **24 35 John Street**, is a stucco hotel that dates from the 1850s, with a drive-through to the stables and carriage house at the rear.

25 47 Pine Street South (best viewed from John Street), ca. 1851
Hill and Dale is important in Port Hope's history, as one of the town's grandest houses, owned successively by three prominent men-about-town: Henry Howard Meredith, a real estate developer; Henry Covert, president of the Midland Railway; and General George Ralston. But it is so difficult to see and has been rearranged and renovated so many times that it's no longer particularly rewarding for the walker-by. The original

Classical Revival house took on some Italianate airs in the 1870s, and at the turn of the century mutated into the L-shaped Edwardian sprawler somewhat visible today. The best view of its four-acre site is here on John Street, facing the double-decker veranda.

26 76 John Street, ca. 1868
When Dr. Weston Herriman bought this house on Port Hope's second-best commercial street in 1871, he added a wing (probably to the south) and set up office and home. The complications of the addition have not entirely been resolved (note the small gable with a bricked-in door underneath, near the main entrance), but in general this is a well-knit ensemble of red brick with just enough yellow brick and iron cresting to be fashionable. With its Gothic-tempered domesticity and side garden, it's a fine addition to John Street's businesslike character.

27 The Carlyle, 86 John Street, 1857
The English-born architect Frederic W. Cumberland turned his hand to just about every going style in his adopted city of Toronto, from classical (Osgoode Hall's centre block) to Gothic (St. James Cathedral) to Gothic-Romanesque (University College). When the Bank of Upper Canada engaged his firm, Cumberland & Storm, to design its Port Hope branch, Cumberland went Italianate. A style that

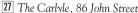
27 *The Carlyle, 86 John Street*   29 *94 John Street*

combined boxy solidity with plenty of flourish in the details, that was "modern" yet harked back to classical models, was ideal for banks and other commercial establishments. (Cumberland may well have been influenced by the popularity of the style for London clubs, especially the Reform Club, built by his mentor Charles Barry.) The little *palazzo* Cumberland built for the bank is both impregnable-looking and delightful, built of so-called white brick from Toronto. The wooden window surrounds were originally painted cream to enhance the stone-like effect. Note the rich double row of brackets and volutes under the eaves. The window treatments decrease in architectural solemnity as they ascend: from pediments on the first floor to curvaceous entablatures on the second to eyebrow-shaped surrounds on the third.

In spite of its prosperous look, the Bank of Upper Canada failed in 1866, and the building was used as a dairy for many years. It is now a restaurant and bed-and-breakfast inn.

28 First Baptist Church, 59 John Street, 1867–68

A well-tempered little church designed by Gundry & Langley of Toronto, with charming sculptures on the label bosses of people, curly-horned rams, leaves, thistles, even a fruit basket.

29 94 John Street, ca. 1835

A rare example of a house that pre-dates the town's building boom from 1840 to 1875. All attention in this prim, symmetrical Loyalist house is concentrated on the doorcase, with its finely fluted pilasters and chinoiserie transom topped by an elongated architrave and outsize cornice. Critics have taken the Loyalist builder to task for too free a hand with the classical orders and for ornamentation so fine it belongs inside the house rather than outside; both true, but in the case of this door, the result is memorable. Probably built as an inn, when John Street was one of the main roads from the lake.

(The robust red-brick vernacular house next door at 96 John Street, which probably dates from the 1880s, makes number 94 look even more delicate by contrast.)

30 74 Dorset Street West, 1877

Dorset Street is a dictionary of nineteenth-century housing styles, beginning with a model Ontario cottage, complete with semicircular window in the gable and a decisive finial. (The porch looks like an add-on.)

31 108 Dorset Street West, ca. 1868

More interesting historically than visually, this house was named Muidar ("radium" spelled backwards) in the 1930s by its owner, Dr. Marcel Pochon. A student of Marie Curie, Pochon was the first manager

[31] *108 Dorset Street West*

[34] *166 Dorset Street West*

of what became Port Hope's largest employer, the pioneering Eldorado radium refinery. From his house on the hill, he could see the refinery, still the most prominent inhabitant of Port Hope's waterfront. (A Crown corporation since 1944, and renamed Cameco in 1988, it now concentrates on the increasingly controversial work of uranium refinement.) Despite an attentively detailed porch, there's a certain going-through-the-motions quality about Muidar as a whole, seen especially in the protruding central bay that ends in a cyclops-like trefoil window and a big, no-nonsense gable.

[32] 150 Dorset Street West, ca. 1869
This board-and-batten cottage was the coach house for a secluded Italianate mansion called Idalia (part of its back is visible at the corner of Victoria and Trafalgar Streets). It was moved to its present site and converted to a house in the late 1970s.

[33] 160 Dorset Street West, ca. 1859
Terralta Cottage was a work in progress for a very long time and should be admired for the charm of its accessories rather than any structural integrity. Its second owner, a prominent local lawyer named Thomas Moore Benson, made substantial renovations in the 1870s to what had been a two-storey Gothic cottage; the tall, blank tower was a twentieth-century mistake. The house's most rewarding vantage point, from

the west, permits a view of the unusual hooded dormers, the slender posts of the portico, and a very pretty Gothic door at the side of the tower.

[34] 166, [35] 172 Dorset Street West, ca. 1860–65
As the houses on the Dorset Street hill become increasingly imposing, these likeable, heavy-lidded neighbours seem to have wandered in from a much plainer street. Typically deceptive Ontario cottages, they look like two-room dwellings from the front but extend dramatically to the rear. With its French doors, two-sided veranda, and uninterrupted hip-roof, 166 Dorset's links with the Regency cottage are clearer. More home-grown, 172 Dorset has a simulacrum of the Ontario cottage's signature peak (in this case it's a triangular dormer rather than an integral part of the roofline). Note the gradually diminishing windows in number 172's tail; builders in Port Hope had to learn early on how to cope with sloping sites.

[36] 188 Dorset Street West, 1904
Port Hope was never an American summer colony on the scale of Cobourg, but some wealthy Americans did settle in for long, temperate summers. One of them, James Schwartz, built a house called Homewood in the fashionable Colonial Revival style. Its bulk, whiteness, and pillared veranda may suggest the American South, but its

36 *188 Dorset Street West*

38 *115 Dorset Street West*

original dark mustard clapboard, high roof, and many-paned dormers represented a revivalist interpretation of seventeenth- and eighteenth-century houses from New England and the Middle States. The original architect is unknown, but Henry Sproatt of the Toronto firm Sproatt and Rolph (the architects of Hart House and Bishop Strachan School) stuccoed over the dark clapboard, painted it white, and probably added the unlouvred shutters. Compared with its neighbour across the street at 175 Dorset, Homewood is relaxed, gracious, and, in spite of its size, surprisingly unpretentious.

37 175 Dorset Street West, ca. 1874
Hillcrest, as this house is called, is often described as Port Hope's only example of the Beaux Arts style. More accurately, Hillcrest is a gigantic Beaux Arts portico grafted onto what was the side of a mid-Victorian villa. The villa was the home of David Smart, an enterprising lawyer, investment counsellor, collection agent, and distiller, who built a big, twin-bayed house that faced the lake to the southeast. An American summer resident named John Schwartz (the brother of James Schwartz, who built 188 Dorset, **36**) revamped the house around 1900 and added the drop-dead Corinthian-columned portico, which is now the front.

38 115 Dorset Street West, 1858
The *Weekly Guide* of October 2, 1858, reported that Thomas Clarke was building a villa "upon the model of the Swiss Cottage" that promised to be a "perfect Gem." The timber construction, broad eaves, and picturesque style may have suggested Switzerland to the reporter, but the house appears to be based on a design by the English-educated architect Gervase Wheeler. Wheeler's plans for a board-and-batten Gothic cottage built in Maine for $2,800 (U.S.) were published in A.J. Downing's 1850 pattern book, *The Architecture of Country Houses*, and the Cone, as this house is called, is a close but not slavish copy. (Clarke, who was associate engineer for the Port Hope, Lindsay and Beaverton Railway, built only the west side of the house; the design was completed in 1875 by a later owner.) The Cone's greyish-mauve colours, which look very modern, are actually in line with Downing's well-publicized preference for soft, unemphatic tones.

39 89 Dorset Street West, ca. 1853
This winsome late-blooming Regency cottage, called Wimbourne, perches on its own little hill with a view of the lake. As well as the *de rigueur* prospect, it has the other Regency hallmarks – a veranda with French doors, an almost square shape, a certain air of informality and leisure. (Like many Regency cottages, Wimbourne was

40 *82 Pine Street South*

43 *64 Augusta Street*

planned as a retirement home, for a tannery owner named William Sisson.) The house's most remarked feature, an unusual truncated gable edged with rickrack-like bargeboard in each side, looks like an adaptation of "Swiss" gables seen in nineteenth-century pattern books. Don't miss the curvaceous cast-iron gratings in the rubblestone basement storey, visible from Dorset Street; they are thought to be from a foundry in nearby Port Britain.

On the hilly side of Pine Street, three houses from different generations bridge from Dorset Street to Augusta.

40 82 Pine Street South, 1876

A relatively unsung and very attractive house, on a piney corner lot. With its three bays, off-centre door, and wide eaves, it falls into the loose category known locally as Port Hope vernacular, but its cachet is in the details: the graceful metal tracery on the transom, the bold treillage on the portico, the cast-stone sills whose brackets echo the paired brackets under the eaves. The so-called white brick, unusual in Port Hope, underlines its urbane character.

41 78 Pine Street South, ca. 1850

The original shape (minus the addition to the north) of this pretty Ontario cottage is outlined by wide brick pilasters at the sides and an angled brick frieze, called dog-toothing, that traverses the side

bays and central gable. Note the simple, urn-topped ironwork railing.

42 74 Pine Street South, 1859

Curvy columns and shingled pediments were modish for early-twentieth-century porches. Behind this porch sits a vernacular house wearing the fashions of an earlier day: three sharp gables with pendants and finials.

43 64 Augusta Street, ca. 1852

A subtle house that owes its appeal to the melding of two architectural streams. The older tradition, Loyalist or neoclassical, accounts for the house's symmetrical arrangement, its flushboard construction, and its position close to the street. If you mentally subtract the little pediment with Gothic quatrefoils, it looks even more like a hold-over from earlier in the century. The entablatures with miniature brackets that top the windows and door are a more picturesque, mid-Victorian detail; so is the sharply pitched roof. Built by William Cawthorne, a watchmaker, it was later lived in by Dr. John Dewar, who was instrumental in bringing Trinity College School to Port Hope.

44 78, 45 82, 46 86 Augusta Street, 1870s–'80s

Three L-shaped, self-confident Victorian villas in a row climb the Augusta Street hill. The most accomplished, 78 Augusta,

48 *95 Augusta Street*   49 *87 Augusta Street*

wants it all and very nearly gets it: a crested and gabled tower that takes on Italianate, Gothic, and Second Empire airs by turns, heavy cast-stone window and door surrounds, and a surprisingly restrained veranda on two sides. Thomas McCreery, who ran what was probably Port Hope's first billiard saloon, built it in the late 1870s.

The house at 82 Augusta is bigger-boned, but with the prettiest veranda of the trio. The most downright, 86 Augusta, looks like a very large version of the bay-and-gable, a popular Victorian style in the Toronto area.

47 92 Augusta Street, ca. 1855
The polygonal central tower (best seen from across the street) looks promising but, like Hill and Dale, this is an "important" local house without much to offer walkers. Successive make-overs and additions have taken their toll, and abundant planting makes it hard to see what remains. Built for Robert Charles Smith, the son of the Bluestone's owner, the Pine House (named for the white pine in front) remained in the Smith family until the Depression.

48 95 Augusta Street, ca. 1850
Known as the Belvedere and celebrated as a particularly fine Ontario cottage, this little house is struggling bravely with an overload of modish features. As if the belvedere, the heavy Greek Revival portico and door,

and the gable with semicircular fanlight were not enough, three tall chimneys stand guard at the sides. Beautifully restored by the twentieth-century architect Napier Simpson, the cottage is a slightly disconcerting example of mid-century taste: it's difficult not to see it as more frosting than cake.

49 87 Augusta Street, ca. 1869
One of Port Hope's most engaging houses. Without the veranda, it would be an attractive, Georgian-inspired stucco building that pleased by virtue of its regularly recurring rectangles: a pattern composed of windowpanes, shutters, sills, sidelights, transom, door. It's the veranda, sweeping around three sides of the house and softening the rectangles with the minimal curves of its simple treillage, that provides the poetry. And, *pace* Victorian theorists like A.J. Downing, who disliked "glaring" white houses, its white-and-green colour scheme just suits its verdant garden.

50 77 Augusta Street, ca. 1850s, additions 1878, 1881–82
At first glance, this looks rather forbidding, like a Dickensian orphanage or workhouse. But walk up to the front door (it has been converted to apartments) and admire the details, particularly the panelled brackets and the contrastingly textured brickwork under the balcony. The original house was given an Italianate flavour in 1878 when

51 *168 Walton Street*

200 and 202 Walton Street

Baron Adolph von Hugel, one of the Midland Railway's managers, ordered alterations from a Peterborough architect, William Petch. Further additions were made in 1881–82 by David B. Dick, a well-known Toronto architect.

Continue on Pine to Walton Street, passing the main entrance to Hill and Dale (**25** above) and (at 39 Pine) its converted carriage house.

51 168 Walton Street, ca. 1865

A dressed-up version of a model Italianate house that appeared in the *Canada Farmer* in 1865 and was copied all over Ontario. The model, described by the *Canada Farmer* as "a straightforward square house," was a symmetrical building with arched windows, quoins, and a projecting frontispiece topped with a pediment. The builders of this house gussied it up with two non-matching bays and a lacy side veranda; then they larded in the full Italianate repertoire of accessories – brackets, dentils, iron cresting, eyebrow window labels – all finely made and integrated into the whole composition. The house was built for the Burnhams, a prominent family in both Port Hope and Cobourg, and remained in the family until 1953 when they left it to the Sisters of St. Joseph.

Head west on Walton Street.

52 200 Walton Street, ca. 1855–60

One of Port Hope's first settlers, James Sculthorpe arrived as a baby at the end of the eighteenth century. Half a century later, he built this smart neoclassical townhouse on a hilly site; from the front, it's not apparent that there are three stories. The florid lyre-patterned cast-iron fence is a nice antidote to the house's spare elegance. Its neighbour, 202 Walton (ca. 1850), is another neoclassical rectangle, banded by pilasters and dog-tooth trim.

The neighbourhood of small brick houses on Church and Baldwin Streets was called Englishtown, because it was a preferred location for retired British military men in the mid-nineteenth century.

53 9 Church Street, ca. 1850

Another Port Hope deceiver, this apparently tiny cottage looks much different from the side. Its lovely Regency door and Tudor-arched transom are very similar to those on the well-known Trick House (see **61** below), and it may have been built by Richard Trick.

54 4–6 Baldwin Street, ca. 1853

This double Regency cottage is an example of Port Hope's penchant – unusual in a town of this size – for semidetached and terrace housing. Sharing a roof did not mean doing without life's pleasing details, such as the lyre pattern on the railing or the

 35 *Baldwin Street*   59 *238 Ridout Street*

crochetwork-like supports for the veranda posts. It was probably built by Robert Youdan, a brick mason, in two parts, with number 6 the first.

55 20 Baldwin Street, ca. 1853
A tidy house probably built by its owner, a carpenter named John Walter. In typical Ontario fashion, he merged a few styles – the heavy eared doorcase and deep eaves of the Greek Revival, the central gable (in this case rather perfunctory) of the Ontario cottage, the Gothic tracery in the round window – to achieve something pleasingly individual.

56 35 Baldwin Street, ca. 1876
An impressive sight at the end of a modest street, this gorgeously turned out Second Empire villa doesn't miss a trick. Among its many finely wrought details: the string course and brackets that underline the coquettish bell-cast mansard roof, the boldly textured window surrounds, the round windows in the octagonal turret, the miniature mansards topping the two porticoes. Even the chimneys sport two colours of brick and moulded fascia. Second Empire roofs often had slate shingles; the wooden ones here mimic a fashionable slate pattern.

57 25 Baldwin Street, ca. 1870s
A vernacular cottage has been updated with concrete "Egyptian" pillars, one of the

novelty revivals fashionable around the turn of the century.

58 236 Walton Street, ca. 1853,
59 238 Ridout Street, 1850s,
60 240 Ridout Street, ca. 1870.
     (Walton Street becomes Ridout Street
     after the first of these next-door
     neighbours.)
Three mid-nineteenth-century houses, all with make-overs. The square Tuscan tower of the Italianate style accustomed Victorians to domestic towers; 236 Walton and 240 Ridout added them to very un-Italianate houses. At first 236 Walton, which acquired its squat central tower about twenty-five years after it was built, looks like a fire station; gradually its honest proportions become appealing and then you notice the bell-cast roof with decorative shingles, the Venetian front windows, and the smart dog-toothed brick cornice. With its taller tower and a veranda to turn master joiners green with envy, 240 Ridout is the more immediately engaging. Its tower, as well as the second storey, was added about 1890. The Ontario cottage between the two has had a less drastic revision; the polygonal porch and generous front windows probably appeared around 1900.

61 254 Ridout Street, ca. 1850
This well-known Ontario cottage, called Trick House, is invariably praised for the finesse of its details. Its builder and first

60 *240 Ridout Street*

61 *254 Ridout Street*

owner, Richard Trick, was a busy local mason. From the dentilled frieze to the brickwork circle under the gable to the quoins to the mysterious blocks in the corners of the windows (an attempt to imitate eared trim?), Trick House demonstrates what a resourceful bricklayer could achieve with his basic building block. The final effect, though, has a slightly make-believe, almost comical quality. Is it due to the staring black-and-white colour scheme, or the basically flat surface, or to lovable, semi-pompous touches like the finial in the gable? Whatever the reason, it's easy to imagine Trick House as the backdrop for an operetta.

62 **284 Ridout Street,** ca. 1850–53
Forge Cottage, as this snug neoclassical house was called, commemorates the occupation of its first owner, the blacksmith Thomas Spry. Blacksmiths were crucial as Port Hope's human and equine populations multiplied in the heady 1850s, and Spry's cottage bespeaks his confidence that pilasters, fanlights, and monumental little doors were well within reach of the working man.

Cross the street and walk back east along Walton.

63 **239 Ridout Street,** 1856
A near-twin of its neighbour across the street at 238 Ridout, **59**.

64 **233 Walton Street,** ca. 1854
In 1971, this Ontario cottage had fourteen rooms and two bathrooms; now, after consolidation of some of the smallest rooms, it has ten rooms. Note the recessed window bays and the stylish portico, echoed by a triangular window in the gable.

65 **213 Walton Street,** ca. 1855–60
The gigantic Gothic treillage on the hip-roofed veranda (which may well have come later, in a belated attempt to render the house à la mode) obscures a simple neoclassical house not unlike 200 Walton (**52**) and 202 Walton across the street.

66 **187 Walton Street,** 1857
Another city-smart house, with the recessed brick panels that grace many Walton Street houses and interesting radiating headers on the windows. Note the dates inscribed on the stone wedges in the top corners.

Turn left at Pine Street.

67 **44 Pine Street North,** 1846
There's no doubt about the date of this splendidly theatrical Tudor house, as it's emblazoned in the middle of the very pointed central gable. Nor about its name, Pinehurst, since it rises out of a copse of fragrant pine trees. The unknown builder was clearly at home with the angular grammar of the Tudor Gothic style: the small

 *44 Pine Street North*

68 *St. John's Sunday School*

stylized gables crammed to capacity by the heavily labelled windows, the buttresses, the delicate window tracery, the boxed porch bristling with finials. Unusual in Upper Canada, where the softer forms of the "medieval" Gothic were more popular, Pinehurst may well have been influenced by J.C. Loudon's 1833 pattern book, *Encyclopedia of Cottage, Farm, and Villa Architecture*. Built for a lawyer, Nelson Kirchoffer, who later became mayor.

68 St. John's Anglican Church, 35 Pine Street North, 1869, Sunday School, 1871

Port Hope's "other" Anglican church was built at a cost of $18,300 by the Toronto architectural firm of Gundry & Langley. Henry Langley's career spanned more than forty years and seventy churches; he made a particular specialty of spires. The one at St. John's stands to the side and is needle-sharp, ringed by projecting boar-like beasties. But the charmer in this ecclesiastical ensemble is the wide-gabled Sunday School to the right of the church, designed by Langley in 1871 and built for $7,500. It bears a strong resemblance to another Gundry & Langley creation, St. Peter's Church on Carlton Street in Toronto (1865), although it is less flamboyantly bichromatic. At the centre of the broad front gable, just enough Gothic detail – crockets, quatrefoils, trefoils, brick striping – propels the eye up the bellcote to

the airy wrought-iron flourish at the top.

In 1873, parishioners could rent pews for $15 per year for a large section, $12 for a small one. Free pews were located at the back of the church.

69 At the corner of **South and Cavan Streets**, the building with the rounded corner was Chalk's Carriage Works, a factory that operated from 1842 to 1934, now attached to a modern apartment building.

Cross the footbridge to the left of the road bridge.

70 Barrett's Terrace, 22–40 Barrett Street, ca. 1860

An unconventional man when it came to his own house (see **71** below), mill owner William Barrett Jr. was pragmatic but not blind to style when he planned housing for his workers. The original ten-unit terrace he erected close to his sawmill and gristmill on the Ganaraska was a long ribbon of brick, castellated from one end to the other, with lyre-shaped posts supporting the identical verandas. Terrace housing is relatively rare in small-town Ontario, but it must have looked familiar to the English operatives and their families whom Barrett imported. The price was appealing too – $10 a month for an eight-room unit in 1880. Today most of the castellation has disappeared, the verandas are no longer

70 *Barrett's Terrace,*
22–40 Barrett Street

71 *16 Martha Street*

identical (although the lyre posts are gradually returning), and there's an additional unit at the east end.

71 16 Martha Street, 1856

Orson Fowler was a nineteenth-century American best known as the champion of phrenology, a popular pseudo-science that judged character by examining the cranium. In 1848, he ventured into architecture, with *A Home for All; or, A New, Cheap, Convenient, and Superior Mode of Building.* Claiming "as a fixed ordinance of Nature" that spherical forms were the most aesthetically pleasing, Fowler went further. They actually caused good feeling: "To gather around a spherical or elliptical table, occasions more harmony and agreeable sensations than around a square one." It seemed only reasonable to Fowler that "the superior mode of building" was the housing form that most closely approached the spherical – the octagon, which he insisted would produce good character, domestic felicity, and lower heating bills. More than a thousand octagons were built across

North America before the fad declined in the 1860s, and at least three dozen are still standing in Ontario.

Port Hope's example, built of scored stucco into the side of a hill by William Barrett Jr., is one of the finest in the province. From his undeniably odd but appealing building, Barrett could survey not only his mills but the terrace housing he had built for his hands. (A true enthusiast, Barrett also seems to have been instrumental in getting two octagonal schools built in Port Hope.) Except for the French doors at the corners and an encircling veranda, the octagon reserves almost all embellishment for the interior: a diagonally placed oval stairwell, stained glass in the octagonal belvedere and on the main floor, and elaborate plasterwork.

An octagon usually indicated the owner's commitment to a Fowleresque blend of pseudo-science, wholesome living, and startlingly modern conveniences: Port Hope's octagon had the town's first indoor bathroom.

135 Queen Street East

St. Marys

"A Well-Settled Stone Town"

St. Marys, stone town, has a lot to offer.

Calm.

Raccoons & cool in the summer. That
burnished colour of the sun on green-veined yellow leaves
where texture mindlessly cups drunk light;
my favourite bridge, the creek, a cleft giant willow fishing
place with rocks. This is idyllic.

David Donnell,
"Up from the River," in *Water Street Days*

Unlike many Ontario towns, whose individuality asserts itself gradually, St. Marys snaps almost instantly into focus: a grey and green composition of water, hills, and stone. Four main bridges stitch together a town that huddles along the Thames River and Trout Creek. Four unexpectedly large churches keep watch on the highest hills. A busy main street divides silent residential blocks, some of which merge abruptly into the pure countryside of barns and silos. The view of the town from the Victoria Bridge is of limestone spires, towers, and turrets climbing the hills.

It was the Thames River – a much less placid body of water than it is today – and the local deposits of limestone that impressed early visitors to St. Marys. In 1848, soon after the town's first mills were built, the Goderich *Huron Signal* saw in the Thames's motion "an emblem of the active industry that now cultivates or adorns its banks. It glides or rather sweeps smoothly, swiftly and clearly over a flat-bed of flag limestone, admirably adopted to building purposes."

The river and building stone notwithstanding, St. Marys was a Johnny-come-lately among Ontario towns. Part of the fertile million-acre triangle called the Huron Tract, the region was discouragingly far from the Great Lakes and the major rivers that were the highways of the early nineteenth century. Unlike many of Ontario's older settlements, inhabited first by the Indians and then more fleetingly by the French, the thickly forested plateau with relatively weak rivers that became Perth County had never been populated. Even the local Indians never stayed, though they hunted there in winter when the mosquitoes were dormant.

By the 1840s, the desirable lakeside land was filling up. British immigrants were arriving in record numbers, and the Canada Company, the British land and colonization enterprise that owned the Huron Tract, was advertising its holdings in rosy-coloured prose. In 1841, the company offered for sale the land that became St. Marys. James Ingersoll, from nearby Oxford County, essentially bought the town and dispatched his brother Thomas to make it a reality. Four years later, about 120 people, most of them English, Northern Irish, and Scottish settlers migrating from neighbouring counties in Canada West, had settled on the Ingersolls' 337 acres.

In 1897 a prize was offered at St. Marys Collegiate for the best essay on the history of the town. The second-prize winner, Maggie Gordon, wasted no time on a lyrical opening. Bluntly she began, "The early history of every country is the same – in every country the pioneer work must be done." Indeed. And the history of St. Marys follows the familiar pattern – the choice of a site near water, the settler who felled the first tree (St. Marys has three contenders), the establishment of the first mills, the first house (**53**, the Ingersoll house at 105–107 Queen Street West), the first fine house (**19**, the present museum at 177 Church Street South), the first school (taught by Gordon Meighen, the grandfather of a future prime minister, for a yearly salary of £6.8s.), the snowballing of civic organization, industry, and social life.

What seems remarkable about St. Marys is how quickly it became itself, and how tenaciously it stayed that way. Its population in 1871 was just over 3,000; it did not climb to 4,000 until 1961 and was just under 5,500 in 1995. Unlike older towns, such as Cobourg or Niagara-on-the-Lake, it apparently never had aspirations to grandeur, much less any real national or even provincial importance. With the Oddfellows' overweening 1879 Opera House as the single debatable exception, St. Marys seems to have been content to be what it was: a market town busy with milling and quarrying businesses.

Not that St. Marys is without local lore or that it did not take itself with appropriate seriousness. As in any self-respecting town, there are legends and near-apocryphal stories. Many towns have one about the settlement's first wedding, probably because of its implied promise of fecundity and growth. In the St. Marys version, the best man, returning from Stratford with the licence, found the bridge (a tree trunk) washed away. With the legal document on one side of Trout Creek and the helplessly fretting couple on the other, the clergyman refused to act. Finally the bride, "inventive as usual in such circumstances," as the *St. Marys Journal-Argus* later described her, suggested wrapping the licence around a stone and hurling it across the river. Which illustrates, aside from the perceived ingenuity of females bent on marriage, the crucial importance of bridges to St. Marys.

More seriously, there is the mysterious, suspiciously papist name of the town. For more than a hundred years, it was believed to have high-toned Family Compact origins in the person of Elizabeth Mary Jones, daughter of Bishop John Strachan and wife of Commissioner Thomas Mercer Jones of the Canada Company. The story had it that in 1845 Mrs. Jones visited the infant village, then called Little Falls, and contributed £10 for the building of a school. In return, a grateful Little Falls renamed itself St. Marys. In reality, as the local historian Larry Pfaff notes, Mrs. Jones's prestige and the promise of £10 may have inspired the village to confirm a name already in use. Recent evidence suggests a less glamorous and more credible namesake: Mary McDonald, wife of John McDonald, who surveyed St. Marys and all of Blanshard Township and tried to name at least one other settlement after his spouse.

Like many towns, St. Marys energized itself by scorning a nearby rival. Describing Stratford as "a locality nearly surrounded by swamps," the leading citizens of St. Marys protested its neighbour's elevation as the district town. A *St. Marys Argus* editorial in 1859 insisted that their youthful town was "already wedded to prosperity, while her sister Stratford, the oldest in the family of villages of the county, is still waiting in hopeless expectancy." At least partly because of Stratford's eventual triumph as the county town, St. Marys left Perth County in 1864 and went it alone as an unincorporated town.

The *Argus* writer had a point: St. Marys was only slightly less populous than Stratford in the 1861 survey (Stratford is now five times the size of St. Marys), and the younger town's superior railroad connections had created a booming grain trade. When William Johnston arrived from Scotland in 1859, St. Marys looked positively hectic. In his *History of Perth County 1825–1902*, he wrote, "On the streets could be seen every day a dozen of grain buyers, all busy, with long strings of loaded wagons pouring into the town from all directions. During autumn the market square was for several hours each day blocked with teams, and extending down Queen Street as far as Wellington was a mass of men and horses, with wheat and other products awaiting an opportunity to move onward."

During the 1860s and '70s, the town supported as many as seventeen hotels, and the leading grain traders (often part of what Larry Pfaff calls the town's Methodist mafia) consolidated their fortunes and commissioned their mansions. The glory days, which were based on the Grand Trunk Railway connections to Toronto, London, and Sarnia, ended when other tracks, which bypassed St. Marys, were chosen as the main Toronto-Sarnia line. The cleverer merchants went into milling or otherwise diversified, but St. Marys lost its edge forever.

Like every place, St. Marys has its local heroes. The attenuated statue of Arthur Meighen (1874–1960), the Conservative prime minister whose St. Marys roots go back to the town's founding, lords it over Lind Park on Church Street. The town mythology also includes the One Who Got Away, in this case an ambitious young Irishman named Timothy Eaton. The future department store magnate arrived in St. Marys in 1860 at the age of twenty-six, joining his older brothers, James and Robert. With James, Timothy opened a dry-goods store on Queen Street, selling boots, hardware, medicine, kitchenware, and farm tools "Cheap and for Cash."

The insistence on cash was a radical departure for a farming society that found it more convenient to barter, but a necessity for a man bent on expansion. In any case, St. Marys honoured the innovation more in the breach than in the observance: Eaton's local accounts show twice as many butter-and-egg transactions as cash. He stuck it out on Queen Street for eight years, adding a clothing store and teaching in the Methodist Sunday School on Church Street. Finally Margaret Beattie Eaton, the presiding genius of the millinery department, convinced her husband that a cash business needed a large manufacturing population, and the couple decamped for Toronto in 1869. Timothy's brothers remained in St. Marys, and Robert Eaton operated his Queen Street grocery and furniture business until 1890.

Other than a few mansions, little remains of the grain merchants' great expectations. It is the local limestone quarries, a utilitarian and very unhectic industry, that have left a more lasting and more pervasive mark on St. Marys. Its memorable buildings, from cottages to grandiose civic structures, are the products of several quarries that lined the banks of the Thames. Mostly rather small operations, on Water Street South and Thomas Street, they were owned by individual masons or groups of masons who built their own stone cottages close to their quarries.

Although the quarries were in active existence for less than seventy years, they seem to have progressed from something like a timeless cottage industry to a modern business. In the nineteenth century, the masons – some but by no means all the proverbial Scottish stonemasons – typically kept slabs close to home to dress and trim during the long winters. At the end of the industry's lifetime, just before World War I, the Bonis plant employed thirty men and used plug drills, motors, a boiler for steam for deep drilling, a compressor, and power derricks. What does not seem to have changed much is the prices. In 1851, cut stone from St. Marys for sills and pilasters was advertised in London, Ontario, at 40 cents a foot, delivered. In 1912, when St. Marys stone had dignified buildings in Toronto, Lucan, and Durham as well as at home, $3.25 would buy a cord of hammer-broken rough stone, and sills and lintels cost only 45 to 50 cents a foot.

Born of water and stone, St. Marys remains true to them in its own contemporary fashion. By the beginning of World War I, building in limestone had virtually ended; the last local example, the Central School at 189 Elizabeth Street, dates from 1914. No longer used for grave, laboriously crafted buildings, the limestone is now burned for cement, and St. Marys Cement is one of the town's major industries. The largest quarries were flooded in the 1930s, creating a justly celebrated swimming area.

Increasingly functionless, the town's founding elements have become more and more purely aesthetic. As Larry Pfaff writes in *Early St. Marys*, the water, "shimmering in the quarries, flowing through the old mill race, and spilling over the dam," has made possible its transition from a milling town to a beauty spot. As have the stone buildings, which – like St. Marys itself – are largely intact, unselfconscious, and blessedly ungentrified.

Water fountain, Queen Street

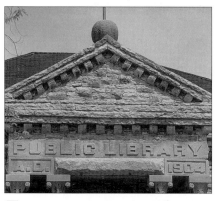

12 *Carnegie Library, 15 Church Street North*

13 *Church Street Bridge*

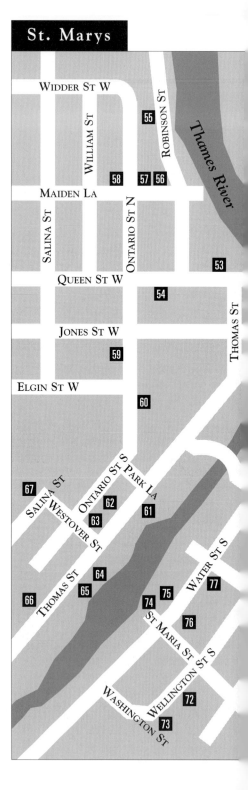

St. Marys

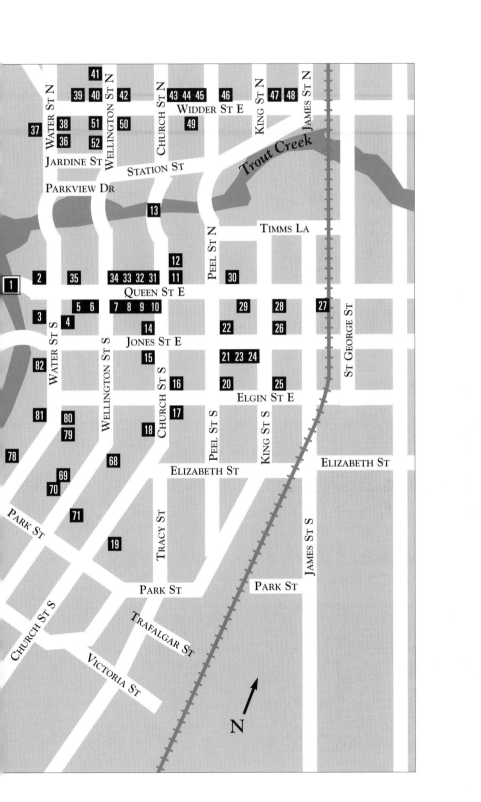

1 *Victoria Bridge, Queen Street across Thames River*

3 *Opera House, 12 Water Street South*

1 Victoria Bridge, Queen Street across Thames River, 1865

St. Marys came into being because the confluence of the Thames River and Trout Creek promised water power for mills. The mills themselves – sawmills, gristmills, cereal mills, woollen mills, even apple butter mills – are gone, but the mill race (the small arch at the eastern end of the bridge built to direct water to the mill property south of Queen Street) remains. Victoria Bridge was designed for $40 by Alexander Niven, a provincial land surveyor, and built by a Scottish stonemason named Alexander McDonald. The stone came from McDonald's own Water Street quarry, and he was paid a very considerable $4,550 for it. Rebuilt in 1984, after surviving two town councils that voted to demolish it and build a concrete replacement, Victoria Bridge is Ontario's second-oldest and second-longest stone bridge.

2 83–91 Queen Street East, 6 Water Street North, 1858, 1855

At the heart of the town's first industrial and commercial district, this is a much-altered ensemble of important early buildings. The gabled house facing the river was built for the miller and businessman William Veal Hutton in 1858; the Huttons were an English family responsible for several significant local buildings. Hutton owned a four-and-a-half-storey gristmill (now demolished) directly across

the street and the four-store commercial building that adjoins his house. The first store in St. Marys, a log building, had been erected on this site in 1843, and Hutton's well-bred replacement, built of regularly coursed limestone by local masons less than fifteen years later, indicates the speed of development in the burgeoning village. (The mansard roof was added to the two stores closest to Water Street in 1884.)

3 6 Water Street South, 1863, 12 Water Street South, 1879–80, 14 Water Street South, 1868

Built over a sixteen-year span by different designers, this commercial row says excellent things about the local limestone quarries and stonemasons. The faux-medieval theatrics of the rough-cut Opera House (number 12) are set off by the beautifully controlled classicism of the earlier ashlar buildings that flank it.

Designed with stores on the first floor, an 800-seat theatre on the second, and meeting rooms for the Oddfellows on the third, the Oddfellows Opera House was so convincing an expression of civic confidence that it was often taken for the Town Hall. Its architect (and lodge member) Silas Weekes gussied up a rectangular building with a quiverful of Scottish Baronial motifs – bartizans, lancet and quatrefoil windows, crenellations, and gables – executed by two St. Marys masons named Fitt and Tobin. (Unfortunately the central gable at

4 *17 Water Street South*

5 *120, 122–132 Queen Street East*

the top that balanced the two over the doors was a casualty of the building's twentieth-century incarnation as a flour mill.) The details are so beautifully conceived and finished, exploiting a range of limestone colours and finishes, that what might easily have tumbled into kitsch is a triumph of the stonemason's craft.

For almost four decades, the second-floor theatre hosted local and touring plays (*Uncle Tom's Cabin* was a guaranteed crowd-pleaser), musicians, and politicians, even moving pictures late in its life. But the Oddfellows never made a financial go of the Opera House and sold it in 1904; for more than fifty years, the building was a flour mill. Restored in the late 1980s by the Lions Club, it now houses stores and condominiums.

The pleasing severity of 6 Water Street South, built by William Hutton, is relieved only by the rhythm of rounded and rectangular openings on the first floor, the graceful flare of the voussoirs, and the projecting keystones on all three floors. Number 14, built by William's brother Theodore to house his dry-goods store, is softer, more Italianate with its rounded windows and doors. Note the contrast between the scabbled (pock-marked) stone blocks of the body and the more finely finished window and door surrounds, cut in a single piece and then incised to mimic voussoirs.

4 17 Water Street South, 1907

The former post office and customs house knits together rock-faced limestone, emphatic sandstone trim, a pattern of rounded and rectangular openings, and a near-Dutch gable into a building whose bluff charm increases the longer you look at it. Designed by David Ewart, chief architect for the Department of Public Works.

Now walk up Queen Street on the north side, looking at the shops on the south side. Unlikely as it sounds in a town the size of St. Marys, the cheek-by-jowl principal streets, Water and Queen, fought it out during the 1850s and early '60s to become the main business section. After initial successes by the Water Street advocates, Queen Street won the day.

5 120 Queen Street East, 1855,
122–132 Queen Street East, 1859

A row of early stores whose pleasure derives almost entirely from sure proportions and finely crafted local limestone. The details are minimal – projecting sills, keystones in the 1859 stores. The compound headers on the windows are typical of the 1850s and less expensive than the massive one-piece lintels more usual in later decades. Built by the first reeve of St. Marys, T.B. Guest.

6 134 Queen Street East, early 1870s

After a row of stone buildings so classic they would look credible in many parts

9 *154–158 Queen Street East*

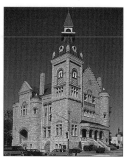

11 *Town Hall,*
175 Queen Street East

of the British Isles from the eighteenth century on, 134 Queen (also built by T.B. Guest) represents an abrupt turn into a regional High Victorian mode. The cast-stone window surrounds, the brackets, and the brick corbels are standard High Vic details; the brick itself, called white brick in the nineteenth century, is pure southwestern Ontario.

7 138–142 Queen Street East, 1868
Notice the discreet refinements that distinguish this stone row from the 1855-59 one (**5**): the subtle corner blocks or quoins, the rudimentary brackets under the cornice, the little "ears" on the voussoirs. The bold storefront framework on the former *St. Marys Journal-Argus* building is wooden. Another row built by the redoutable Guest, who left it to his eldest son, on condition that he not marry into a certain St. John family.

8 150 Queen Street East, early 1870s
The Grand Central Hotel was one of the town's dozen and a half hotels during the 1860s and '70s, when Queen Street was clogged each autumn with "a mass of men and horses" buying and selling grain. Number 152 Queen was originally the carriageway to the stables at the rear of the hotel.

9 154–158 Queen Street East, 1897
Two red-brick storefronts making the most

of turn-of-the-century embellishments: stained glass, rock-faced lintels, and extroverted wooden cornices.

10 166 Queen Street East, 1850s
This is where Timothy Eaton tried unsuccessfully to sell the locals on cash buying, from 1861 to 1869.

11 Town Hall, 175 Queen Street East, 1891
When the frame Town Hall burned in 1889, Dr. John Mathieson, the chairman of the St. Marys building committee, exhorted the town council to build not "for now, but for years or generations to come," choosing ornamentation neither exaggerated nor plain but "of a lasting and permanent character." Which only goes to show how much permanence is in the eye of the beholder, since the new Town Hall is every inch a period piece.

The period in question favoured medieval details like stepped gables, towers, turrets, sandstone-rimmed round arches, and sandstone-and-limestone chequerboard trim. George Gouinlock, a Toronto architect who later designed the Canadian National Exhibition buildings, upped the picturesque quotient with rock-faced limestone and a twisted belfry in imitation of the campanile of Santa Croce, Florence. Unfortunately, his interest in the Richardsonian Romanesque look doesn't seem to have extended beyond the Queen and

12 *Carnegie Library, 15 Church Street North*

14 *First Baptist Church,*
34 Church Street South

Church Street façades. The style's accessories, best suited to complex horizontal structures, are here applied to what is essentially a tall rectangle.

The Town Hall's romantic exterior belied its pragmatic inside, which housed jail cells and the town fire engine as well as the usual public hall, city offices, and police court.

12 Carnegie Library, 15 Church Street North, 1904–05

At the turn of the century, the St. Marys Library had 3,000 books without a proper home. But when Andrew Carnegie volunteered $10,000 to build a library (one of 125 he endowed in Ontario), not everyone leaped at the American philanthropist's offer. Some townspeople had qualms about Carnegie's reliance on sweated labour and his use of the infamous Pinkerton Detective Agency to quash strikes; more businesslike types worried about committing St. Marys to annual operating costs of $1,000. Finally put to a vote in a municipal election, Carnegie's offer squeaked through by thirty-five votes.

The St. Marys architect J.A. Humphris adjusted the favoured Carnegie classical plan to the local limestone. Smoothly dressed stone would have been a likelier choice for the style, but the fashion was for rough-cut stone, which had the added appeal of matching the Town Hall. The endearing result looks rather as if a fabric

artist had knitted a Palladian building in nubbly grey worsted. The line of rounded corbels outlining the pediment and the cornice is another neighbourly nod to the Town Hall, and the Romanesque-style columns with their vegetal forms are lovely.

13 Church Street Bridge, 1884

The most poetic of the town's bridges, the Church Street Bridge was designed by William Williams and built for $3,800 by local masons. The English-born Williams, the pre-eminent architect in St. Marys during the 1880s, was a man of parts: during the same decade, he also functioned as town clerk, insurance agent, and money-lender. His low-slung, double-arched bridge was thoroughly repaired and upgraded in 1979.

Return south on Church Street, crossing Queen Street.

14 First Baptist Church, 34 Church Street South, 1902

Less celebrated than the churches further up the hill, and less admired than it should be, this is a plucky recasting of a medieval style by the versatile J.A. Humphris. From the front it looks to be one-half of a steep gable plus a chunky little tower topped by four bartizans. The view from the side, as it climbs the Jones Street hill, is different again, and also rewarding.

16 *St. James Anglican Church,*
65 Church Street South

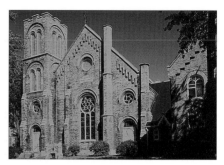

17 *St. Marys United Church,*
85 Church Street South

15 46 Church Street South, 1871

In a century when shopkeepers often lived next to or above the shop, bank managers did the same. After 1889, when the Bank of Montreal relocated here, the small pedimented door led to the bank; the one behind the boxy portico led to the manager's house. The projecting central block outlined by the brick mock-quoins is attractive, but something – perhaps the uninspired brackets and cornice – hints that business came first here.

16 St. James Anglican Church,
65 Church Street South, 1858

Shortly after its consecration in 1859, the *Hamilton Spectator* judged St. James a "plain but handsome" structure with a "much needed" belfry not yet built. (The "plain and unpretending" interior apparently had only honesty to commend it.) The local Anglicans had built their Gothic Revival church, largely with their own labour, for $4,800; Archibald Lampman, father of the poet, was the first rector. The much-needed belfry, designed by William Williams, did not appear until 1886 and it is indeed the ensemble's beauty mark: modestly crenellated, turreted, and making handsome use of several different limestone finishes. The parish hall, built in rock-faced limestone, dates from 1907.

17 St. Marys United Church,
85 Church Street South, 1879

After St. James's cool grey stone and pointed arches, set well back on its broad lawn, the United Church (née Methodist) shoulders up close to the sidewalk, round-arched and wearing no-nonsense yellow brick. All of which suits the church where the most go-getting businessmen in nineteenth-century St. Marys came to worship. Nonconformist denominations favoured the Italianate style because of its supposed freedom; the attractions here include, beside the style's signature round arches in singles and pairs, a bold corbel table, a turret or two, and lovely limestone drip moulds and other trim. A Brantford firm, William Mellish & Son, designed the church; the 1893 Sunday School was the work of D.G. Baxter.

It's worth walking around the back to the door in the limestone addition to see the interior, a grand room ringed by rounded pews and focussing on an immense Casavant organ. As dictated by Methodist teaching, nary a painting or statue disturbs the impressive calm; even the stained glass is abstract.

18 100 Church Street South, 1863

The gable aspires upwards, while the heavy lintels, protruding sills, and quoins keep this stone Ontario cottage firmly grounded. A fine house for a Methodist merchant: it was built for Timothy Eaton's older brother and business partner James, when the two were running a dry-goods store

19 *177 Church Street South*

20 *67 Peel Street South*

together on Queen Street. (The entrance porch was added in this century.)

19 177 Church Street South, 1854

How fitting that George Tracy's Castle in the Bush, as this ambitious early house was called, has been the St. Marys Museum since 1959. Not only was it the first house of any elegance in St. Marys, but it was probably responsible for the presence of Robert Barbour, the master builder who created some of the village's most beautiful structures.

When Tracy, an early settler and landowner, was ready to build a limestone mansion, he is said to have advertised in New York State newspapers for craftsmen. According to the Tracy family story, Barbour, a Scottish-born mason working as a contractor's foreman in Rochester, New York, answered the advertisement. The rest, as far as St. Marys is concerned, is architectural history. Barbour stayed for the rest of his life, shaping the local limestone and brick into humble cottages, Georgian commercial buildings, schools, and grand villas.

A characteristic example of Barbour's work in the 1850s, the Tracy house has his signature lintels (less massive here than on some of his later buldings) but not the quoins that would distinguish much St. Marys stonework in the next decade. Whether Barbour actually designed as well as built this house is unknown. The three-

storey, twin-gabled plan with a recessed doorway is strikingly similar to a house in A.J. Downing's popular American pattern book *The Architecture of Country Houses* (1850), and Barbour may have varied it, adding the unusual two-storey umbrage or recessed veranda. (The same American building is generally considered to be the inspiration for a well-known Port Hope house, the Cone, at 115 Dorset Street.)

Retrace your steps on Church Street and turn right on Elgin.

During the boom of the 1860s and '70s, the grain speculator George Carter so dominated the scene that some called St. Marys "Carter's Corners." That was hyperbole, but it was literal truth when applied to the block circumscribed by Jones, King, Elgin, and Peel Streets. From 1869 to 1883, Carter erected four fashionable houses here for himself, two daughters, and a son: the bold businessman was also a Methodist patriarch determined to keep his son and sons-in-law in the family business and close at hand.

20 67 Peel Street South, 1883

The last of the Carter buildings was designed by William Williams for Carter's son, James, and his wife, Mary Box. A graceful two-sided veranda that stretched between the two main gables has been replaced by a modern porch, but otherwise

22 *217 Jones Street East*   24 *236 Jones Street East*

this remains very much as built: a proud, tall house whose many up-to-the-minute details – some Queen Anne, some William Williams – seem not so much applied as part of its structure. The arrowhead iron fence and the slate roof patterned in hexagons and rectangles are noteworthy, but nothing beats the glorious ribbed chimney-stacks, the finest in St. Marys.

21 218 Jones Street East, 1914

Not part of the Carter family compound, this is the only Tudor Revival house in town. All the hallmarks of this doughty style are here: parapeted gables, clusters of many-paned windows, a red-brick skin, mock half-timbering on the sides. Even the drainpipes are put to graphic effect. Built by a London, Ontario, architectural firm, Watt and Blackwell.

22 217 Jones Street East, ca. 1875

The house built for George Carter's daughter Hatty and her husband, Clarence Freeman, probably by the prominent London, Ontario, firm of William Robinson, who also built Carter's house at 224 Jones. Yellow brick, also called white brick, was a favoured London material, prized for its availability as well as its resemblance to stone. The Freeman house is a variation on a favourite Ontario model, a squarish building relieved by a projecting central bay topped by a gable. (The plan for just such a "straightforward square" Italianate house

appeared in the *Canada Farmer* in 1865.) Note the line of rounded openings that begins with the front door, continues to the windows on the second floor and in the gable, and ends with the bargeboard itself.

23 224 Jones Street East, 1869

George Carter's elaborate verandas, his crested summer house, and the carriage house are visible now only in archival photographs; this denuded Italianate cube fronted by a modern porch is all that remains of the patriarchal mansion. When Carter died in 1889, his business was apparently thriving, but in the early 1900s, a series of financial catastrophes ensued. His son, James, and his son-in-law Clarence Freeman committed suicide, leaving Carter's remaining son-in-law, Henry Rice (see 24 below), to oversee the final days of the business, which collapsed in 1921.

24 236 Jones Street East, 1881

Local legend has it that when Henry Lincoln Rice married Charlotte Carter, he was reluctant to give up the life of a classicist for the family grain business. Perhaps to sweeten the pot, George Carter presented the Rices with this stylish mansion as a wedding gift. Assessed soon after it was built at $2,000, it included a full set of Second Empire features (a style that had recently peaked in larger centres) and many interior luxuries such as ornate plasterwork and six marble fireplaces. The

25 *253 Elgin Street East*   26 *31 King Street South*

architect was William Williams, who does not seem to have found the Second Empire style entirely congenial: the veranda undercuts his soaringly handsome tower, and the lone dormer in the main mansard needs company. For the first half of this century, it was the home of a local writer, the poetaster Dr. Thomas Sparks.

25 253 Elgin Street East, 1886

What distinguishes this Italianate house is its red-brick embroidery. Using whole and half bricks, William Williams, the architect who is responsible for virtually all the bichromatic brick decoration in St. Marys, stitched in rows of crosses, string courses, two different styles of window headers; even the chimney is embellished. Coloured brick was championed by John Ruskin, who saw it as a "truthful" substitute for the polychrome marble of Italian churches, and the stripes that circle the front door's transom do suggest the Italian originating impulse. (On the other hand, they also recall the name given to this style by its detractors: "streaky bacon.")

The house was built for Alfred H. Lofft, a dry-goods merchant, for $2,200, and the *Argus* commented on April 15, 1886, "No section of the town has improved more during the last few years than that neighbourhood, and when the fine houses of Mrs. Hill, Mrs. Armstrong and Mr. Lofft are completed, it will be in a position to compete with any other portion of town."

26 31 King Street South, ca. 1857

Stone and wood were the most accessible building materials in early St. Marys, and this salmon-pink brick house, now painted bone white, was only the second brick dwelling in town. (The first is Lauriston Cruttenden's house at 36 Ontario Street North.) Its owner, David Smith, is listed in the 1861 census as a "gentleman" with $24,000 in capital. Built close to the street in the custom of the time, the house originally had a veranda that shaded all three bays. (The doorcase, inspired by eighteenth-century models and a touch too delicate for the house as a whole, was added in the 1920s.)

Follow Jones Street east to James Street and turn left.

27 Water Tower, James and Queen Streets, 1899

Looking like a medieval donjon or keep, complete with loopholes – the long slim openings from which to shoot arrows – and fine string courses, the 75,000-gallon water tower served a very up-to-the-minute municipal water system when it was built and remained in use until 1987.

28 252 Queen Street East, 1849, 1869

An appealingly un-organic witness to changing architectural fashions. In 1848, a twenty-five-year-old Irish-born carpenter named John Sanderson arrived in St. Marys;

28 *252 Queen Street East*

32 *155 Queen Street East*
31 *161 Queen Street East*

he had walked twenty miles from the train station in Ingersoll, carrying all he owned, including his tools. A year later, he built a small cottage of roughly cut stone (the gabled section to the west). Two decades later, now the owner of a thriving Queen Street lumberyard, Sanderson attached a two-storey Italianate box of regularly coursed limestone; the finely crafted details include the high, splayed window headers with sandstone keystones. At the turn of the century, the entrance porch (like a minia-ture of the main house, with its bracketed cornice, rounded panes of glass, and wood-en wedge that mimics a keystone) appeared, as well as the veranda treillage and the by then old-fashioned gable on the original section.

29 234 Queen Street East, 1850s
An early limestone store, with the shop-keeper's residence on the second floor. Many St. Marys buildings are built on a downward slope, with "hidden" stories behind; this one is built into a rising hill. Note the trail of very large stones near the chimney, a characteristic of 1850s buildings.

30 219–221 Queen Street East, 1870s
A store built of flushboard, with a board-and-batten wing to the side that probably served as the shopkeeper's house. The 1870s were late for the bold Greek Revival returning eaves on the main building, but

the style's off-centre door left lots of room for the generous shop window.

As you re-enter the business district, cross to the south side for a better view of build-ings across the street.

31 161 Queen Street East, ca. 1854
An early and very appealing limestone store, from the slender columns on the ground floor to the pilastered dormers at the top. The indented door between two large display windows is a typical arrangement.

32 155 Queen Street East, 1883
Three decades after number 161 was built, a smart store needed much more in the way of architectural bells and whistles. This one accommodates decorative brick, vermicu-lated quoins, four round windows with handsome cast-stone surrounds, brackets, even an iron grace note on top of the Palladian window.

33 147 Queen Street East, 1872
Behind this straightforward brick boom-town façade, Robert Eaton, brother of Timothy, and his son operated a store until 1890.

**34 Andrews Jeweller, 135 Queen
Street East,** 1884
"William Andrews' Palatial Jewelry Esta-blishment," as the St. Marys *Argus* called it in 1886, is a testament to the Victorian

 135 Queen
Street East

37 106 Water Street North

penchant for excess: from bombé glass and wooden trim on the first floor, to carved stone window surrounds on the second, to a mansard roof, cresting, urns, and a clock from the Seth Thomas factory in Connecticut on the third, topped off by a tower. Designed by William Williams, the building still houses a jeweller's shop, and the original syrup-coloured walnut fittings inside ("a model of artistic taste and beauty," according to the *Argus*) are well worth a visit.

35 115 Queen Street East, 1855,
109–113 Queen Street East, 1904
Another good example of two different eras cheek by jowl. Number 115 Queen is a sober early store built of coursed limestone rubble; 109–113 is also restrained, but in the red brick fashionable at the turn of the century. Note the swag decoration on the frieze, one of the classical motifs popular with Queen Anne–style builders. The first floor held a general store, the second a "China Hall" or crockery shop.

Turn north up Water Street past Parkview Drive and Jardine Street.

36 99 Water Street North, ca. 1870
Robert Barbour built this and three other nearby houses for Fanny Moore Adam, a widow and innkeeper. The heavy lintels and dramatic quoins are Barbour leitmotifs. The porch is not original, but the pilastered

door, raked limestone door sill, and lovely half-round Tuscan pilasters on the wall are.

37 106 Water Street North, ca. 1900
An unassuming clapboard house made captivating by reason of its gable. As the nineteenth century waned, bargeboards became simpler, and the builder's attention turned to the area at the peak of the gable, above the so-called collar-tie. A highly textured concoction of diamonds, triangles, and circles, this one compounds the delight by continuing below the collar-tie, with a shingled trapezoid divided into three more triangles.

38 107 Water Street North, ca. 1870
Another of the houses built by Robert Barbour for Fanny Moore Adam, this one was rented out to her sister Jane Stafford and her family. It's tempting to call this squarish, hip-roofed, self-possessed little house a Regency cottage; perhaps more accurately, it's a vernacular building that suited the local materials and climate as well as Barbour's talents. The panelled door, doorcase, and six-over-six windows are all original.

39 111 Widder Street East, 1850s
The smart door is a later addition, but the cottage itself, built of rather rough stone, without quoins and with the windows topped with compound headers, is an early and likeably sturdy piece of work.

41 *146 Wellington Street North*

44 *191 Widder Street East*

40 **130 Wellington Street North,** 1890
Gray Gables, as this limestone hulk was called, is anomalous in St. Marys for its size and ambition. At the same time, it hasn't quite decided what it wants to be: Richardsonian Romanesque (the rocky façade, rounded windows, sandstone trimmings), Château style (large, relatively flat surfaces, steep slate roof, the rounded stone corbels), or something else. The architect, George Gouinlock, who designed the Town Hall on similar principles, seems to have admired Richardsonian Romanesque details without bothering much about the style's dependence on complicated, intersecting masses. As a result, his mostly rectangular building at some points looks affectingly plain, at others almost absent-minded. The Wellington Street façade, with the sandstone-lined gable and Romanesque porch columns, is the most attractive. Built for $10,000 for a local department store magnate, Robert Dickson.

41 **146 Wellington Street North,**
ca. 1880
One of this town's most uninhibited pieces of folk art began life much more primly with the gabled front that faces Wellington Street. On the veranda side, a woodworker made a joyful spectacle with bargeboard, turned posts, superb brackets, and all manner of smaller ornamentation. On the veranda treillage, note the alternation of the open type, where the spindles create

the design, and the solid, where the spoke-shaped voids form the pattern.

42 **St. Marys Presbyterian Church,**
147 Widder Street East, 1879–80
The Gothic Revival style with a tin-topped steeple makes for a very French-looking Presbyterian church. Note the stone corbel tables (the stepped arrangements of smallish brackets, more frequently brick in nineteenth-century churches) that pleasingly define nave and gables. Designed by a Toronto firm, Gordon & Helliwell, Architects.

43 **183 Widder Street East,** ca. 1915,
44 **191 Widder Street East,** 1900,
45 **197 Widder Street East,** 1895
Three big-boned Queen Anne villas with a strong family resemblance bestride the Widder Street hill. The structures are the same: a gabled, projecting three-storey bay with a balconied porch slung across the main front. After that, the fun of comparison begins: two have porches that wrap around the side, two have stone-rimmed elliptical windows in the bay, two have fanciful dormers in the main roof, etc. The most glamorous of the trio, number 191, flaunts a generous assortment of the Queen Anne mix of medieval and classical accoutrements: Ionic columns supporting the rounded porch, rocky lintels and sills, several kinds of shingles, a picturesque triple-flued chimney, and rooftop crenellations

47 *249 Widder Street East*

48 *261 Widder Street East*

that end in Viking-like punctuation points. But that still leaves plenty to admire in its more sedate siblings, particularly in the gable and window treatments. Number 197 (the most "classical" of the houses) was built for David Maxwell Sr., a prominent manufacturer of farm equipment whose hay rakes were nationally celebrated; number 191 was built for his son and business partner David Maxwell Jr.

46 Holy Name of Mary Catholic Church, Peel and Widder Streets, 1892–93

Like the architects of the neighbouring Presbyterian Church a decade earlier, Post & Holmes, the Toronto architects chosen by the Catholics of St. Marys, had a magnificent hilltop site and local limestone at their disposal; Post & Holmes also chose a Gothic Revival style but with a rockier skin, according to the fashion dictates of the 1890s. The preponderance of the steeple gives the church a narrow-shouldered look, and the side roof, with two rows of pointed dormers *and* decorative tiles, is far too busy. But Holy Name of Mary is never less than workmanlike and sometimes very fine, as in the frontispiece and tower that exploit a whole vocabulary of pointed arches, one on top of the other.

47 249 Widder Street East, 1871

Built for Thomas Fogg, a manager of the Grand Trunk Railway, this stylish house is not entirely what it seems. Apparently made of red brick (now painted white), it is actually brick veneer, one layer thick, over frame construction. And the chunky pedimented window headers on the second floor are metal factory-made units that snap on and off. The door, however, is genuine walnut, made for the boss in the Grand Trunk Railway's Sarnia carpentry shops.

48 261 Widder Street East, 1881

The house of Frances McCracken, gentleman, follows a standard Italianate model; the original shutters (actually used in the nineteenth century to moderate extreme heat or cold), the recessed door, and the brick quoins that mimic stone are attractive features in excellent repair. Unlike its neighbour at 249 Widder, this is a true brick house, with walls of three-brick thickness.

Retrace your steps two blocks.

49 196 Widder Street East, 1873

Looking very countrified on a street notable for more showy, citified buildings, this clapboard house was built by two Scottish contractors, James Craig and James Hamilton, for Craig and his family. In addition to their carpentry firm (which worked on the Opera House), Craig and Hamilton ran a planing mill that provided the doors, windows, and wooden trim, such

50 *109 Wellington Street North*

52 *92 Wellington Street North*

as the finials and sinuous bargeboard in the side gables. Its most diverting piece of woodwork, the veranda, was probably added at the turn of the century by its second owner, another carpenter named Michael Tevlin.

50 109 Wellington Street North, 1874
No wonder Dr. John Hugh Mathieson inscribed his name (albeit misspelled as Matheison) on the glass transom: his entrance porch with its fretwork decoration and shutters-cum-door is a robust little hymn to the High Vic virtues of security, domesticity, and pride of ownership. The veranda treillage and railing is graphic and unusual; note the economy-size balls on the railing.

Mathieson obviously had strong feelings about architecture: his own house is an example of Robert Barbour's brick masonry and, as chair of the building committee for the Town Hall, he probably championed the architect George Gouinlock, whose work he was in a position to know well (130 Wellington, also designed by Gouinlock, is just across the street).

51 106 Wellington Street North, 1869
From the front this looks like a handsome hip-roofed cottage, with finely dressed quoins and matching door and window surrounds set in rougher stone walls. The view from Widder Street reveals a much

more sizeable house that slopes down a hill, a feature that required the hand of a master builder, in this case Robert Barbour. This is the finest of the four houses Barbour built for Fanny Adam; she rented it to her sister Margaret Beattie and her merchant husband, Alexander.

52 92 Wellington Street North, 1890
The childhood home of poet David Donnell, who was born in this "well-settled stone town," as he called it, in 1939; his father Arnold Donnell taught classics at St. Marys Collegiate. Without the portico, this is a well-behaved but typical local merger of Gothic and Italianate elements. What lifts it above the ordinary is the sculpted wooden porch and particularly its blossoming wrought-iron balcony.

Return to Queen Street and cross Victoria Bridge.

53 105–107 Queen Street West, 1843, 1914
About two years after Thomas Ingersoll and his brother James founded Little Falls, soon to be St. Marys, Thomas built the settlement's first house, across the river from his sawmill and gristmill. After clearing the land, he quarried the stones from the river; the side wall to the west shows some very hefty boulders and the rough lintels and sills typical of the earliest masonry. In 1914, a storey was added to the original one-and-

54 *144 Queen Street West*

56 *157 Maiden Lane*

a-half-storey house, but the front remains much as built by Ingersoll.

54 144 Queen Street West, 1865
Even the chimneys are limestone in a house full of admirable touches. Among them: the neoclassical door and balconied portico (an 1880s improvement), the exaggeratedly delicate bargeboard on the side gable, compared with the heartier variety on the front, and the prettiest pendant in town. Built for James MacKay, a St. Marys pioneer storekeeper and hotelier.

55 108 Robinson Street, ca. 1870
With its location on the Thames River, the very large windows from which to admire the view, and an air of self-possessed informality, this house suggests the Regency cottage. St. Marys was settled after the style's high point in the first half of the century and, in general, not by the leisured classes who typically built Regency cottages, but the flavour is here. Built by John Henry Clark, gentleman, along with an orchard to the north and the splendid rubblestone carriage house visible from Robinson Street. (Now converted to a house, its address is 107 Ontario Street.)

56 157 Maiden Lane, ca. 1917
A very jolly grafting of Queen Anne accessories – variously shaped shingles, the sunburst motif in the gable, the rafters on the dormer, the dentils that underline the

stained glass and rim the porch, a dormer whose "skirt" extends to the porch – on a clapboard vernacular building. Queen Anne builders favoured extravagant asymmetry but this house is symmetrical.

57 163 Maiden Lane, ca. 1894
One of the last stone houses in St. Marys. The large round-headed windows in the main gable are give-aways to its date, but otherwise this undemonstrative L-shaped house might have been built at any time since the town's founding. The fine-boned porch with its minimal treillage and the heavy stone sills are particularly appealing.

58 60 Ontario Street North, ca. 1855
A very simple "first generation" (i.e., without quoins) stone cottage with compound window headers, built for William Blackwell.

Head south on Ontario Street.

59 52 Ontario Street South, 1858
Built for a prominent Catholic settler, Patrick Whelihan, this stone house has the town's only elliptical fanlight, now obscured by a modern porch.

60 89 Ontario Street South, ca. 1870
Unfortunately for walkers, Mount Pascoe, as one of the grandest houses in St. Marys was called, is difficult to see from either Ontario Street or Thomas Street. The

61 *181 Thomas Street*

63 *216 Thomas Street*

original owner, a lawyer named C.S. Jones, positioned his yellow-brick mansion, a mélange of Georgian and Italianate elements capped by a chic mansard roof, on the peak of a hill in a four-acre park. As the local historian Larry Pfaff notes, Mount Pascoe seems to address itself to another local landmark built on a facing hill, the St. Marys Museum: in 1870, it was owned by Jones's parents-in-law. Like the museum, Mount Pascoe was built by master mason Robert Barbour; the design came from a pattern book by Samuel Sloan. A later, long-time owner, William Dale, was a two-time mayor of St. Marys and a distinguished classicist who taught the writer Ralph Connor at St. Marys Collegiate. Dale is also the subject of James Reaney's play *The Dismissal.*

Cross to Thomas Street via Park Lane to see a good selection of stone cottages built by masons who worked (and often owned) the small quarries that lined this part of the Thames River.

61 181 Thomas Street, 1863
Built by a Scottish stonemason, Alexander Grant, and his son John as their home, this is very nearly the paradigm stone cottage. The neatly coursed stones and the delicacy of the moulded and pilastered door are balanced by the massive lintels and quoins; the hip-roof puts a very satisfying cap on it all. John Grant followed in his father's

footsteps, working on the Opera House, the Victoria Bridge, and the Andrews jewellery store, among others.

62 210 Thomas Street, ca. 1884
Appropriately enough, the stone town's premier carpenter and mason, Robert Barbour, lived in three houses on the street known for its stone cottages; two are still standing. Swinton House, as the Barbours called this Ontario cottage, was the builder's last residence. (He committed suicide in 1898 at the age of seventy-six.) Something of the shoemaker's-children principle may have been in operation here: the house is well designed and built but lacks the finishing touches enjoyed by Barbour's clients.

63 216 Thomas Street, ca. 1865–66
Barbour's penultimate house is far more appealing. The little windows in the gable have their own rather exclamatory headers and protruding sills, and the simple bracketed doorcase is charming.

64 243 Thomas Street, ca. 1870
A cottage built by another accomplished mason, George Falconer. Note the curved lintels and the voussoirs in the peak.

65 257 Thomas Street, ca. 1880
This brick *bijou* was the house (and probably the work) of the architect J.A. Humphris, who designed the Carnegie Library, the First Baptist Church, the additions to

66 *Westover Park, 300 Thomas Street*   66 *Carriage house*

Westover Park across the street, and very probably its wonderful carriage house. His own house was something else again, a tidy orange box banded by mock quoins and window headers in yellow brick, its fancy cornice regularly dripping pairs of brackets. (Ignore the modern garage.)

66 Westover Park, 300 Thomas Street, 1864–67

For a house designed for the "quiet afternoon" of its owners' lives, Westover Park has seen much enlargement and activity, including adaptation as a Roman Catholic seminary in the 1940s and now as a country inn. When only in his forties, William Veal Hutton sold his house and successful milling business on Queen Street and retired with his parents and two brothers to the new house built by another brother, Joseph Osman Hutton. William and Joseph Hutton lived here until their deaths (in 1906 and 1910, respectively), refining and elaborating their vast garden. Of Westover's nineteen acres, seven were actively cultivated, including a celebrated greenhouse, now demolished, and the very Victorian "mound," or artificial hill, to the left of the house.

Lavish as their holdings were, the Huttons' double-gabled house, probably adapted from plans for a suburban villa in the *Canada Farmer* of 1864, was just that: an unpretending, utterly solid suburban villa. Its most attractive features are the three-dimensional bargeboard, the finely framed window above the bay, and, of course, the regularly coursed ashlar and monolithic lintels that strongly suggest the hand of the Huttons' near neighbour Robert Barbour.

The real scene-stealer at Westover is the carriage house, designed in 1911 presumably by J.A. Humphris, a superbly busy building whose façade is a quilt of odd-shaped pieces of planking, stone, shingling, even stained glass. So-called Stick style buildings, of which this is a simplified late-blooming Canadian version, were fashionable in the United States at the end of the nineteenth century; this one has the elaborately decorative timbered surface but not the complicated, cross-gabled shape.

Return to Westover Street and walk two blocks west.

67 Ardmore Park, 186 Salina Street South, ca. 1853–55

Joseph Hutton's first house in St. Marys was a limestone Regency cottage romantically sited on an eleven-acre property. As at Westover Park, its regular courses (unusual for the 1850s) and deep lintels are reminiscent of the work of Robert Barbour, but the builder is not known. Nor is Hutton's reason for selling it almost immediately, in 1855. A subsequent owner, the Irish painter and lawyer Edward Taylor Dartnell, enlarged the house, landscaped

68 *127 Wellington Street South*

74 *Stone house on the St. Maria Street extension west of Water Street South*

the park, and may have given the house its Irish name, Ardmore Park. The two-storey tower was added at the turn of the century.

The following walk on Wellington Street South and Water Street South is an additional loop that features a handful of stone cottages, picturesque verandas, and some early commercial structures.

68 127 Wellington Street South, ca. 1895

Behind the veranda is a vernacular Italianate house with the Palladian window that local carpenters favoured in the first decades of this century. But it's hard to keep your eyes off the veranda, a most diverting piece of wraparound crochet-work.

A cluster of modest turn-of-the-century houses at this end of Wellington Street are decked out with well-preserved wooden trim.

69 146 Wellington Street South (ca. 1900) has a handsome example of barge-board in its last stage, when all the action took place above the collar-tie. The porti-co at **70 164 Wellington Street South** (ca. 1905) is dominated by a sunburst of spindles. **71 165 Wellington Street South** (ca. 1870) is a plain cottage fronted by a veranda very typical in early-twentieth-century St. Marys, its treillage a dainty strip of spindles.

72 317 Wellington Street South, 1860s
The one-and-a-half-storey house that Isaacher Murray, a stonemason, built for himself could hardly be simpler. The modern door interrupts the regular march of lintels over windows and door, but otherwise the exterior is probably unchanged (note the side wall, its austerity broached by only two windows).

73 345 Wellington Street South, 1860s

No one in St. Marys was better acquainted with grandiose stonework than James Elliott, the master mason of the Opera House. But when it came to his own house, he opted for a simple stone Ontario cottage with a high basement and central peak.

74 Stone house on the St. Maria Street extension west of Water Street South, ca. 1850

Built for Gilbert McIntosh, a woollen miller whose mill was to the west of the house. The main building, a little strong-box whose lintels and quoins seem to grow out of the very fabric of the house, is noticeably more rustic than the wing, which dates from the 1860s. That decade preferred its stonework regularly coursed, its quoins and lintels more emphatic. McIntosh's mill, which employed up to twenty people and could turn out about eighty yards of cloth a day, was one of the businesses that languished when Queen

75 *254 Water Street South*

78 *136 Water Street South*

Street became the town's main axis; it went bankrupt in 1870.

75 254 Water Street South, ca. 1880
A charmer, with all kinds of attentive detail – a gable lined with rickrack, a sloped portico with brackets *and* dentils, two glass Gothic doors that open only from the inside.

76 253 Water Street South, ca. 1900
A frame house with Queen Anne leanings. Its vaguely Chinese veranda is a deft mélange of the stock trimmings of the day.

77 223–225 Water Street South,
   ca. 1855
A large-windowed store (number 223) plus smaller-windowed storekeeper's residence (number 225). Part of its urbane look derives from the ashlar masonry on the front, including the frieze that runs across the front and ties house and store together.

78 136 Water Street South,
   1860
If the Brothers Grimm had collected folk tales about Ontario stonemasons, one or two might have taken place here. The gabled front is built of broken-coursed limestone, the sides of coursed rubble. The recessed doorcase, the pedimented lintels, the Gothic window crammed into the peak and surmounted by a keystone add up to an endearing, albeit slightly spooky house. Even the chimney is a diverting piece of

stone patchwork. The original owner was a stonecutter named James Whitson.

79 111, 80 105 Water Street South,
   early 1860s
Two early stone cottages that have been modified with porches and, in the case of number 111, a dormer.

81 84 Water Street South, 1850s
One of the last reminders of the many commercial buildings on Water Street, this was a general store also believed to be the town's first self-standing, full-service bank. (Earlier banks had been part of other businesses, with limited hours.) The Bank of Montreal operated here from 1862 to 1889.

82 48–50 Water Street South,
   1921, 1857, 1869
Three modest, efficient buildings that span a half-century. The limestone building in the middle is the oldest, built in 1857 as a cobbler's shop, with the second floor probably for living quarters. The wooden building began life in 1869 as a house, an indication of the close mix of residential and commercial structures at the time. And, a St. Marys rarity, the diminutive 1921 building made of pressed concrete was a warehouse for fruit, which arrived on the CPR just behind it.

City Hall

Stratford

Meat, Potatoes, and "a Pleasing Air of Comfort"

Tyrone Guthrie, the Stratford Festival's first artistic director, had a genius for publicity, and over the years he burnished his version of the festival's beginnings in 1953 to a fine sheen. In Guthrie's story, a boy from a bucolic Ontario town was inspired by the proverbial high school English teacher with a passion for Shakespeare. The boy, whose name was Tom Patterson, came home from World War II with a naive and audacious idea: he would mount a first-class professional Shakespeare festival in sleepy Stratford.

The truth was that Patterson, who was an expert in municipal sewage systems, had attended two professional stage productions in his life and knew almost nothing about Shakespeare. The idea for the festival really began not in Patterson's visionary rambles along the Avon River but on a tipsy evening at a meeting of the American Waterworks Association. There Patterson and another civil servant talked with Stratford's mayor about ways to boost their city's tourist industry. Patterson recalled, "The basic interest was in Stratford. It wasn't in Shakespeare or literature."

Both Patterson's pragmatism and his civic devotion are typical of Stratford, a town of 27,000 that has steadfastly refused to have its head turned by the presence of a major international festival in its midst. Visitors often assume that the Shakespearean names for Stratford's schools and wards and some of its streets are part of the festival's marketing plan, but they, and the Shakespearean Gardens, preceded the festival by many years. Some priorities never shift in this agricultural district; the welcoming road sign as you approach Stratford gives the Stratford Festival and the annual Ontario Pork Congress equal billing.

Stratford's Shakespearean connection dates from the early 1830s, when the British directors of the land and colonization enterprise called the Canada Company named a dot on a map for the playwright's birthplace. The third of the Canada Company towns, Stratford was halfway between its more favoured older siblings, Guelph and Goderich, and was planned to be no more than a stopover on the road to Goderich. On July 11, 1827, Dr. William "Tiger" Dunlop, the company's "Warden of the Woods and Forests," became the first white man to walk the banks of the nameless river at the site that would become Stratford. As the surveyor in their party, Mahlon Burwell, recorded, it was a typical Stratford day: "It rained and continued to rain until 1 o'clock p.m."

In fact, Stratford's abundant rain and snowfall would be an important component of the settlement's prosperity: the city's location on a plain a thousand feet above sea level makes it the highest city in Ontario as well as the wettest in southern Ontario. The extra five inches of precipitation produced an exceptionally fertile soil, but Dunlop and his party had no thought of a permanent settlement. The place where the river, first called the Little Thames, crossed the Huron Road remained more or less a collection of bark-covered huts for travellers until 1832. In that year an Irishman named William Sargint built the town's first proper building, the Shakespeare Inn. Within five years, the Little Thames had been rechristened the Avon, and Stratford on Avon, Upper Canada, was launched.

The town's growth was not meteoric, and the satire in a 1900 novel, *Committed to His Charge*, by two Stratford sisters, Robina and Kathleen Lizars, about a town called Slowford-on-the-Sluggard was probably well aimed. Some of "Slowford's" problems were obvious. The political agitations of the 1830s discouraged emigration and westward expansion. Far from major waterways at a time when the most reliable transportation was by water, Stratford was swampy, mosquito-ridden, subject to cholera epidemics. It competed for population and services with nearby St. Marys, as well as with its other Canada Company relatives, Guelph and Goderich. And Stratford was very much the company's neglected child. Although company officials in 1834 had commissioned the surveyor John McDonald to design a plan for the city with a population of 35,000, the company did almost nothing to stimulate Stratford's growth. It built a mill and appointed a land agent, but the lion's share of amenities was reserved for Goderich. Elite settlers were lured to the Lake Huron port, and Stratford got a mixture of Irish, Scottish, and German emigrants, with a smattering of English tenant farmers and farm labourers.

When W.H. Smith visited Stratford in 1845, he was hard put to say more for it in his *Gazeteer of Canada* than that it had a population of 200 and mail three times a week. In addition to the usual mills, it had three shoemakers, two tailors, two doctors, and other purveyors of life's necessities. But, as

W. Stafford Johnston, the historian of Perth County, writes, "In a rough and hard-drinking society, the importance of a place could be measured by its liquor outlets." Stratford claimed one distillery, one brewery, and two taverns. Goderich by contrast had three distilleries, two breweries, and five taverns.

W.H. Smith returned to Stratford and its "natural advantages" in 1852 but found little to encourage him. The buildings, he wrote, were generally inferior: "This, however, is not surprising, as an inland place, surrounded by bad roads for a large portion of the year, is scarcely likely to partake largely of a cheerful character; the inhabitants, no matter how enterprising they may be by nature, most frequently, when subjected to the depressing influences of local drawbacks, find their natural animal spirits lowered."

Smith despaired too soon. Stratford was just on the verge of raising its revenues as well as its animal spirits. In 1853 it became the county seat of the newly formed Perth County, and enthusiastically caught the decade's railway fever. Offering bonuses to rail companies, Stratford welcomed "a welter of railways," in the words of its historian Adelaide Leitch (*Floodtides of Fortune*). Changing names, owners, and sometimes gauges, railways came and went with bewildering speed; at one time, Stratford was the intersection point for three of them. Luckily for the city's looks, the most important company, the Grand Trunk, positioned its various depots away from the river and the city centre. Even more luckily for the city's economy, the Grand Trunk moved its locomotive repair shops to Stratford in 1871, and the railways remained the town's biggest employer until the 1950s.

Small wonder that the mayor's chair ordered for Stratford's new City Hall in 1899 has a locomotive carved on its back, or that the stained glass on the landing in the Perth County Court House features a train. The railways formed an important part of Stratford's personality, giving it an industrious, craftsmanlike culture that included a wide-ranging apprenticeship school, a "University of the Mechanical World" recognized throughout the railway world. And the railways brought thousands of new townspeople. By 1874, the population had jumped to 6,000, up from 3,500 in 1859. When Belden described Stratford in his *Illustrated Atlas of the County of Perth* in 1879, he noted some of Ontario's best business blocks, streets lined with shade trees and "a pleasing air of comfort."

The town Belden saw is still largely intact, and in some ways even more pleasant than in its Victorian glory days. The river that snakes through Stratford has been central to its history, supplying power, transportation, and recreation. Horses raced on the Avon's frozen length in winter, large baptismal groups were immersed in it, and, if you believe the local talk, at least half the people of Stratford were conceived along its shores. Reclaimed in this century from neglect and industry, the Avon has never been prettier. The 173 acres of parkland along the river and Lake Victoria contain gardens, islands, walking paths, tennis courts, and boats and canoes for rent. Two Shakespearean touches in this pastoral landscape are the swans that have been patronizing the Avon since 1918, and the Shakespearean Gardens between the Avon and the Court House.

But Stratford is not really a beauty spot, in spite of what the festival's glossy brochures will tell you. It remains the robust, refreshingly dowdy market town it has been for over a century, and that accounts for a large part of its appeal. Its failure to be picturesque is partly a function of its age: like the other Canada Company towns, Stratford developed in the solid middle decades of the century after the fine-boned Loyalist and massively elegant Greek Revival styles had had their day. Along with the perennial Ontario favourite, Gothic Revival, Stratford's paramount styles are Italianate and Queen Anne. The showy Second Empire fashion of the 1870s was slightly *de trop* and put on airs. In the eyes of Stratford's burghers, a domesticated Italianate building was solid and just prosperous-looking enough; Queen Anne's lavishness and fantasy were scaled down to match the local sensibility.

At least as influential as Stratford's mid-century beginnings was its psyche: the practical merchants, railway men, and retired farmers who peopled the town were relentless renovators and improvers rather than aesthetes, people who didn't trouble overmuch about a house's proportions when it came to adding garages and dormers. There are very few blocks in Stratford where well enough has been left alone, with the attendant loss in charm.

A key part of Stratford's style derives from one of its chief building blocks: the buff-yellow brick of southwestern Ontario, called white brick in the nineteenth century. Not everyone liked it: "Horrid white brick," Oscar Wilde sniffed when he saw Toronto in 1882, "with its shallow colour spoiling the effect of the architecture." But for much of nineteenth-century southwestern Ontario, a yellow-brick house was a matter of necessity.

Nineteenth-century Ontario builders never shared the American affection for wood, and a series of disastrous fires in London and Toronto in the first half of the century confirmed their belief in brick. The clay used in those early brickyards was often Erie clay, which a 1906 Bureau of Mines report claimed covered western Ontario with a "mantle" that ranged in depth from one foot to at least 130 feet. Most important for the look of Ontario, bricks made from it emerged from the kiln a subdued yellow.

Erie clay also produced red bricks, but only from the top layer of clay, when rain and snow had washed away the lime but left the reddish iron. The abundant supply of yellow bricks combined with a much smaller cache of red bricks largely determined the appearance of southwestern Ontario cities and towns such as London and Stratford. Often renouncing even the showiness of accent colours, builders in these centres emphasized the bricks' resemblance to stone with a painted yellow or buff trim the same shade as the bricks. These reassuringly monochromatic, utterly solid-looking houses, often Italianate or Gothic, are typical of the first few generations of Stratford houses.

By the turn of the century, fashionable home-owners were tired of the local product and ready for something more exotic: red brick, which they imported from around Toronto. In addition to its novelty, red brick suited the warmly romantic Richardsonian Romanesque and Queen Anne styles in favour at the time. But even when Stratford heeded fashion it remained, in the words that *Weekend* magazine used to describe its pre-festival personality, a "meat and potatoes town...a genteel but shabby railroad switching center."

Shabby is no longer accurate, and the railroads left Stratford in the early 1950s, taking 2,000 jobs with them when steam was replaced by diesel. Today the town has a mixed industrial base, with automotive and luggage factories predominant. But the kernel of *Weekend's* description is still true of a downright town that loves its river, its parks, even its theatre festival, but keeps them in commonsensical perspective. In *Floodtides of Fortune*, Adelaide Leitch tells a favourite Stratford story of two old women who walked by the Festival Theatre's mammoth parking lot during a performance of *Richard III*. They noted about a dozen unoccupied parking spaces, and one woman gloated to the other, "You see! I told you this thing would never last!"

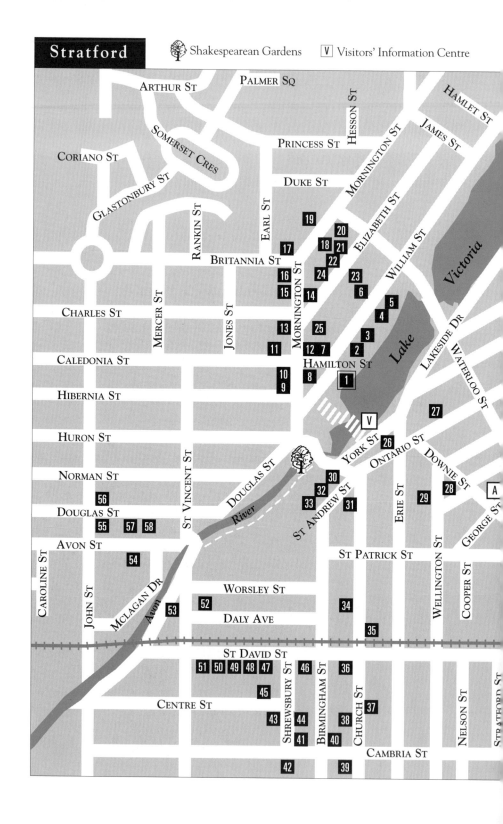

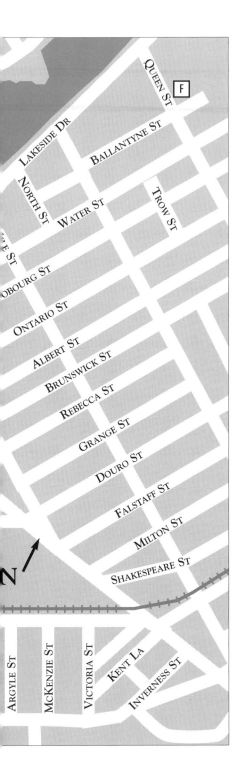

30 *Perth County Court House,*
1 Huron Street

4 **5** *101, 109, 113 William Street*

Lake Victoria

1 *53 William Street*

5 *113 William Street*

Beginning at the Visitors' Information Centre, cross the bridge and turn right on William Street.

1 53 William Street, 1880
A handsome Italianate house in Stratford's trademark yellow brick, built for Samuel Robb, registrar. The detail lavished on the veranda alone, from the bevelled posts topped with shelves and dentils to the incised trim on the arches to the dentilled and decorated frieze above that, is a good sampler of late-Victorian motifs and techniques.

2 63 William Street, 1875
Built by a family of carpenters named Todd, this modest board-and-batten cottage just suits its lakeside setting. Originally its front-facing gable presented a bolder profile; the second-storey "wings" were punched out later.

3 69 William Street, ca. 1876
The bell-cast roof on the entrance porch lifts this house's spirits, as does the line of lovely pendant-dripping brackets that supports the deep eaves (best seen at the side closer to number 63). Otherwise it's a serious house, its brackets borrowed from the Italianate style, but its mostly straight lines and symmetry hark back to a vernacular Georgian. (The addition to the side is newer, as evinced by the brick colour.) In 1877, this property was home

to ten people, one cow, four horses, and one dog.

4 101, 109 William Street, 1907–08
A jolly pair of near-twins sit side by side on the lake. In a compromise typical of vernacular Ontario architecture, lots of *au courant* details – the second-floor windows like open books placed downward, the classical porch with oversize dentils and clusters of colonettes like bowling pins – were applied to a plainish yellow-brick body. Number 101 was built for Thomas Henry, a plumber who became Stratford's mayor; 109 was intended for a contractor named Paschal Pigeon.

5 113 William Street, before 1857
William "Boss" Easson built a house next to his waterside sawmill and furniture warehouse and was renowned for supervising his workers from his first-floor bedroom. In 1876, he tarted up the original house into a top-heavy Second Empire belle, and the assessment jumped from $1,600 to $8,000. Easson's Frenchified taste included coloured glass, elaborately moulded plaster ceilings, and five fireplaces. Avon Castle, as his house was called, was a Conservative gathering-place, and Sir John A. Macdonald danced here. (Easson also built a row of cottages that stretched from number 113 to Waterloo Street, for his mill workers to rent.)

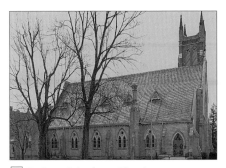

8 *St. James' Anglican Church,*
41 Mornington Street

9 *36 Mornington Street*

6 **114 William Street,** ca. 1855
Rev. Ephraim Patterson, the first incumbent of St. James' Church, moved into this hip-roofed Ontario cottage in 1857. The pilastered, classical doorcase lends a touch of *gravitas* to the simple, one-storey house.

7 **11 Hamilton Street,** 1890–91
Kathleen and Robina Lizars, the daughters of Judge Daniel Lizars, wrote their anecdotal, semi-fictional histories *In the Days of the Canada Company* (1896) and *Humours of '37* (1897) in this house, as well as a more scandalous Stratford *roman-à-clef* about a certain Anglican rector in Slowford-on-the-Sluggard (*Committed to His Charge*, 1900). Their house (with an altered front door) has a flat-featured, rather puzzling quality. You look in vain for an organizing principle, but the point here is more the impressive range of materials deployed by *fin-de-siècle* builders: standard red brick, decorative brick, sandstone, two kinds of shingles, two kinds of planking, stained and clear glass.

8 **St. James' Anglican Church,**
41 Mornington Street, 1868–70
The Stratford Anglicans waited thirty years for their yellow-brick church, worshipping successively in the Shakespeare Inn, the log schoolhouse, a frame church on the present site, and a red-brick church so unsightly that Stratfordians tried to prevent visitors from seeing it. (Perhaps

for this reason, no picture of the second church exists; it was demolished in 1867.) For their third church, the parishioners commissioned the celebrated Toronto church architects Gundry & Langley. They chose the so-called Decorated Gothic style, described in the local paper as echoing "the earliest and purest style of Gothic architecture." In theory that meant ogee curves, elaborate ornamentation, and unexpected vistas; what that became at St. James' was a vertical, asymmetric, but by no means highly decorated church. The tower was added in 1909; the modest turret on the non-tower side is a nice touch. The prices of materials and labour are illustrative: the architects were paid $300, yellow brick from nearby Brantford cost $595, painting and staining $246, excavating and teaming $110. The interior of St. James' is difficult to see except during services, but royalists should make the extra effort and enter through the parish hall: the bright blue carpet in the chancel was made for the coronation of Elizabeth II in Westminster Abbey and sold afterwards to a number of lucky parishes.

9 **36 Mornington Street,** ca. 1880
One of the prettiest versions of a typical Stratford house, the L-shaped yellow-brick Italianate. This one has a vertical and very *soigné* look, with the slim windows encompassing the two-storey bay and the storm door and flossy veranda

10 *46 Mornington Street*   11 *14 Caledonia Street*

stashed neatly into the angle of the L.

10 46 Mornington Street, 1863
When Thomas Birch, tinsmith, arrived in Stratford in 1857, the village had only three brick houses. His own Ontario cottage has several chic touches: the steeply pitched hip-roof, the strip of bichromatic diaperwork under the eaves, the proud chimney-stacks, the yellow-brick quoins, and the rounded Italianate windows and door that were newer than the pointed Gothic. The grandiose curved portico replaced the original.

11 14 Caledonia Street, 1905
Complicated but rarely complex, Queen Anne houses are eager to be liked. This one, with the requisite tower, balcony, porch, bay, and dormer sheathed in red brick and shingles, is a particularly pleasing example. The oval window embraced by a drip mould and keystone (on the side next to the balcony) is the kind of elegant Palladian detail that Queen Anne builders liked to domesticate – in this case, by setting it in shingles.

12 71 Mornington Street, 1921
In *Craftsman Homes* (1909), the American designer Gustav Stickley praised the bungalow as a "primitive dwelling" whose "low broad proportions and absolute lack of ornamentation" made it at home anywhere. This one, with its little shed dormer peep-

ing out from the massive roof, the exposed rafters, and the mixture of materials – a novelty striated brick popular in the '20s, stucco, and wood – is a typical example of this doughty style. Dr. Lorne Robertson built it for his parents, Dr. and Mrs. J.A. Robertson; the Drs. Robertson practised briefly with Norman Bethune.

13 90 Mornington Street, 1865
Two bays, one pointed gable with airy treillage, and a trefoil underneath add up to a classic Gothic cottage. The neoclassical door was not part of the picturesque package but remained an Ontario favourite. The Stratford Festival owned this house and actor Mervyn Blake lived here; it was apparently his suggestion that the steps be modelled in the shape of the festival stage. Ignore the dubious portico.

14 109 Mornington Street, 1877
A delightful house blending bay-and-gable with Italianate brackets. Best of all is the elaborate veranda, especially the storm porch, whose round door is rimmed by cording and delicate little corded pillars, then embraced by rounded windows. If a storm porch could aspire to the condition of a petit four, this is it. Appropriately, the house's first owner, John Gibson, was a baker and confectioner. Its neighbour number 119 has a very similar plan minus much of the charm.

15 *122 Mornington Street*

18 *153 Mornington Street*

15 122 Mornington Street, 1875–76
Three Gables, as this house was inevitably called, looks more formidable without the loopy bargeboard that originally softened the gables. Note the tactful dimensional effects achieved with brick on the window surrounds on front and sides, the pilastered doorframe, and the quoins.

16 126 Mornington Street, 1879
This high straight house with its tiny ineffectual gable (a typical Stratford touch) looks featureless at first, but try to see it early or late in the year, before the vine obscures a handsome series of arcades and corbels on the front and sides. The doorcase looks like a twentieth-century classical revival afterthought.

17 2 Britannia Street, 1900–01
Finely situated at the crossroads of Mornington and Britannia Streets, this Queen Anne house flaunts the usual mix of classical (pillared porch, pediments, Venetian window) and medieval (fairy-tale tower, decorative brickwork) elements. So-called white brick was an unusual choice for a Queen Anne house; most tended to be red brick or wooden in Canada. Built for a dentist named W.R. Hamilton.

18 153 Mornington Street, 1879
Theoretically the Gothic gable aspires heavenward, but all the slanting lines on this copybook cottage – the gable, the main roof, and the veranda, even the finials on the bargeboard – seem to point downward, the better to emphasize its sheltering function.

19 186 Mornington Street, 1873–74
John Corrie, who described himself variously as a hotelkeeper, road inspector, contractor, and gentleman, built himself a reserved yellow-brick house whose elegantly framed windows are best seen at the sides. Around 1939, a subsequent owner attempted an Ontario version of Tara with this massive pillared portico and swollen doorcase with a broken pediment.

20 72 Waterloo Street, 1859
Stratford's earliest settlement was to the south of the Avon; this is one of the first houses built north of the river. Always a bit out of date in the cautious Ontario way, it was originally a Loyalist-type house built on property that stretched to the river. The gable with the Gothic ogee-topped window came later, after the Gothic craze had passed. Built for an attorney named John Sidney-Smith, the house was kept in the same family for more than 125 years.

Elizabeth Street between Waterloo and Mornington is a block of mostly plain-Jane houses, but in the middle a companionable yellow-brick quartet is worth admiring.

22 *54 Elizabeth Street*

25 *5 Elizabeth Street*

21 62 Elizabeth Street, 1905

Queen Anne builders were indebted to picturesque styles for their irregular massing and variety of window types and sizes, but they turned classical when it came to the details. This house sports Tuscan pillars, dentils, a swan's-neck pediment, swags, and garlands; the rosettes at the top of the oriel window are especially fetching.

22 54 Elizabeth Street, 1897

The prettiest of the four, number 54 has the same basic structure as number 62 but contrives to look taller and slenderer. Where its neighbour's trimmings derived from the classical side of the Queen Anne style, this one is a potpourri of late-Victorian bits and pieces: the round Romanesque windows, the collar-tie bargeboard in the gable, the dainty portico and side porch laden with Eastlake-style knobs, spindles, and circular forms. The posts that resemble table legs are another bow in the direction of the English furniture designer Charles Eastlake.

23 55 Elizabeth Street, 1878

The hip-roof rises to a little black lace cupola that is more seductive than the rest of this rather serious house. The brick "frame" under the cornice that curves and then runs down the sides and is emphasized by the length of the brackets is a graceful touch.

24 48 Elizabeth Street, 1897

The builder nodded to fashion with the Romanesque windows, but saw no reason to give up a good thing – in this case, the chunky Ontario cottage – just because it was thirty or more years behind the times.

25 5 Elizabeth Street, 1896

Built by R. Thomas Orr, a leading Stratfordian and one of the prime movers behind the local parks system, this affable house is a sampler of Queen Anne traits: the dark red brick lightened by painted white woodwork, the roomy classical porch with twin Tuscan columns set on pedestals, the pediment hung with shingles, the free and easy mix of English vernacular elements (the oriel window and trim that hints at half-timbering) with classical (the prettified ornaments in the pediments and the dentils in the main pediment).

Return to downtown Stratford, admiring the early gravestones scattered on the lawn of St. James', crossing the bridge to York Street, and then walking through York Close to the north side of Ontario Street.

26 North side of Ontario Street between Church and Erie Streets

In 1863, the Stratford council prohibited frame buildings on Ontario Street; by 1879, Belden's *Illustrated Atlas of the County of Perth* found "some of the finest business blocks" in the province on Ontario Street.

64 Ontario Street

28 City Hall, Wellington and Downie Streets

Many of the buildings in this first block were built in the 1860s, when the curved windows of the Italianate fashion coexisted with the restraint and symmetry of the older neoclassical style. Individual details catch the eye: the sturdy High Vic brackets on the shopfront frieze of number 34, the bichromatic strip of diaperwork on numbers 22–24 and 26 that ties together a yellow-brick and a red-brick building, the door set in the corner at number 54 (formerly the Albion Hotel, built in 1855). But the block as a whole, with a certain unstrained unity in diversity, adds up to more than the sum of its parts.

27 North side of Ontario Street between Erie and Waterloo Streets
More extroverted and firmly knit together, the next block of Ontario Street is a sturdy red-brick row. Some of the third stories were added in the 1880s, while other buildings date entirely from that robust decade, and the rhythm of brackets, piers, strips of ornamental brickwork, and windows of every shape at the same elevation makes for a richly dimensional block. Note that, beginning with number 78, the buildings come in groups of two.

Return to the beginning of this block and turn sharply left onto Downie Street.

28 City Hall, Wellington and Downie Streets, 1899
In the early morning of November 24, 1897, between bookings for a Scottish concert and a Hibernian ball, Stratford's combined city hall, market, and theatre burned beyond repair. The replacement, designed by the Toronto architects George King and John Wilson Siddall, takes possession of its triangular site with an almost bewildering busyness, manipulating two curved rectangles, a triangle, and a hexagon into a Ruritanian fantasy. Strictly speaking, the City Hall belongs at the Jacobean end of the Queen Anne spectrum, but the shape, the flag tower, the white-painted scrollwork, and the finials give it a jovially ersatz Mittel Europa feel. The dark red brick was the third choice: the architects wanted buff-coloured brick and the councillors pined for the even paler brick of the original Italianate hall, but when the local brickyard over-fired its batch of so-called white, red won the day. In *Floodtides of Fortune*, Adelaide Leitch described the result (before the trim was painted white) as "an enormous, russet-brown plum pudding squatting in the middle of the square." Note the terracotta seals on both sides of the main door celebrating Industry and Enterprise with bas-reliefs of a train and beehive.

29 *38–46 Wellington Street*

30 *Perth County Court House, 1 Huron Street*

29 38–46 Wellington Street, 1880

The space behind City Hall was a market until 1913 and is still ringed with late-Victorian commercial buildings. Like a great piece of red basketwork dominating Market Square, the Worth Block is one of Stratford's most satisfying buildings. Built as a hotel by William Worth, it retains the original slate roof whose sheen acts as a foil for the earthy bricks. The brickwork itself is a bravura, captivating design involving chequerboards, latticework, corbels, Romanesque arches, pilasters, and piers.

Retrace your steps along Wellington and Downie Streets, turning left at Ontario Street.

30 Perth County Court House, 1 Huron Street, 1885–87

When you approach Stratford from the east, Perth County Court House is visible for miles. The light, bright profile is first apparent, then the bold colour scheme: the mauvy shade of Credit Valley sandstone, yellow brick, rusty terracotta and painted wood. When local judges complained that jailyard odours and poor ventilation in the original courthouse-cum-jail were making them ill, the county council hired the London architect George Durand to build a new complex. The courthouse he designed is a mélange of Italianate, Queen Anne, and Richardsonian Romanesque elements. The Richardsonian Romanesque round

arches, contrasting textures, and massive stone foundation dominate, but this is not a heavy, ground-hugging building typical of the style. Its height and colour scheme, the jaunty heft and flare of the openwork tower, the proliferation of terracotta details give it a sunniness not usually associated with courthouses. The allegorical terracotta roundels and plaques repay close inspection, particularly the "benediction" roundels above the main door. Inside, there's a cornucopia of late-Victorian decoration in mint condition: encaustic tile floors, symbolic stained glass, the carved oak staircase. Durand himself designed the ecclesiastical-looking jury box and prisoner's box and the Eastlake pews in the butterscotch-and-cream-coloured courtroom.

In one short block, St. Andrew Street exemplifies quite a lot of civilization and its discontents. With the side of the Court House in full view, the library, archives, jail, St. Andrew's Presbyterian Church, and the high school stand in line, each offering its own version of peace, order, and good government.

31 Stratford Library, 19 St. Andrew Street, 1902, 1926

Like many Ontario libraries, Stratford's started as a Mechanics' Institute, designed to encourage adult education for the working man. Those egalitarian origins made an awkward match with the American mil-

32 *Stratford-Perth Archives,*
24 St. Andrew Street

36 *136 Church Street*

lionaire and sweatshop proprietor Andrew Carnegie, who offered $15,000 to erect a library building. After much resistance, the library board finally prevailed and an ungrateful citizenry accepted Carnegie's largesse, but his name never appeared on the building. The Edwardian Classical structure, the oldest Carnegie library in Canada still in use as a library, acquired its new front in a 1926 expansion designed by a Stratford architect, J.S. Russell. (The front door originally faced St. Andrew Street.) The change from the turn-of-the-century vigour of the original orange brick with dark mortar and rusticated stone to the smoother, pinker bricks and cool grey cut stone favoured by the 1920s is visible from the side.

32 Stratford-Perth Archives, 24 St. Andrew Street, 1910

One of the town's unsung charmers, the former registry office plays little sister to the Court House. Dressed in the same yellow brick, sandstone, terracotta, and wood, with a sandstone door that mimics the Court House door, all firmly banded in rusticated stone and brackets, it may be less accomplished but ends up being more lovable.

33 Stratford Jail, 30 St. Andrew Street, 1886

Designed as a companion to the Court House by its architect, George Durand,

the jail has a surprisingly domestic front. Ontarians were quite used to having their jails in the centre of town, but Durand's architectural euphemism may suggest the end of an older, more bare-faced acknowledgment of the fact of imprisonment. Originally the jail looked even more genial, with shutters, finials, and the trim painted dark red to match the Court House; today, the modern round awnings and white paint consort oddly with the barred windows.

Turn onto Birmingham Street, then left on St. Patrick and right on Church Street.

34 112 Church Street, 1863

A fair variety of styles are living harmoniously here: a Gothic Revival peak and window, classical pilasters and double cornice, and – the latecomer – a Tudor storm porch with an almost Oriental swing to its bargeboard.

35 123 Church Street, 1877–78

The plan for this popular Italianate house with the protruding frontispiece appeared in the *Canada Farmer* in 1865. Early in this century it became a hotel where a room and home-cooked meals cost $8 a week.

36 136 Church Street, 1863

The front-facing gable with the large doorcase placed at the side is a Greek Revival arrangement here trimmed with Gothic

38 *182 Church Street*

41 *220 Cambria Street*

Revival bargeboard and treillage; the veranda that takes an unexpected turn to the side is part of the home-made charm.

37 169 Church Street, 1879

A tall, perfectly proportioned Italianate charmer with an Eastlake porch tucked modestly to the side. For once the characteristic Stratford gable that perches at the very top of a bay is detailed enough that it doesn't look perfunctory.

38 182 Church Street, 1892

This bluff red-brick house looks like an overblown bay-and-gable that sprouted side additions. The stained glass, the round Romanesque window, and the rusticated brick chequerboards set into the façade are all turn-of-the century touches, as is the Queen Anne sunburst in the gable. The irresistible entrance porch is in the Eastlake style, here slightly enlarged to suit this house. The first owner was Thomas Ballantyne, a cheese dealer who founded the Black Creek Cheese Factory and became Speaker of the Ontario legislature.

39 208 Church Street, 1889

Fir Holme, as this house was called, was built as an angular, late-period bay-and-gable with a tiny entrance porch trimmed with bargeboard. By 1900, a porch that swept around two sides of the house was considered essential; this custom-made version sports a front pediment, a pleasant

rounded intermission at the corner, and dressed limestone bases from nearby St. Marys. As you turn onto Cambria Street, admire the two tall chimneys with the pleated insets in the chimney walls made by diagonally set bricks.

40 200 Cambria Street, 1895–96

Slightly more vertical than the big-boned Queen Annes on this street, this is a Queen Anne nonetheless, anchored to its corner lot by the characteristic corner tower. Derived from the *tourelles* of the Loire Valley châteaux, the home-grown version here is handsomely ringed with a row of sandstone corbels.

41 220 Cambria Street, 1895–96

A "hideous crystallization of the worst parts of Victorian architecture" was how a recent owner, Mrs. Wallace McCutcheon, described her house, perhaps affectionately. She also complained that it was "Queen Anne in front and Mary Ann behind," a reference to the bad late-century habit of squandering all the interesting massing and ornamentation on the front. Actually, this delectable mountain has more in common with the weighty, round-arched Richardsonian Romanesque style than with Queen Anne. The immense arch over the front door topped with a trio of smaller, rather Moorish arches, whose lines are continued by the round windows in the flanking towers, makes a bold Richardsonian statement.

42 *227 Cambria Street*

43 *48 Shrewsbury Street*

Note the rusticated brick chequerboard above the main arch and the use of rounded and rusticated bricks in the arch itself. James Stamp designed it for Thomas Trow, a surveyor and the grandfather of Mrs. McCutcheon.

42 227 Cambria Street, 1873
The three bravura Gothic gables clamour for attention, but below them, this is a yellow-brick house in the Italianate style with rounded door and windows. The veranda lines are still visible on the brick. Alexander Hepburn, a Scottish-trained builder and architect who became Stratford's city architect in the 1880s, built it for a farmer named William McGuigan.

On your way down Shrewsbury turn back to see how 227 Cambria's triple gables close off the street.

43 48 Shrewsbury Street, 1872,
  second storey added 1879
One of Stratford's finest houses, seen to best advantage when sun and shade play across its subtle, dimensional effects, all achieved in brick. Although the second floor was added seven years after the first, only a change in brick colour on the second floor facing Centre Street gives the game away. Note the eared surround of the first-floor window opposite the bay, which is then topped by a Tudor label; the window directly above it has its own equally grave, elaborate, eyebrow-topped frame. The very deep cornice that finishes with pinking trim and the double corner lot are other grace notes.

44 43 Shrewsbury Street, 1890
Playing country cousin to number 48's city mansion, this endearing Italianate box has an undeniable family resemblance to the sophisticate across the street. Its rooflines and broad-ribbed cornice echo the slope of the veranda roof and the crochet-like strip of treillage underneath it; even the asymmetry of the door contributes to the unpretentious appeal.

45 20 Centre Street, 1891
Unique in Stratford, this very American-looking house is full of distinctive aspects, beginning with the side entrance and the narrow clapboard. Its balloon-frame construction, an efficient method invented in the U.S. in the 1830s that placed the frame of the house mostly on the outside, was often used for pattern-book houses. This one, however, is believed to have been designed by an architect; the detail around the first-floor window on the street side alone, with its pilasters, moulding, frieze, and bell-cast little roof, makes that a plausible guess. Notice how the windows on the next two floors decrease in size and detail while they continue the basic two-part structure. Built for David Davidson Hay, a merchant and politician from nearby

48 *325 St. David Street*

51 *351–353 St. David Street*

Listowel who served as the registrar for North Perth.

46 265 St. David Street, 1864–66
An Italianate house politely sectioned off with quoins and a string course was no longer quite the thing by the turn of the century. This one's owner, Joseph Walsh of Walsh Bros. Grocers, added its huge, unconvincing Beaux Arts carapace sometime after 1897, making the central tower look like a very inadequate party hat.

47 313 St. David Street, 1873
In 1873, the Stratford *Beacon* reported, "Tenders for Mr. J.G. Smith's new residence, St. David Street, were opened on Saturday and Mr. Thos. Orr's being the lowest, was accepted at 5,390 dollars for the whole work." The classical porch (which was probably added around 1913) obscures the architect Alexander Hepburn's handsome variation on the Italianate plan published in the *Canada Farmer* in 1865 and built throughout the province. Other refinements on the basic pattern include a prettily pillared front door, the double brackets supporting the deep eaves, the panel-trimmed cornice, and the double round-headed second-floor windows finely outlined by brick and stone eyebrow headers.

48 325 St. David Street, 1938
A very likeable Georgian Revival house, built for Dr. H.B. Kenner on the foun-

dations of an 1866 house. The doorcase with its swan's-neck pediment and pilasters, the steep roof, tall side chimneys, dormers, and modillion cornice are all typically Georgian; the rough stone is not, but it effectively counterpoints all the civilized symmetry.

49 335 St. David Street, ca. 1869
The first and simplest of three Gothic Revival houses built within a few years of one another, this typical Ontario cottage is the work of a carpenter named James Moore, who lived here with his family.

50 343 St. David Street, ca. 1870
A slightly more elaborate Ontario cottage, built by and possibly for another carpenter, James Greenley. Greenley appreciated the changes that could be rung on two colours of brick: in addition to the same diaper-work in the frieze as seen at number 335, he devised the recessed plaques under the windows, the bold headers above them, and a distinctive brick pattern in the place of quoins. A subsequent owner, Thomas Orr, added the classical portico sometime around World War I, as well as the Queen Anne–style windows on the first floor and an addition to the rear.

51 351–353 St. David Street, ca. 1867
St. David Street's *pièce de résistance* is a smashing many-gabled house, built by John Holmes, a contractor also responsible for a

 100 Daly Avenue

54 51 Avon Street

trio of local churches: St. James' Anglican, St. Joseph's Catholic, and Knox Presbyterian. Holmes put his ecclesiastical experience to good use here, with an ogee curve above the main door (echoed in all the second-floor windows), an oriel window, trefoils in the bargeboard, and exclamatory finials. (The original verandas probably echoed the main door's ogee curve too.) Even the graphic use of yellow-brick trim had churchy origins: the English writer John Ruskin recommended what he called "constructional polychromy," a brick stand-in for the flat surfaces and multicoloured stone and marble designs of Italian churches. Fashionable colonial architects followed suit in the 1860s and '70s, for houses as well as churches, and Ontario's stocks of red and yellow bricks made possible the style's vivid effects.

52 100 Daly Avenue, 1896

Dun-Edin – the name is inscribed on a sandstone plaque on the bay nearer the door and signed by its proud maker, R.B. Barber, Arch. – was built for a jailor named Hugh Nichol, but this house is far from dour. Like most Queen Anne builders, the Stratford architect Robert Barber preferred cheerfulness to dignity: the asymmetrical, vaguely Chinese entrance porch, the bay with the Juliet balcony that addresses itself to St. Vincent Street, the oddly abrupt, solid bargeboards all contribute to the jaunty total.

53 42 St. Vincent Street, 1874

When the proportions are impeccable, just a soupçon of detail on the gable and the recessed door is all that's necessary. The flowing bargeboard and finial are original.

Cross the Avon and turn left.

54 51 Avon Street, ca. 1875

A bracketed Italianate house adapted to a local variant (the "Stratford" storm porch still with its original glass) and a fashionable Second Empire roof with no loss of charm or poise. Every bell and whistle is tacked into the appropriate place here, from the brick diapers set precisely between the brackets to the double string course that marks the slight difference in height between the storm porch and the two pretty bays. From 1883 to 1919, this was the Annie MacPherson Home for Boys, designed to bring destitute English children to the Gospel and fresh Canadian air. Apparently some remained unimpressed by all this architectural good behaviour: a Stratford souvenir pamphlet of 1898 assured readers that "the altogether unworthy ones are returned to England."

55 171 Douglas Street, 1891

The symmetry of the two matching bays is not a Queen Anne characteristic, although the red brick with white painted woodwork, the corner brackets, and the gables hung with shingles and filled in with spindled

56 *170 Douglas Street*

57 *159 Douglas Street*

and fretted ornaments (available for $7 or $8 from a catalogue or a local planing mill) are. Queen Anne designers made a specialty of chimneys, so suggestive of domesticity and solidity, building them tall and proud and emphasizing their presence on the external wall: this house is most attractive on the John Street side, where the decorative bricks set in an arcade point to the chimney within. The designer was a Stratford architect, Harry J. Powell; the original owner was James Stamp, a builder, who rented it to William Maynard, a banker.

56 170 Douglas Street, 1924

Nothing but the best for Gordon Rankin, owner of Rankin Ice Cream Parlour. He commissioned an architect from Toronto, stonemasons from Scotland, and limestone from Indiana for his Tudor Revival house. The double-gabled symmetrical front, the large expanses of steep roofs, the casement windows, the combination of rough stone and stucco added up to a nostalgic style that appealed mightily to prosperous Ontarians in the 1920s. The woodwork, with all gumwood trim, was done by Stratford's celebrated furniture company, McLagan's, and the master suite had one of Stratford's first showers.

57 159 Douglas Street, 1876

The attention-grabber here is the veranda with the keyhole-shaped arches, one of the bolder devices in the Queen Anne repertoire and probably added some twenty years after the house was built. The corner brackets in the bays that meet to form a kind of protective hood are almost identical to those next door at number 171; such typical Queen Anne accessories could be bought ready-made for $3 or less. Originally the home of Judge John A. Barron.

58 151 Douglas Street, 1868

The date, the three gables, and the lovely ogee curves in the windows in the smaller gables suggest that this house was built by John Holmes, the church builder who built 351–353 St. David Street (51 above). (When the trees are in leaf, you may have to venture up the driveway for a better view.) Built for a barrister named Robert Smith, the house acquired its distracting porch early in this century.

Conclude by going back across the bridge on St. Vincent Street to the path that leads to the Shakespearean Gardens. When the path ends at the schoolyard, keep going until you enter the gardens. A long thin primrose path of dalliance between the Court House and the Avon, they include a perennial garden, an herb garden, an Elizabethan knot garden, and a garden planted with varieties mentioned in Shakespeare's plays. The 1910 smokestack is the remainder of the E.T. Dufton woollen mill, which occupied this site from 1874 until it burned in 1919.

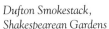

Dufton Smokestack,
Shakespearean Gardens

$\boxed{\text{F}}$ *Festival Theatre*

The Stratford Festival's two main theatres are not on the walking tour, but both have historical interest. In the case of the Festival Theatre, the design is a very particular solution to the notoriously difficult thrust stage – and a salute to the festival's beginnings.

$\boxed{\text{A}}$ Avon Theatre, Downie Street, 1901
Behind its nondescript 1967 façade and modern use as the Stratford Festival's second stage is an equally nondescript turn-of-the-century building and a rich history of vaudeville, straight theatre, and moving pictures. Built to replace the theatre in the original Town Hall by one of Stratford's most active impresarios, Albert Brandenberger, it was called Theatre Albert and probably designed by a Stratford architect named Harry J. Powell. The 1,100-seat theatre opened for business with *The Female Drummer* and hosted all the big-name touring companies of the day, from Maude Adams to the Dumbells. Unlike the Festival Theatre, Theatre Albert was (and remains) a conventional proscenium-arch theatre with adequate stage dimensions (thirty-two by fifty-four feet) and a small-ish orchestra pit.

By 1910, Brandenberger had renamed it the Griffin and billed it as "The House of Polite Vaudeville and Motion Pictures." In the 1940s it became the Avon moviehouse; in 1956 it returned to its theatrical beginnings with Jean Gascon's production of three Molière farces.

$\boxed{\text{F}}$ Festival Theatre, 1956
No doubt about it, the Stratford Festival's main stage *looks* festive, as well as very much a creature of its decade. Partly a parasol, partly a crown, it remains a radical departure for theatres. Tanya Moiseiwitsch and Tyrone Guthrie, the festival's designer and artistic director respectively, designed the challenging thrust stage, which for the first three seasons was enclosed by an enormous tent. The tent and seating were designed by the late Robert Fairfield, the designer of the Ontario pavilion at Expo 67. Commissioned to build a permanent theatre around the original stage and amphitheatre, Fairfield was highly conscious of what he called "the buoyant charm of a temporary shelter" and the public's "alarming affection" for the sweltering tent. His circular design is a homage to the tent's "mystic personality" as well as an example of the fifties' love of novelty forms.

Common Architectural Styles

Warning: Ontario builders were incorrigibly conservative and unorthodox. Dates are approximate, especially the "closing" date, since individual builders carried on with a favourite style long after it was passé. Descriptions aim only for the hallmarks of one style, but in reality, a "typical" Ontario building could combine traits from three or four different styles.

Georgian 1784–1860

Upper Canadian builders remained loyal to Britain's premier eighteenth-century style long after it passed from favour in the Old Country. In Britain the style was symmetrical, robust, and decorated with columns, pilasters, porticoes, and other classical trimmings. In Ontario, the style was symmetrical, robust, and, in a pioneer society with a harsh climate, much plainer. Typically built of red brick or frame, the Ontario Georgian has a boxy shape, a central door often simply topped with a rectangular transom, many-paned windows, a steepish roof, and large chimneys placed at the edges of the roof.

Loyalist 1800–50

Between the sturdiness of the Georgian and the massiveness of the Greek Revival, there was a lighter, graceful intermission, called Loyalist in Canada. An international style called Adam in Britain (after the architect brothers Robert and James Adam), Louis XVI in France, and Federal in the United States, this is basically a finer-boned continuation of Georgian.

231

Similarly committed to symmetry and restraint, the
Loyalist house can be distinguished from the Georgian
by a greater daintiness, shallower planes, gentler roof
pitches, a fondness for oval forms and arcades, and classical ornamentation that sometimes looks more like
cabinetwork than architecture. The Loyalist door,
framed by the characteristic elliptical fanlight, fluted
pilasters, and sidelights, tends to be more prominent
than the self-effacing Georgian.

Regency 1820–70

British officers stationed in hot countries from Australia
to India brought back the idea of an informal, low-slung
house with deep eaves and verandas. Combining the
aristocratic cachet of the officers, fashionable Romantic
notions of closeness to nature, and a casual pragmatism,
the so-called Regency cottage caught on in some of the
coldest outposts of Empire. Ideally situated with a view
or in a large garden, the Regency cottage minimizes the
indoor-outdoor distinction with multiple French doors,
a relatively unimportant main door, and verandas on
one, two, three, or four sides. A one-and-a-half-storey
version with a central peak is called the Ontario cottage.

Greek Revival 1830–60

Considering themselves the spiritual heirs of Athenian
democracy, the Americans fell so in love with Doric
columns, porticoes, and pediments from about 1830 to
1850 that the architect Alexander Jackson Davis complained that it was impossible to distinguish between
churches, banks, and courthouses in a typical
American town. Upper Canadians were wary of temple-front buildings that trumpeted republican values,
but a certain number of memorable Greek Revival
buildings insinuated themselves into Ontario, frequently through American settlers. Public buildings
are distinguished by very heavy mouldings, porticoes,

pillars (Doric and Ionic more often than Corinthian), and horizontal rooflines. Domestic buildings when grand shared many of those characteristics, but a more typical and modest Ontario Greek Revival house is marked by a front-facing gable, disproportionately massive door placed at the side, and prominent returning eaves.

Gothic Revival 1840–90

The style considered by many the pre-eminent Canadian architectural style goes by several names, all telling. The most common name harks back to its medieval and "barbaric" origins with the non-classical Goths. "The English style" suggests its close connections with the mother country, and Augustus Pugin's term "Pointed or Christian Architecture" nods to its central visual clue, the pointed arch, and its relation to the High Church forms of Christianity. European interest in the high medieval style began with the proto-Romantic movement in the eighteenth century but really flourished beginning in the 1820s and '30s. Imported to Upper Canada, at first it was a romantic top-dressing, with pointed arches, crenellations, and crockets applied to neoclassical bodies. As the fashion progressed and became more scholarly, Gothic's irregular massing and the unity of certain forms of ornament, window tracery, and church organization followed. Used in the towns for churches but also for houses and more rarely for public buildings.

Italianate 1850–90

The nineteenth century considered this a "modern" style, neither a classical revival (such as Greek Revival) nor a picturesque revival (such as the return of Gothic). In reality it was related to both classical and picturesque; its immediate forebear was the Renaissance house of Tuscany, recently seen as a

model for the London men's clubs. In Ontario, the
flexible type could be a squarish bracketed house or a
more irregular one with the characteristic tower. (A
very popular model, published in the *Canada Farmer*,
could not forgo the so-called Ontario peak.) The
brackets were *de rigueur*, so much that the style was
sometimes called the Bracketed style. Look also for
round-headed windows, often in pairs; plans both
symmetrical and L-shaped; cupolas or square Tuscan
towers, sometimes called campaniles.

Second Empire 1870s

Second Empire (also called the French style and sometimes the Renaissance style) is one of the few styles
that came and went with dispatch in Ontario. With
infrequent exceptions it was a modish creature of the
1870s, used in large cities for public buildings, chic
townhouses, and modest row housing. The relatively
few Second Empire buildings in the towns are typically elaborate houses (and firehalls in Perth and
Cobourg). Named for the grandiose building projects
of Napoleon III (1852–70), most notably the enlargement of the Louvre, Second Empire is immediately recognizable by virtue of its mansard roof, whether
straight-lined, concave, or convex, a rediscovery of a
seventeenth-century form popularized by François
Mansart. Other earmarks are advancing and retreating
planes, symmetry, and lavish ornamentation that
includes sculptural mouldings, columns, quoins, iron
cresting, and slate roofs.

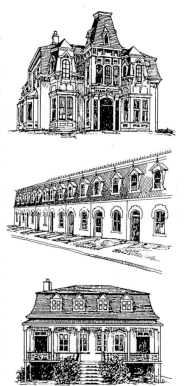

Romanesque Revival 1870–90

By the mid-nineteenth century congregations neither
Anglican nor Catholic were looking for alternatives to
the Gothic style for their churches. Although its
medieval origins were equally papist, the Romanesque
style looked attractive, especially to Presbyterians.

Characterized by smooth surfaces (often red brick), towers, corbel tables, and the essential round-arched windows and doors, the style made its appearance in the towns almost exclusively in churches.

Richardsonian Romanesque 1890–1900

A modification of the Romanesque Revival, named for the influential American architect Henry Hobson Richardson (1838–86). In contrast to the smooth-surfaced civility of Romanesque Revival, Richardson made something altogether burly, irregular, and horizontal out of rock-faced stone (alone or in combination with brick), rounded windows and doors so deeply set as to be cavernous, chunky columns, and foliate decoration, whether in stone carving or terracotta.

Queen Anne 1880–1915

This misnamed style would hardly have pleased the eighteenth-century English queen in its free-for-all mixing of the picturesque (irregular form, gables, towers, turrets) and the classical (Palladian windows, classical orders, and other trimmings). Originally an English return to the (idealized) medieval vernacular house devised by the British architect Richard Norman Shaw (1831–1912), the style is sometimes called Shavian Manor and had great popularity in the New World. A hospitable, sprawling look that suits the broad lawns of Ontario towns, Queen Anne has deep porches, towers, complicated rooflines, a multiplicity of materials. Look for fishtail shingles, stained glass, and spooled (or Eastlake) porches.

Beaux Arts 1900–45

A monumental fashion that swept the United States at the turn of the century but left small-town Ontario mostly undisturbed. Inspired by and named for the

École des Beaux-Arts in Paris, whose classical curriculum formed a generation of architects, the style tended both to the pure Greek model and to the highly decorated Roman and Renaissance forms. As an example of the first type, grandiose white temple-front houses were built by Americans as summer houses in Cobourg; the former library in Perth, elaborately decorated with two pedimented and pilastered sides, represents a more Frenchified version of the classical.

Edwardian Classical 1900–30

A dignified, classically based style used for houses as well as institutions, Edwardian Classical appears most notably in the towns as Carnegie libraries, thanks to Andrew Carnegie's well-known predilection for classical revival styles. Look for red brick accented with stone, deep eaves with dentils, prominent entranceways, grandiose classical elements such as voussoirs and keystones, and heavily banded (sometimes called channelled) walls, corners, and surrounds.

Glossary

acanthus a honeysuckle-like flower used in classical ornament, most typically in a CORINTHIAN CAPITAL.

apse in ecclesiastical architecture, the vaulted extension (semicircular or polygonal) to the NAVE.

arcade a series of ARCHES supported by PIERS or columns, either open, as in a roofed gallery, or blind (see BLIND ARCADE), as in several Niagara buildings.

arch a curved structure used in doorways, gateways, etc. as a support for the weight above it.

architrave 1) the main beam resting on top of a column; 2) the various decorative parts, such as plain or moulded trim, surrounding a doorway or window.

ashlar masonry of squared and finished or CUT STONE with a smooth or tooled face.

balustrade a row of balusters with a rail used on a terrace or balcony.

bargeboard a decorative edge, often fretted (see FRETWORK), on a GABLE edge or EAVES line.

bartizan a TURRET placed at the angle of a PARAPET or the top of a tower.

base course, baseline a defining external feature such as a stone foundation or projecting brick COURSE that marks the floor of a building's first storey.

bay describes the division of a front or façade by openings (windows or doors); for example, a house with two windows and a door has a three-bay façade.

bay-and-gable a late-nineteenth-century Toronto double or row house featuring a polygonal two- or three-storey bay topped with a sharp gable trimmed in bargeboard; the fashion reached the towns, although usually for more expansive single houses. The term was coined by Patricia McHugh (*Toronto Architecture*).

bay window a window set in a projection having several sides, usually a part hexagon or octagon in plan, but occasionally rectangular or, more rarely, triangular.

bead-and-reel classical moulding of alternating beads and reels.

belfry 1) a bell tower; 2) the part of the steeple where the bell is hung.

bell-cast a curved roof profile flaring out at the bottom.

bellcote a framework on a roof from which to hang bells, typically with either a GABLE or a SHED ROOF.

belvedere a glazed structure projecting above a roof, affording a good view, hence the name, or lighting an attic or roof space.

bichromatic having two colours, usually referring to the use of red and yellow (called white in the nineteenth century) brick.

blind arcade a series of ARCHES projecting slightly from a solid wall.

blind arch an ARCH projecting slightly from a solid wall.

board-and-batten vertical wood siding formed by wide boards with projecting narrow strips (battens) covering the joints.

bombé swelling or curving outward.

bond an ornamental and structural pattern of brickwork facings created by laying bricks lengthwise as STRETCHERS and endwise as HEADERS in layers called COURSES. Types of bond include COMMON, ENGLISH, FLEMISH, and STRETCHER.

boomtown façade a false front masking a roofline, associated with the frontier.

boss a knoblike decorative element.

bracket a projecting support, or apparently so, at EAVES, doorways, and sills.

broach spire a usually octagonal spire rising from a square tower without an intervening PARAPET.

broken pediment see PEDIMENT.

broken-coursed masonry using stones of varying sizes arranged in parallel but differently sized horizontal COURSES.

buttress an attached pier projecting from a wall, thus strengthening it; designed to resist the outward thrust of roof vaults in Gothic and Gothic Revival buildings.

campanile Italian for bell tower, frequently used to describe the square tower in an Italianate building, with or without bells.

capital crowning feature of column or PILASTER.

casement window a window hinged at the side to swing open.

cast stone late-nineteenth-century concrete, used in moulds for window SURROUNDS and other decorative effects.

chamfer a bevelled corner.

chancel the area around the altar of a church.

chimney pot a pottery or metal device, often spherical, topping a chimney to improve the draft and minimize smoke.

chinoiserie various Chinese motifs, most commonly a rectilinear pattern in a window, TREILLAGE, or BARGEBOARD, the divisions offset as in an Oriental screen.

clapboard horizontal wood cladding of overlapping thin boards.

collar-tie a horizontal brace on the BARGEBOARD of a GABLE, used increasingly from the 1860s.

colonette a small column.

colonnade a row of regularly spaced columns supporting an ENTABLATURE.

common bond brickwork laid with several COURSES of STRETCHERS alternating with a course of HEADERS, often five courses of stretchers to each course of headers.

compound header a strengthening element atop openings, composed of different pieces of stone or brick. See also SOLDIER LINTEL.

corbel a projection of stone, brick, or timber to support weight, or for decoration.

corbel table a line of CORBELS bordering a wall or GABLE.

Corinthian the most elaborate of the Grecian orders, with a bell-shaped CAPITAL decorated with ACANTHUS leaves.

corner boards vertical boards at the corners of a frame building.

cornice 1) in classical architecture, the topmost portion of an ENTABLATURE, above the ARCHITRAVE and FRIEZE; 2) ornamental moulding that projects along the top of a wall, pillar, or building, usually of wood or plaster; 3) the projecting member forming the upper feature of a DOORCASE, or the decorated overhang at the EAVES.

course the line in which bricks are laid, or a horizontal division of stonework.

coursed rubble rough stone laid in more or less horizontal courses.

crenellation alternating raised portions and indentations at the top of a wall, usually on the roofline.

cresting an ornamental, lacy finish along the top of a screen, wall, or roof, often of ironwork, sometimes of wood.

crocket a hook-like Gothic ornament, carved to resemble leaves and plants, and typically used on steeply vertical surfaces such as SPIRES and GABLES.

cruciform cross-shaped.

cupola a structure, often domed, projecting above the roof, similar to a LANTERN or BELVEDERE, but usually serving as a ventilator.

cut stone sometimes called sawn stone, split and squared stone as opposed to RUBBLESTONE or FIELDSTONE; the most refined type of cut stone is ASHLAR.

dentils small rectangular blocks, resembling teeth, often seen decorating the lower part of a CORNICE.

diaperwork surface decoration of small, repetitive motifs, frequently crosses in Ontario towns.

dog-toothing an ornamental, repetitive arrangement of small triangular shapes resembling a row of canine teeth.

doorcase the frame of a doorway, which may include the moulding around SIDELIGHTS and TRANSOM as well as the door.

Doric one of the Greek architectural orders, ideally with a plain CAPITAL, fluted column (see FLUTING), and no base.

dormer a window projecting from a sloping roof, usually in a small enclosure. The name derives from the French verb for sleep.

dressed stone stone, usually limestone or sandstone, treated with chisels and hammers to create various textures.

drip mould a protective moulding around the top of a window, ARCH, or door, curved or rectangular (when rectangular, called a LABEL).

drop 1) the lower extension of a FINIAL on a BARGEBOARD and often decorated with a turning at the base; 2) a similar turned device, of acorn or turnip shape, used on BRACKETS and the lower ends of BARGEBOARDS.

ears lateral projections of the trim around the top of a DOORCASE or window SUR-ROUND, often seen in Greek Revival buildings; sometimes called shoulders.

Eastlake a decorative style that produced knobbed, spindled, and latticed VERANDAS, BARGEBOARD, and BRACKETS on late-nineteenth-century houses. Named after British decorator and architect Charles Lock Eastlake (1836–1906). (See also SPINDLEWORK.)

eaves the lower edges of a roof projecting beyond the wall of a building.

egg-and-dart classical moulding alternating ovals and arrowheads.

English bond brickwork with alternating COURSES of HEADERS and STRETCHERS.

entablature in classical architecture, the horizontal element above the columns, comprising in ascending order ARCHITRAVE, FRIEZE, and CORNICE; a wide and important moulded band.

eyebrow dormer, eyebrow frame a dormer or frame shaped with a wide curve resembling an eyebrow.

fanlight a semicircular or elliptical window over a door, with radiating glazing bars suggesting a fan.

fascia 1) in classical architecture, one of the faces in an ARCHITRAVE; 2) a horizontal wooden board below the EAVES or, by extension, a horizontal moulding.

fieldstone uncut, undressed stone as found in fields.

finial a pointed ornament usually seen at the apex of a GABLE.

Flemish bond bricks laid with HEADERS and STRETCHERS alternating in each COURSE.

flushboard horizontal wood siding with a flat or flush surface.

fluting a type of decoration consisting of long, round grooves; the vertical channelling on the shaft of a column.

French doors double doors, with windows extending the full length or almost full-length.

fretwork cut-out ornamental woodwork, usually from a plain board with the pattern of voids created by a narrow-bladed fret saw, which could be used around tight curves.

frieze 1) in classical architecture, the middle member in an ENTABLATURE; 2) more informally, a decorated band attached to the wall surface.

frontispiece the principal entrance BAY of a building.

gable the enclosing lines of a sloping roof.

gambrel roof a GABLE roof having a double pitch or two slopes on each side, with the lower slope steeper and the upper one more gentle.

Greek key an ornamental, repetitive motif formed of vertical and horizontal straight lines.

half-timbering a construction method in which the frame and principal supports are exposed; the interstices may be stucco, brick, etc.

hammerbeam a type of wooden roof supported by horizontal BRACKETS, much like a COLLAR-TIE with the centre removed.

header the short end of a brick.

hip-roof a roof sloped on all four sides.

impost a member set in the wall at the point where an ARCH begins and ends.

Ionic an order of Greek architecture, its CAPITAL decorated with ramshorns.

Juliet balcony a small balcony.

keystone 1) the central stone of a masonry ARCH, usually sloped on both sides to form the key of the structure, which prevents the collapse of the arch; 2) a large, central piece in a LINTEL.

label a projecting rectangular moulding around an opening, designed to repel rain.

lancet a sharply pointed Gothic ARCH, resembling a lancet or spear.

lantern a small structure raised above the roof, of various shapes, with windows.

leaded windows panes of glass, often diamond-shaped or rectangular, set in lead strips (called cames).

light a single window or the subdivision of a window opening into separate glazed areas.

lintel a horizontal timber, stone, or arrangement of bricks over an opening that carries the weight of the structure above.

mansard roof a HIP-ROOF of GAMBREL form, i.e., with all four sides with steeper slopes towards the EAVES and a gentler slope towards the ridge.

medallion a circular decorative element.

metopes in a DORIC ENTABLATURE, the panels between the TRIGLYPHS.

modillion a flat BRACKET with scrolls at both ends.

Moorish arch horseshoe-shaped ARCH.

mutules the blocks projecting slightly below the SOFFIT of a CORNICE.

nave the main area of a church, sometimes flanked by aisles.

ogee an ARCH formed by two convex arcs above two concave arcs.

oriel window a BAY WINDOW found on upper stories only.

Palladian window an ARCH-headed window flanked by SIDELIGHTS.

palmette a fan-shaped decoration modelled on a palmated leaf.

parapet the extension of a wall above the roofline, usually at the GABLE end.

pediment a low-pitched triangle ornamenting the front of a building, door, porch, or window. A broken pediment appears to have the apex of the triangle chewed off. A swan's-neck pediment is also broken, but the broken lines are sinuous.

pendant an elongated decorative knob hanging from a BRACKET, BARGEBOARD, etc.

pier a solid masonry support that protrudes slightly from the façade.

pilaster a rectangular column attached to a wall and projecting only slightly from it, often conforming with one of the classical orders.

pinnacle a sharp termination to a TURRET or a BUTTRESS.

porte-cochère a roofed carriage entrance.

portico a porch with pillars or columns.

quarry-faced stone also called ROCK-FACED and popular at the turn of the century, stonework in which the squared block is left with a bulbous face.

quatrefoil a four-lobed figure used in Gothic Revival windows and decorative sculpture.

quoins a projecting corner feature, often stone but occasionally brick or even wood (from the French *coin* for corner).

raked masonry masonry that has been DRESSED to create a striated surface.

raking cornice the CORNICE on the sloping sides of a PEDIMENT.

rafter a long timber piece used to support a roof.

relief joints in masonry, prominent mortar with a rounded profile.

returning eaves the extension of the EAVES CORNICE around the corner at the GABLE ends, typical of the Greek Revival style.

reveal the side of an opening cut through a wall, for doors or windows.

rock-faced see QUARRY-FACED STONE.

rosette a flat, small circular decoration trimmed with rose petals.

rotunda a round building or room, often with a dome.

rough-cast a rough plaster made of lime, water, and cow's hair; as a finishing touch, gravel is "cast" on by the plasterer.

roundel a round decorative element, such as a plaque or window.

rubblestone rough, broken building stone.

rustication a masonry technique using massive ASHLAR blocks cut to project boldly from the margins, typically used on the bottom part of a building.

saltbox (roof) a roof with a short front slope and a long back slope, so named for its resemblance to an old-fashioned salt container.

sash the wooden assembly of a window, containing the glass; a sash window opens at the top and bottom.

sawn stone see CUT STONE.

shaped gable a GABLE with multi-curved sides.

shed roof a single slope, like a lean-to roof.

shelf 1) a horizontal projection around all sides of a VERANDA post; 2) a small, protective projection at the top of a window or door.

sidelight a glazed panel adjacent to a door.

soffit the under-surface of eaves.

soldier lintel a straight-topped row of upright bricks used as a COMPOUND HEADER.

spindlework decorative woodwork of repetitive turned ornaments or spindles. When these are relatively short, the more correct term is "spoolwork."

spire the tall pointed termination to a church tower.

steeple a church tower and its SPIRE, or an ornamental tower terminating in diminishing stages.

stepped gable a gable with stepped sides.

stretcher the long side of a brick.

stretcher bond bricks laid lengthwise every COURSE.

string course a moulding or projecting COURSE running horizontally on a building surface, usually between stories.

surround the decorative and (sometimes) protective casing around a window or door.

swan's-neck pediment see PEDIMENT.

terracotta fine-textured clay fired at very high temperatures, used for cladding and for relief decorations such as plaques.

tracery the design in a window composed of various LIGHTS.

transept the transverse arm or arms of a church, usually crossing the NAVE at the entrance to the CHANCEL.

transom the upper LIGHT of a doorway or window, generally of rectangular shape.

trefoil a three-lobed figure used in Gothic Revival decoration.

treillage decorative trim, wooden or sometimes ironwork, used on VERANDAS.

triglyphs in Greek architecture, vertical blocks in a DORIC FRIEZE divided in three by two vertical grooves; the panels between the triglyphs are called METOPES.

Tudor arch a late-medieval ARCH, less acute than a LANCET, that begins with a broad curve and rises to a point.

Tudor label a rectangular, projecting moulding above a window, door, or ARCH.

turret a small tower.

Tuscan the simplest of the Greek orders, ideally unfluted DORIC columns with a base.

tympanum a flat wall surface within either a PEDIMENT or an ARCH.

umbrage a recessed porch shaded by the continuation of the house's roof.

Venetian window a three-part window with a larger centre LIGHT and narrower SIDELIGHTS.

veranda a roofed open structure across the front, side, or back of a building, at times encircling, or almost so, the lower storey of a house; a large porch.

vermiculated stone stone blocks incised with channels resembling worm tracks.

volute a scroll or spiral occurring in IONIC or CORINTHIAN CAPITALS.

voussoir a wedge-shaped stone forming a component of an ARCH.

Many of the definitions in this glossary are reproduced or adapted from Architectural Terms *by Marion Walker Garland and* Rogue's Hollow *by Peter John Stokes, and used with the kind permission of the authors and the Architectural Conservancy of Ontario.*

Suggestions for Further Reading

GENERAL

Adamson, Anthony. *The Gaiety of Gables: Ontario's Architectural Folk Art.* McClelland & Stewart, 1974.

Arthur, Eric, and Stephen A. Otto. *Toronto: No Mean City.* University of Toronto Press, 1986.

Beckman, Margaret, Stephan Langmead, and John Black. *The Best Gift: A Record of the Carnegie Libraries in Ontario.* Dundurn Press, 1984.

Blake, Verschoyle Benson, and Ralph Greenhill. *Rural Ontario.* University of Toronto Press, 1969.

Blumenson, John. *Identifying American Architecture: A Pictorial Guide to Styles and Terms, 1600-1945.* Norton, 1987.

Blumenson, John. *Ontario Architecture: A Guide to Styles and Building Terms, 1784 to the Present.* Fitzhenry & Whiteside, 1990.

Brosseau, Mathilde. *Gothic Revival Architecture.* Parks Canada, 1980.

Byers, Mary, and Margaret McBurney. *The Governor's Road: Early Buildings and Families from Mississauga to London.* University of Toronto Press, 1982.

Cameron, Christina, and Janet Wright. *Second Empire Style in Canadian Architecture.* Parks Canada, 1980.

Clerk, Nathalie. *Palladian Style in Canadian Architecture.* Parks Canada, 1984.

Dendy, William. *Lost Toronto.* McClelland & Stewart, 1993.

Downing, Andrew Jackson. *The Architecture of Country Houses* (1850). Dover, 1969.

Downing, Andrew Jackson. *Victorian Cottage Residences* (1873). Dover, 1981.

Fermor-Hesketh, Robert, Editor. *Architecture of the British Empire.* Vendome, 1986.

Gowans, Alan. *Building Canada: An Architectural History of Canadian Life.* Oxford University Press, 1966.

Gowans, Alan. *The Comfortable House: North American Suburban Architecture, 1890-1930.* MIT Press, 1986.

Gowans, Alan. *Looking at Architecture in Canada.* Oxford University Press, 1958.

Greenhill, Ralph, Ken Macpherson, and Douglas Richardson. *Ontario Towns.* Oberon, 1974.

Hall, Roger, and Gordon Dodds. *Ontario: 200 Years in Pictures.* Dundurn Press, 1991.

Kalman, Harold. *History of Canadian Architecture.* 2 volumes. Oxford University Press, 1994.

McBurney, Margaret, and Mary Byers. *Homesteads: Early Buildings and Families from*

Kingston to Toronto. University of Toronto Press, 1979.

McBurney, Margaret, and Mary Byers. *Tavern in the Town: Early Inns and Taverns of Ontario*. University of Toronto Press, 1987.

McHugh, Patricia. *Toronto Architecture: A City Guide*. McClelland & Stewart, 1989.

MacRae, Marion, and Anthony Adamson. *The Ancestral Roof: Domestic Architecture of Upper Canada*. Clarke Irwin, 1963.

MacRae, Marion, and Anthony Adamson. *Cornerstones of Order: Courthouses and Town Halls of Ontario, 1784-1914*. Clarke Irwin, 1983.

MacRae, Marion, and Anthony Adamson. *Hallowed Walls: Church Architecture of Upper Canada*. Clarke Irwin, 1975.

Maitland, Leslie. *Neoclassical Architecture in Canada*. Parks Canada, 1984.

Maitland, Leslie. *Palladian Style in Canadian Architecture*. Parks Canada, 1984.

Maitland, Leslie. *The Queen Anne Revival Style in Canadian Architecture*. Parks Canada, 1990.

Maitland, Leslie, Jacqueline Hucker, and Shannon Ricketts. *Guide to Canadian Architectural Styles*. Broadview Press, 1992.

Jeanne. *At Home in Upper Canada*. Clarke Irwin, 1983.

Poppeliers, John, et al. *What Style Is It? A Guide to American Architecture*. Preservation Press, 1983.

Rempel, John. *Building with Wood*. University of Toronto Press, 1972.

Rifkind, Carole. *Field Guide to American Architecture*. New American Library, 1980.

Tausky, Nancy A., and Lynne DiStefano. *Victorian Architecture in London and Southwestern Ontario*. University of Toronto Press, 1986.

Whiffen, Marcus. *American Architecture Since 1780: A Guide to the Styles*. MIT, 1992.

Whiffen, Marcus, and Frederick Koeper. *American Architecture, 1607-1976*. Routledge and Kegan Paul, 1981.

Wright, Janet. *Architecture of the Picturesque in Canada*. Parks Canada, 1984.

INDIVIDUAL TOWNS

Cobourg

Guillet, Edwin C. *Cobourg 1798-1948*. Business and Professional Women's Club of Cobourg, 1948.

Spilsbury, John, Editor. *Cobourg: Early Days and Modern Times*. Cobourg Book Committee, 1981.

Goderich

Wallace, Dorothy. *Memories of Goderich*. Corporation of the Town of Goderich, 1977.

Merrickville

Turner, Larry. *Merrickville: Jewel on the Rideau*. Petherwin Heritage, 1995.

Niagara-on-the-Lake

Field, John L. *Niagara-on-the-Lake Guidebook*. Renown Printing, 1989.

Mika, Nick, Helma Mika, Nancy Butler, and Joy Ormsby. *Niagara-on-the-Lake*. Mika, 1990.

Stokes, Peter John. *Old Niagara on the Lake*. University of Toronto Press, 1971.

Paris

Parr, Joy. *The Gender of Breadwinners: Women, Men, and Change in Two Industrial Towns 1880-1950*. University of Toronto, 1990.

Smith, Donald A. *At the Forks of the Grand*. Volume 1, Paris Centennial Committee, 1956. Volume 2, Paris Public Library Board, 1982.

Perth
McGill, Jean S. *Pioneer History of the County of Lanark*. Clay Publishing, 1968.

Turner, Larry, with John J. Stewart. *Perth: Tradition and Style in Eastern Ontario*. Natural Heritage, 1992.

Picton
Cruickshank, Tom, and Peter John Stokes. *The Settler's Dream: A Pictorial History of the Older Buildings of Prince Edward County*. Corporation of the County of Prince Edward, 1984.

Lunn, Janet, and Richard. *The County*. Prince Edward County Council, 1967.

Port Hope
Craick, W. Arnot. *Port Hope Historical Sketches* (1901). Haynes Printing Co., 1974.

Craick, W. Arnot. *Little Tales of Old Port Hope*. Guide Publishing Company, 1966.

Cruickshank, Tom. *Port Hope: A Treasure of Early Homes*. Bluestone House, 1987.

St. Marys
Pfaff, L.R., and C.M. Pfaff. *Limestone Legacy in St. Marys: The Story of the Huttons, Millers and Gentlemen*. Thames Printing, 1989.

Wilson, L.W., and L.R. Pfaff. *Early St. Marys*. St.-Marys-on-the-Thames Historical Society, 1981.

Stratford
Johnston, W. Stafford, and Hugh J. M. Johnston. *History of Perth County to 1967*. County of Perth, 1967.

Leitch, Adelaide. *Floodtides of Fortune: The Story of Stratford*. City of Stratford, 1980.

Index

The text in this book is set in Goudy, which was
designed by Frederic W. Goudy in 1915.

Designed by James Ireland and Sara Tyson

Typeset by James Ireland Design Inc.

The drawings on pages ii-iii, 233 (bottom),
234 (top), 236 (bottom), 237 (top and bottom), and
238 (bottom) are by Pat Stephens.

Other drawings on pages 233-38 are reproduced
with permission from *The Buildings of Canada:
A Guide to Pre-20th-Century Styles in Houses,
Churches and Other Structures*, by Barbara Humphreys and
Meredith Sykes, illustrated by Michael Middleton,
copyright The Reader's Digest (Canada) Association Ltd.